Salo's Song
A Jewish Wartime Romance

Salo's Song

A Jewish Wartime Romance

BARBARA ESSER

Translated by Colin Berry

VALLENTINE MITCHELL
LONDON • PORTLAND, OR

Sag beim Abschied leise Servus by Barbara Esser
first published in 2002 by Kremayr & Scheriau,
Vienna/Munich, © Barbara Esser 2002.
All rights reserved.

First published in 2005 in Great Britain by
VALLENTINE MITCHELL
Suite 314,
Premier House
112–114 Station Road, Edgware,
Middlesex HA8 7BJ

and in the United States of America by
VALLENTINE MITCHELL
c/o ISBS, 920 NE 58th Avenue
Suite 300
Portland, Oregon 97213-3786

Website: www.vmbooks.com

Copyright © 2005 Barbara Esser

British Library Cataloguing in Publication Data

A catalogue record for this book has been applied for

ISSN 0 85303 522 9

Library of Congress Cataloging-in-Publication Data

A catalog record for this book has been applied for

Printed and bound in Great Britain by Antony Rowe Ltd, Chippenham, Wiltshire

To my distant relative Ilse Tysh, full of years,
whose life story is the basis of this book

BARBARA ESSER

Contents

Preface

The death of my sister has altered my life as it approaches its end. Marianne died in November 1999. I did not want her to go before me. Her survival and her rescue from the Nazis had given my existence its purpose and justification.

She had visited me early in the year, as she used to every spring. Since she had emigrated to Canada no week went by without our telephoning one another and writing letters – and no year went by without one of us visiting the other. The last time she was in London, she brought this strange cough with her. It sounded quite different from one associated with a cold: metallic and dry. Just listening to it was painful. Early in the evening I poured her dry martini. This aperitif at six was a tradition that she kept to rigidly. Marianne didn't take a single sip. I noticed her full glass, saw her huddled up on the sofa and heard the rattle in her lungs. I knew what awaited her.

Marianne was like a daughter to me. She came to England in 1939, after I had fled here first. She was only fourteen. I brought her up, worked to keep her, cooked, sewed and cared for her. I tried to explain to her what could not be explained. In those days I lived just for her.

Now she is gone, pictures from the past that I tried for so many years to preserve in my innermost being suddenly rise up again before me. At night, they force their way into my dreams, recalling the happy and sad scenes of my life. The strange thing with age is how the deepest-buried memories work their way towards the surface as the years pass. My contemporaries tell me the same. Memories push their way to the fore like some ill-bred lout. Sometimes they bring old friends and happy laughter, but often sadness and pain.

After my sister's death I began a course of treatment at the London Holocaust Centre, hoping to rediscover my will to live. Whether it is worth it at eighty-five, I don't know. But one thing that I have come to realize is the importance of remembering. 'Memory', a Jewish rabbi once said, 'is the secret of redemption.'

No one dominates my memory as much as Fred. It is almost 20 years since he failed to wake up one morning, yet no day passes without my thinking of him. When he came to London, in May 1939, he still had his Jewish name, Salomon, in his passport. Friends called him Salo. Later he changed his first name and his surname, like most Jewish emigrants. His past, though, could not be sloughed off. It followed him to the end.

The scene of our first meeting in Hyde Park, and the recollection of this man so turned in on himself, have been etched into my memory. Salo was then only thirty-three, yet he moved like an old man whose infirmity makes his movements slow. He walked with the aid of crutches. He had arrived in London two days earlier, on 22 May 1939. His brother Moishe had only hinted on the telephone that something had happened to him, and that he himself had hardly recognized him when he saw him again.

Salo had wasted away to just forty-two kilos. He wore a pinstripe suit that was too big for him, and apparently not his. He stood before me strangely stiff, his scraggy neck sticking out of a collar that was far too wide, and had to be held closed with a tie. The skin of his face stretched over the cheekbones. Perhaps I stared at him for a moment with the mixture of horror and fascination with which one looks at people with some stigma or defect. This man, so obviously concerned to give a distinguished impression, reminded me of fatally ill patients whom I had looked after when I was a nurse at home in Aussig, in Bohemia.

The moment he bent to kiss my hand and revealed his bony scalp, I knew something frightful must have happened to him. Perhaps I sensed too that even my worst fears could not approach the reality of what he had experienced. Only years later did he tell me what had really happened.

We went to have coffee, and as I said goodbye later, he asked when he could see me again. I invited him to one of my traditional Friday-evening dinners as soon as he had recovered his strength.

I was sure I wouldn't see him for some weeks. Two days later, early on Friday evening, there was a ring at the door. There he stood, with his hair freshly Brylcreemed, again in the same borrowed suit, leaning on the crutches and with a bunch of red roses in his hand. He was almost an hour too early, and stayed longer than all the other guests.

He is still with me.

List of Illustrations

1 Growing Up in Bohemia

My lipstick has almost run out. It's time I got a new one. At my age vanity is not what it was, but I still never go out with pale lips. It is one of the many carefully cultivated rituals that become entrenched over the years like the lines on a face. Before I met Fred I hardly used make-up. But Fred liked it when I painted my lips glowing red. 'You have a lovely mouth,' he would say. 'You shouldn't hide it.' I always found my mouth a little bit too big. Like my breasts. 'When they were giving out breasts', my grandfather teased me as I was growing up, 'you kept shouting, "Over here!".' Who I had inherited my generous dimensions from in this department was a mystery to my mother, who was very petite. But the big mouth, she said, was definitely from my father. And the thick eyebrows. I have wondered what psychological traits I owe to him. I have never found out, as I never knew my father.

To judge from the few photos I saw of him, he must have been a good-looking man. His black hair was combed back in a bold sweep, a few strands always falling over his high forehead and bobbing before his eyes, which I was told were deep brown and strangely appealing. He must have fixed this gaze on my mother when he met her for the first time. Grete was then sixteen, and the gentle, classical beauty that I so admired later, was already emerging in her face. Her parents had taken her to the municipal theatre in Aussig, the large, mainly German, town in the Elbe valley in Bohemia. This man sat two rows in front of them. He didn't see much of what was happening on the stage, she told me decades later, with a smile that still showed how flattered she was, because he stared at her constantly. In the interval he had spoken to her parents, introduced himself as the owner of a shirt factory, and asked whether he might some time take their daughter out.

Shortly after her eighteenth birthday, she accepted his proposal of marriage. I think she loved him very much because she never spoke a word against him. It must have hurt her deeply that he deceived her shortly after their wedding. And not just once. After six years of marriage, when she was twenty-four and six months pregnant with me, she divorced him. In those days, in 1914, that was unheard of, but in Türmitz, the suburb of Aussig, where everyone knew everyone, it verged on a scandal. My mother took her maiden name of Schnitzer again. After the divorce she got no money from her husband; he left her only her engagement ring. She moved from Teplitz, where she had lived with him, back to Türmitz, to the house of her parents, who were less than delighted. After all, besides two sons, they had two more unmarried daughters, and they were plagued by the fear that their newly returned daughter and her newborn child would bring the stigma of unmarriageability to all three girls.

But by the time I had begun to take stock of the world around me, my mother had married again. Her new husband was eighteen years older than she. He had known my mother by sight for years, although he had never dared approach her – partly because of the big difference in their ages. My father – it was always natural for me to call him my father – had a complex all his life about his appearance. In the First World War his right eye had been damaged, and since then the lid was screwed up. He thought his face, with a large hooked nose in the middle of it, looked too unmistakably Jewish, and was ashamed of it. Later he was convinced that his appearance would be his undoing because it fitted fatally into Nazi racial typology.

Fritz Lönhardt was his name, and he asked my grandfather for my mother's hand in marriage. My mother later told me that he had said, 'I have loved your daughter for years from afar. I can guarantee her financial and emotional security – and I promise to adopt little Ilse straight away'. My grandparents gave their consent. Did my mother marry him for love? At first, I suspect, it was an alliance for security based on respect, which grew into a deep attachment. Later, I think, it developed into genuine love. When their lives came to depend on it, my parents always supported one another.

My father was a major in the Austro-Hungarian army, and

until it was disbanded at the end of the First World War, he was responsible for the Italian prisoners of war (POWs) held in the large camp in a garrison town not far from Aussig. The town was called Theresienstadt. Over twenty years later many of my relatives and friends would be imprisoned in the same camp, in the model Jewish ghetto of the Nazis.

In those days, back in 1918, we lived outside the walls of the camp, on the first floor of a barracks. I still remember how, when just four years old, I tried to catch butterflies in the garden. My little hands were too clumsy and my movements not agile enough. My mother still didn't like it. 'They know you want to catch them, that's why they flutter away so fast,' she said. I believed her, and said aloud so that all the butterflies could hear me, 'I don't want to catch you at all.' I thought it a clever way of deceiving them, but it didn't work. 'Anyway, if you do catch them, they won't live long,' said my mother. 'Look at them when they are free. In captivity they lose all their beauty. Their little wings break, and their colours lose their brightness.'

Later, I often recalled her words when I thought of Father and Mother shut up in a ghetto. Right to the end, I was told, my mother smeared red colouring on her cheeks, not to make herself beautiful but to survive the next *Selektion*. She had dampened the red bags of ersatz coffee with saliva to release the colouring. Other women pricked their fingers with a needle and spread the drops of blood on their cheeks and lips.

I cannot recall having a sense of danger as a child. At the end of the First World War the POWs were gradually released. They were exhausted and hungry. In those days hunger was ever present. There were repeatedly hunger demonstrations in Bohemia. Many soldiers in the Austro-Hungarian army had deserted from hunger, and formed so-called 'green bands' that roamed the Bohemian woods and lived by stealing food.

Released Italian POWs in Theresienstadt were also on the lookout for something to eat, and had come into our house. Mother hadn't noticed. I remember the scene exactly, as a group of them suddenly stood before me in the kitchen. Their appearance did not frighten me so much as arouse my curiosity. One of the soldiers had found a glass bowl full of eggs in the cupboard and was about to get it down. The bowl slipped from his grasp and smashed on the floor, and all the raw eggs broke.

There he stood, the poor, hungry soldier, in a slimy puddle of egg white and yolk. I must have laughed aloud at the sight, along with his comrades. Suddenly my mother was in the room. She saw the mishap, and me standing happily among the ragged soldiers. She grabbed me with a jerk and shut me in my room. It was the first time I had seen her really frightened. Usually she radiated deep confidence, in which you could almost snuggle up as if under a warm blanket.

My mother telephoned from the officers' mess to her father in Türmitz, which was only twenty miles away. Being a factory owner, he already had a telephone at that time. 'This is no place for a child,' she told him, and asked him to take care of me until the situation calmed down. That same day my grandfather trotted over from Türmitz in the horse-drawn carriage. Theresienstadt was in utter turmoil. Prisoners of war were roaming everywhere, some of them armed. On the way to Türmitz a number followed us on bicycles. Grandad's old nag had a bad limp, and our pursuers were catching up. As they got nearer and nearer, Grandfather grabbed me from the carriage, squeezed me into the ditch and threw himself over me like a living shield. I shall never forget the feeling, with Grandfather wheezing on top of me, his beard, which tickled my ear, and how he whispered it would all be all right. I felt as safe as in Mother's tummy. In fact, once they had made sure there was nothing edible or of value in the carriage, the soldiers went off without touching a hair of our heads.

I must have been six when my deep sense of security was first briefly shattered. We were now living again in Türmitz, where my father, who had previously worked as a chemist in a sugar refinery, had bought a tar factory. At first he had only three workers, but the staff soon grew rapidly. We lived on the second floor of a house built at the turn of the century that stood right on the market square. It was a beautiful flat, with four rooms and ornamental plaster ceilings, parquet flooring and a large green-tiled stove in the main living room. It wasn't quite luxurious, though, as, instead of a modern toilet, it had only an earth closet that regularly froze in the winter. A Jewish grocer had a shop on the ground floor. Every few days he would roast the coffee beans that were delivered in large jute sacks, and the aroma of freshly ground coffee would waft up the stairwell – a smell that even today takes me back to my childhood. From our windows we looked on to a roundabout, bordered by huge oak trees, where the trams connecting Türmitz and Aussig turned round.

I had many playmates in the neighbourhood. In the house behind ours lived a friendly little man, Mr Šwechla, who worked as a miner in one of the nearby coal mines. Almost every year saw a new arrival in the Šwechla family. Altogether the parents had managed in eighteen years of married life to produce sixteen sons and daughters. This wonderful fecundity amazed me all the more as I then firmly believed that the babies were brought by the stork. How could it come about that they were delivered next door while nothing of the sort happened to us, even though I dearly wished for a sister and left a lump of sugar on the window sill every evening?

Martha, one of the youngest of this huge family, was my best friend. She was exactly the same age as me, and had long pitch-black hair, for which I envied her, as I did her many brothers and sisters. She usually spent all day with me, going home only at bedtime, when she had to share a bed with two of her siblings. Sometimes she let me be a hairdresser and play with her thick mane. I was allowed to plait her pigtails and loops, which always ended crooked with just a few strands of hair, and to brush her hair till it gleamed like silk. Like all little girls, we loved dressing up. Searching for material and clothes, we crept into my parents' bedroom, which was not allowed. Breathing heavily, we raised the massive lid of the linen chest, which was quite large enough to swallow us both up, and began removing the contents layer by layer. Pillowcases edged with lace, heavy damask tablecloths and fine linen napkins with pillow lace, came to light, accompanied by a slightly musty whiff. I had just wrapped a tablecloth around my neck like a shawl when my eye fell on the monogram in the corner of the hem, where the letters 'GW' were embroidered. And this monogram, I discovered, was on all the other linen too. I was quite sure because I could already read individual letters of the alphabet. 'G' was the initial of my mother Grete. But what did 'W' stand for? After all, our name was Lönhardt.

Heart pounding, I ran to my mother, who was sitting drinking coffee with my father in the living room. My safe little world was suddenly rent apart. 'I don't understand, Mummy, why there is a W on our linen. Did you steal those things?' For me, the only explanation was that my mother was a thief. Father and Mother exchanged meaningful glances. 'Go outside for a moment,' ordered my father. I shut the door behind me and heard them arguing in lowered voices, but could not make out a word. Suddenly the door opened again. Father crouched down in front of me at my eye level, as he did whenever he had something important to say. 'I am going to tell you the truth,' he said, adding that I was old enough to hear it. I gave a start. If growing up meant one had to take on unpleasant truths like being made to put on a scratchy old pullover, I would happily forgo it. I glanced at my mother, who gave me an encouraging smile. 'You had another father,' he went on. 'But he wasn't a very nice man. He didn't make your mother happy, so she divorced him before you came into the world. When I met the two of you, you were a tiny little girl. I didn't just fall in love with your mother – I fell in love with you too. I picked you out because you are something very special.' Fritz Lönhardt took me in his arms and kissed me on the head.

That was when he began to prepare me for life. After that, he never hid the truth from me whenever I asked. And he never let me face it alone.

As for the mystery of where babies came from, though, I was left in uncertainty for a long time. The tale about the storks was demolished by fellow pupils at school. I had no idea how my mother struggled to have another child. Every year in spring she went away for three weeks to Franzensbad, leaving me behind with Father and our servant girl. I was told it was for a rest. Only years later did I learn that she hoped the mud baths there would improve her chances of conceiving.

I was eight when she was at last expecting a child, and was immensely happy. The pregnancy was accompanied by so many complications that, fearing the birth would be as difficult, she sent for a midwife, who came especially all the way from Halle in Saxony. She had been recommended by a close friend who lived there, who with her help a few years before had borne a lump of a boy called Hans Fürth. This Hans from Halle was later to play an important role in the life of my as yet unborn sister.

My life was changed by Marianne's arrival. Up till then I had been the little girl. Now, I was suddenly the big sister, to whom, after her birth, the tiny dark-haired bundle was entrusted. The doctor ordered Mother to have six weeks' strict bed rest. And so, helped by our servant, I was able to carry the baby around and bath her, taking her to my mother for breast-feeding. In the afternoons, I put Marianne in the pram and pushed her through the park in Türmitz.

One day in early summer the June sun had driven away the sulphurous haze that often spread over the Elbe valley like a murky and evil-smelling baldachin, and there was a cloudless blue sky. The smell of lilac and jasmine was in the air. A few elderly men were sitting on a park bench waving their walking sticks around and discussing politics at the tops of their voices. Marianne was the loudest of all with the ear-splitting yelling coming from her basket-weave pram. 'She must be hungry,' one of the old men said. 'Perhaps her nappy is full,' suggested another. 'Or she has a tummy ache,' thought a third. A sniff was all that was needed to clarify the matter. I had a nappy with me, although I knew how to change it only from watching other people. We laid Marianne on the bench, and the old men stood around and argued about how to put it on, and where the safety pin went. 'When I was young, you did it like this,' said one of the white-haired old gentlemen. 'Nonsense, that would never hold!' claimed his friend. When I took Marianne home, she had a complete tangle around her tummy. Mother laughed, but was careful to praise my efforts too. After that, I often changed my sister, and in a peculiar way she was also my child. That remained so to the end.

Marianne's arrival also changed my religious identity. Only a handful of Jewish families lived in Türmitz, although in Aussig they were about a tenth of the population of 50,000. We were not practising Jews, and I had been inside a synagogue only twice, once for a bar-mitzvah and once for a wedding. Like many Jews in Bohemia and Moravia, we were largely assimilated, much to the chagrin of the orthodox. In my early years I never felt at all Jewish. Awareness of a vaguely separate identity was first awakened when I went to school. On the way I was teased several times by other children, who tore the grips from my hair and shouted, 'You

7

Jews killed Jesus.' When these incidents became more frequent and I came home crying, my mother got our servant girl to go with me to school and collect me afterwards. This strange form of anti-Semitism came from a mistaken interpretation of the New Testament that many Catholics believed at the time. Some Catholic politicians developed absurd conspiracy theories that the Jews were striving for world domination.

The English say, 'If you can't beat them, join them.' That is what we did. After my sister was born my father decided to have us both baptized as Catholics. 'You'll see, this stupid animosity will stop just as soon as it gets around that you have been christened,' he promised. And in fact from then on I belonged with the others – at least at first. Like the quite widespread mixed marriages of Jews and non-Jews in the area, conversion to Christianity was a common mark of assimilation. Giving up religious practice and custom seemed to many Jews an acceptable price for the supposed privileges of equal rights and social integration. My father, a convinced agnostic, thought it a good bargain.

At first open anti-Semitism in Bohemia was hardly noticeable. After the end of the Habsburg monarchy and the founding of the Czechoslovak Republic, political debate was shaped by the tensions between German Bohemians and Czechs. The new government in Prague had had all the statues of the Habsburg emperors removed in the Sudeten German towns. In Aussig, where more than 80 per cent of the inhabitants were German, Kaiser-Josef Square was renamed School Square. Czechoslovak legionaries had tipped the statue of Emperor Joseph II off its plinth. Czech was made a compulsory subject in German schools. We sang the Czech national anthem 'Kde domov muj …' ('Where is my home, my Fatherland …'), which we learned by heart, and had the day off school on the birthday of the state president, Thomas Masaryk. Plays in Czech were performed for three months of the year in the Aussig Theatre.

Sometimes cultural identity comes more to the fore in small, closed worlds. In Aussig, which had scarcely lacked for club life before, there were over 300 associations. My father founded two liberal associations, the Jahn Gymnastics Club and the Aussig Rowing Club. He himself was a member of the 'Schlaraffia', a Jewish-influenced lodge, whose members met for highly secret meetings and greeted one another meaningfully with the word 'Lulu'. There were also many political associations, and in some places the mood in German areas of Czechoslovakia degenerated into an oppressive chauvinism. The social democrats, who had got a good half of the votes in the local elections in 1919, lost their appeal. Six years later more people in Aussig voted for the National Party and the National Socialists than for the social democrats.

My grandfather was very worried. He was the deputy mayor of Türmitz, and a committed social democrat. Every Sunday morning he invited a dozen men from politics and business to a buffet lunch in his Victorian villa. My grandmother beat thirty eggs in a large bowl and cooked scrambled egg in several frying pans at once. There were also tinned sardines and Hungarian wine. Father always took Marianne and me with him – and Hans, the son of his sister-in-law Hilde. Cousin Hans, a slightly built boy with a fair crop of hair and wise blue eyes, was about the same age as Marianne and was proud to be allowed to escort the Lönhardt girls. Unlike the family he had married into, Hans's father Robert was a strict practising Jew. He observed all the Jewish holy days with great fervour, spending them several times a year with his equally devout widowed mother. He was unbelievably proud of his son Hans, who was always first in his class at school. He always said, 'One day he will be president of Palestine. He's bright enough, and as pious as a rabbi.' With us, Hans was anything but pious. We spent a lot of time together with him, mostly with Grandfather. In the meantime we moved house, and now lived a stone's throw from Grandfather, in a beautiful house with a garden that my father had had built.

Grandad Gustl was the guardian of a little paradise that drew children from all around. He owned a molasses factory, and was always experimenting with fodder mixes for animals and – like Noah – kept at least a pair of every kind of farmyard animal for the purpose: two pigs, two sheep, a bull and a cow, two goats and about 250 hens, a dozen geese, and of course cats and dogs. His garden had 400 gooseberry and 200 raspberry plants, seven plum trees and half a dozen other types of fruit. The shelves in his cellar groaned with cider, plum purée, jams and compôte. As a refrigerator, he had a coffin-like metal container, with a block of ice that was delivered each week.

Grandfather had given us children one of the plum trees. We were allowed to pick the fruit, and could do what we liked with it. 'You can eat it, make jam or sell it to your parents,' he suggested. Most ended up in our stomachs, which blew up like balloons. The rest we converted to money.

Perhaps because my grandfather had accepted me as the child of a divorcee before I was born or because he had thrown himself over me unhesitatingly to protect me from the Italian prisoners of war, or for whatever reason, our relationship was something special. Although a dignified figure with a white beard and always dressed in made-to-measure suits, he remained a lad at heart, and always had some crazy idea or other. Once he pressed lighted candles into the hands of Hans, Marianne and me and fixed a starched handkerchief on the back of his trousers with a safety pin so that it stuck out like a hare's bobtail. Then he dashed around the table shouting, 'Set fire to my snozzle!' We followed him and tried to set his 'snuffer' alight. This went on until Grandmother suddenly appeared in the door and cried out in horror, 'Gustl, are you mad?' 'Why?' he responded, gasping for breath 'We're having a grand old time.'

When Grandpa Gustl went away with his wife Hedwig, and had to leave the dog alone in the house for two days, he took one of the weights from the grandfather clock, and went off to the butcher and got him to cut a chunk of meat of the same weight. He hung it on the clock chain and wound it up as far as it would go, so that the food came into view about eight hours later at the level of the dog's snout. And it worked.

I admired him for his crazy ideas and the natural way he conspired with his grandchildren against the whole world of grown-ups. When my father punished me by withholding pocket money, Grandpa secretly slipped me some. When my parents went to Tunisia for three weeks, I was allowed to stay with my grandparents, and Grandpa Gustl kept me off 'sick' from school for a few days, even though of course I was perfectly well. No one knew; it was one of our many secrets. When I was seven, I wrote a list of my favourite people on a long piece of toilet paper. Toilet paper ranked almost with writing paper in our home, and – sometimes my father's attempt to inculcate modesty went over the top! – we were allowed to use it for its intended purpose only on Sundays. The rest of the week, old newspapers had to do. And so I sat for a long time with the valuable roll in front of me, and struggled to decide whether I should put my mother at number one or my Grandpa Gustl. It seemed something like betrayal when I finally put him at number two.

The buffet lunch at Grandfather's on Sundays was a ritual loved as much by us grandchildren as by our fathers. While world politics was being discussed in front of the fire in the drawing room, Marianne, Hans and I fought over the empty sardine tins in the room next door, and for the privilege of soaking up the remaining oil with bread. The older I got, the more often I listened at the door to hear part of the conversation. I often heard my father's voice standing out, and he spoke differently from the way he spoke to me. His words suddenly had an anxious undertone.

He had changed since his serious illness. Papa had invented various asphalt mixtures and held a number of different chemical patents. He extended his factory every year, and had risked his health for his work. It was still not clear how things would turn out. Lately he had complained of a painful tongue. He must have known what that meant. The chemical industry was associated with a dreadful scourge that was much feared. In the long run, the heavy tar vapours that Father inhaled in his laboratory, working from dawn to dusk on new formulae, were life-threatening. Amazingly, they were then thought of as beneficial to TB sufferers in small doses. We regularly had patients from the chest clinic in the mountains near the Elbe for a week-long cure in the factory, to strengthen their bronchial tubes by breathing in the black fumes.

Eating had been causing my father pain for some time. His tongue had swollen to a thick lump. Eventually he consulted a doctor, who made the devastating diagnosis: cancer of the tongue in the secondary stage. The same day he was sent to a professor in Vienna who was regarded as a leading expert in the field. When we met him at the station on his return, he was terribly disfigured. Metal splints led from his ears into his mouth and ended in two hypodermic needles that were inserted into the tongue on both sides. Behind the ears, the splints, filled with radium, were fixed to the skull.

Father had to wear this radium apparatus for three months. He lay in bed unable to speak, and could take only liquid nourishment. The lymph nodes under his arms had swollen to the size of tennis balls. Sometimes we heard him cry out with pain. When I sat beside his bed, he wrote on a scrap of paper, 'Next time I'd rather kill myself.'

He survived, although he never recovered completely from this ordeal. It also dawned on him at that time that we would one day have to live without him. This worry never left him afterwards – and it was later to prove well-founded.

Even though he tried to hide them, I sensed his dark thoughts. But I didn't ask him about them. There were enough exciting and new things in my life to distract me. At ten, I joined the Falcons, an international socialist youth federation. They were well-disposed to the Jews, and had close links with Jewish-socialist youth organizations all over Europe. We were like Scouts and Guides with political ideals, expressed in various mottos like, 'We say what we think without flinching' or 'We never talk about others behind their backs'. The Falcons in Bohemia tried to awaken class consciousness among working-class youth and opposed the militarism and chauvinism of the post-monarchy period. Political fervour aside, though, they wanted to have fun too. Dressed in uniforms with light- blue shirts and blouses and dark skirts or trousers, we had little feasts by the campfire and three-week long summer trips to Lindau, the Rhineland and Austria. For me this was the essence of adventure and growing up.

A still greater passion was the one I developed for sport. Everyone at that time took part in some kind of collective sport. Most members of the Jahn Gymnastics Association, founded by my father, were Jewish. Anyone who wasn't a Jew was taken to be a socialist. I went there for athletics training. I also joined the Aussig rowing club. Our club HQ was in Wannow on the Elbe – right next to the far more imposing boat-house of the so-called Rowing and Ice-skating Club. And although we shared the same sport, worlds separated us. For even then the rowing club next door did not admit Jews, whereas in our club they were welcome. I was twelve when I began rowing – and as one of three girls infiltrated a male domain. Once a week we met for training in the boat-house by the Elbe. In the fours we rowed around the broad bends of the Elbe, with Schreckenstein Castle, perched on a sandstone rock, rising up above. We passed the great pleasure steamers bound for the harbour at Aussig, the huge barges and the rafts made up of tree trunks. On the way we stopped to rest at a little inn on the banks of the river that had the best ice-cream in Bohemia. We occasionally also stopped at one of the straw-berry fields, picking a few pounds of fruit and squashing at least as much again. At weekends we rowed longer stretches, either downstream to the German border or upstream to Melnik. Overnight we stayed in youth hostels.

And of course the first exciting encounters with the other sex were in the offing. Unfortunately, the boys who liked me were ones I just saw as club chums. Then there was Herbert, a handsome lad who seemed to pick out fastidiously those few words he deigned to utter, exuding as he did so an air of almost casual superiority that always filled me with languid feelings. But this Adonis completely ignored me.

I had already had my first kiss at thirteen. The young gentleman was called Erich Fischer, the red-headed son of a professor from Dresden covered in freckles, whom I had got to know on one of the trips with the Falcons. This red falcon sent glowing letters to me at home. I wasn't especially in love, but it seemed to me a sign of maturity.

A few weeks before my eighteenth birthday, my child-hood, which until then had had relatively few problems, came to a rude end. On the evening of 6 November 1932, we all gathered by the new radio in the living room, my parents, grandparents and Marianne, who was for once allowed to stay up. Following a vote of no confidence, there were new elections for the German Reichstag. 'Today,' my father announced with what at the time I thought exaggerated pathos, 'will decide our future.'

We received the German radio, which was then still allowed. Accompanied by constant crackling, the tense voice of the announcer came through the aether with the first results. My father suddenly began to count up like crazy, jotted down columns of numbers on a pad, noting the percentages for the Nazis and the votes for the social democrats. He so dearly wanted Germany, where there were almost daily bloody clashes between the National Socialists and supporters of left-wing parties, to come to its senses. No chance! True, the Nazi Party had lost a good 4 per cent of its votes, but it remained the largest party. A third of Germans had voted for Adolf Hitler.

Father got up from his chair, suddenly unusually weary, and with a tired movement switched off the bakelite receiver. For a moment there was silence. No one said a word, and Marianne pressed herself closer to my mother and me. 'That', said my father finally, 'is the end of us.'

2 Gathering Clouds

When I go into my living room in the morning she is already there. She has always been there. Her picture has hung for many years in the same place above my small desk. I have the impression she looks down on me and on my life, laid out before her in a glass display case. In the picture she is a young girl. She has a pretty face, but on some days her eyes look strangely weary, and too sad for her age. Sometimes I think I detect a sceptical expression, at others a hint of boredom. But perhaps I imagine it, and these are just blurred images that one projects on to the screen of one's own life.

The girl is me. I was twenty when Malva Schalek drew this pastel portrait of me. It was in the summer of 1935, and the coppery light of late afternoon flooded our conservatory, as I sat, perched on a stool, and tried to gaze fixedly at nothing. Was there anything duller than sitting for a portrait? I wasn't allowed to talk, and the artist herself said nothing. My parents had wanted to have this picture of me, and Malva wanted to repay their hospitality for having her stay with us for several weeks.

She was our house guest on and off in summer, when she travelled from Vienna to Aussig with her easel, brushes, crayons and oil paints to spend the humid time of year in the cool valleys around the Elbe. Malva was a cousin of my mother's. Her mother Balduine was the oldest sister of my Grandma Hedwig. Malva's uncle, Joseph Simon, a brother of my grandmother, had helped her set up in Vienna at the beginning of the century. Peppi, as we all called him, moved in the best circles. He had been the banker of Katharina Schratt, the actress from the court theatre and mistress of the Emperor Franz Joseph, and had become the owner of the Theater an der Wien. He was not only a close friend of Johann

Strauss; in 1887, when Strauss was married for the third time, to Adèle Deutsch, Joseph's sister-in-law, the two became related by marriage. These family links would prove important for me too, many years after Peppi's death.

Peppi had at that time set up a studio for his niece, Malva, in the attic of his theatre and introduced her to Vienna society. Malva soon made a name for herself with her portraits and interior scenes. She did portraits of many families of the Jewish *haute bourgeoisie*, and painted a picture of the boudoir of Katharina Schratt that still hangs in the old Town Hall in Vienna.

I remember Malva as a modest, introverted person; she spoke little, and in practical, everyday matters she showed an almost touching helplessness. She had a stomach complaint, and always had to follow a careful diet, and when, as often happened, we were invited somewhere, she left most of her food untouched. Our cook prepared light meals for her and put her food through a mincer so that it was easier to digest.

Abstemious in her personal life, in which she had no place for a man, she gave herself totally to her art. She preferred doing portraits of children. She painted my sister Marianne, the children of many of my parents' friends and the offspring of the Petschek and Weinmann families, the two wealthiest Jewish families in Aussig. It was in her pictures that Malva, a person of few words, found a free and rich language that caught the particular characteristics of her subjects, handled their feelings with empathy without exposing their inner life. Malva's portraits of my mother and Grandpa Gustl hang in my entrance hall, that of Uncle Herbert, my mother's youngest brother, in my living room. Sometimes, looking at these pictures, one feels that they conceal emotions, like memories of times shared with those who are long dead.

Malva portrayed a Jewish middle-class world, with its pride in status often achieved through much effort and with its supposedly successful assimilation into wider society. Many of her sitters she was to draw again later in another place, in the concentration camp in Theresienstadt, where she was deported in 1942. Grandma Hedwig was also taken there with her younger brother Armin; likewise Aunt Wog and Uncle Otto, my father's brother and sister.

No one could foresee all this in 1933. Should one hold it against people that they trust in what is good, and hope it will see them through dark, troubled times? My father, ever the sceptic, was branded a pessimist. 'Fritz, you see everything too black,' they said, trying to appease him. So often when he spent the evenings or Sunday lunch-times eating with friends and family, he spoke passionately about how he saw the future. While the others wavered between disbelief and confidence, he had begun to change the way he planned his life – and mine.

My father looked at Germany where, just two hours away by train, the thin veneer of civilization had cracked, with such apparent lack of resistance that I cannot understand it to this day. In April 1933 a boycott started of Jewish shops, doctors and lawyers. Non-Jews who ignored it had to reckon with being punished. In May the books of Jewish authors and opponents of the regime were publicly burned in Berlin and other university cities. In June the Social Democratic Party was banned, and its entire assets confiscated, while SPD members were banned from professional employment. A part of the SPD leadership fled to exile in Prague. In Germany there was only one political party: the NSDAP.

National socialist mentality did not stop at frontiers. It existed in Czechoslovakia too, being organized at first in the DNSAP and the Deutschnationale Partei. Both parties were banned by the Prague government in autumn 1933. It was even forbidden to listen to German radio in Czechoslovakia. But the Nazis soon found a new cover. On 1 October the former PE teacher Konrad Henlein founded the 'Sudeten German Homeland Front'. Many officials of the forbidden Nazi parties were involved in its foundation, and of course took their followers with them. 'Henlein', said my grandfather, 'is a very evil character. He will sow discord between Germans and Czechs.'

After 1918, when the Czechoslovak republic allotted the Germans of Bohemia and Moravia minority status, the term 'Sudeten German' soon became a political concept. Although most of the Germans in Czechoslovakia had no connection with the Sudetes, middle-sized mountains in the borderland between Silesia and Bohemia, those from the Erzgebirge and the Elbe valley, from northern Bohemia and northern Moravia, and those from the area around Eger and from southern Moravia, all included themselves under this heading. What had initially denoted more a cultural identity increasingly developed into a unifying national movement after Hitler came to power. When this later on grew into a nationalistic frenzy, it made the Jews strangers in their own country.

At first the lines of division were concealed. In our German Reform Realgymnasium for Girls, non-Jewish pupils sometimes demonstratively sat apart from girls who came from homes where the parents were Jews or socialists. We knew that two of the teachers did not like Jews, so we avoided them as far as possible, as we did classmates who suddenly took to wearing knee-length white socks. One of these had always invited me for her birthday up to then – and it was obvious why she didn't any more.

'Perhaps we should buy white socks too,' I said bitterly to my friend Traute Fehres, who was from a family of committed socialists. 'Forget it,' said Traute, 'I bet you there are no more to be had in the whole of Aussig.'

The white socks were a sign of nationalistic sympathies. Even the members of the German Gymnastics Association of Aussig, which the Czechs had banned for a while, wore them with their grey suits. Jews were of course barred from this association, which none of us had any wish to join anyway. We avoided them, as we avoided those bars and shops in Aussig that we knew were frequented by Nazis. In this way – or so it seemed on the surface at least – we could go on living reasonably, because in Bohemia anti-Semitism did not flare up wildly the way it did in Austria, for example. It was more a case of small smouldering fires, which many hoped would one day peter out of their own accord. Until then, one had just to keep away from them.

My father did not share this view. I recall how I came home from school one Wednesday in the summer of 1934. It wasn't an ordinary day because in the morning I had sat the last exams for my school leaving certificate. In a few weeks I would at last have my matriculation certificate. Life had seldom seemed so full of promise as on that day. It was as though I was standing on a station with a large suitcase, with thousands of lines leading in every direction under the sun, and could board any train, change where I wanted, travel hither and thither as I chose. I felt inexpressibly free.

My first destination was clear. I wanted to go to Prague, that vibrant city, and study medicine at the German university. Even as a child, I had always wanted to be a doctor. Poor Marianne had to play at being a patient countless times so that I could play the doctor, putting bandages on her and covering her caringly with sticking plasters. The subject interested me as much as the idea of helping people. I already had the desire to make things all right. Perhaps also to help myself, because as I was often told, almost as a reproach, I empathized too much with the misery of others. Unfortunately I have never really overcome this.

At the age of twelve I had stopped eating meat. The sight of dead hares and ducks which my father's business associates brought back from hunting and hung in our cellar repelled me. Father was incensed at my boycott of meat. At home we didn't eat kosher, let alone go without meat. My mother, though, had some understanding and also the diplomatic skill to sell my vegetarianism to my father as a decision that would benefit my health, as all the meat he indulged in just didn't agree so well with Marianne and me. My favourite food from then on was apricot dumplings with brown melted butter, sugar and cinnamon.

I was supposed to have this on my last day at school that Wednesday. 'Your mother is doing your favourite,' said my father as he welcomed me home. 'We'll eat it together, and then you and I will go somewhere in private because I have to talk to you.' I sensed that somehow his words lay heavy on his tongue, and that he was having to force them out. What was going on? What had happened?

I ran into the kitchen. Mother embraced me as best she could with her hands covered in dough. 'Would you like to help me, Ilsuschka?' she asked. 'It will speed things up. Marianne should be here in a moment.' While we wrapped the pitted apricots in little balls of dough, I told her for the hundredth time of my high-flown plans in Prague. My mother was always like a friend with whom I shared secrets that my father must never know. Her goodness and her understanding for the sensibilities of growing girls had made her my ally. She knew about unhappy infatuations and being kissed for the first time, about problems at school or quarrels with friends. Today, though, she was strangely quiet. When I tried to find out from her what Papa wanted from me, she was evasive. The big decisions – we were still living in a patriarchal world – were the man's province. Like most clever women, my mother knew how to influence my father behind the scenes, often so subtly that he didn't notice. But to all appearances, he decided.

As we ate and talked about all sorts of unimportant things, the room was electrically charged with my parents' tension. Eventually Father and I withdrew to the living room. This was also our music room. I had learned to play the piano on the baby grand that stood there, and Mother had many times accompanied me on the guitar and sung at the same time. She had a beautiful soprano voice that sounded through the whole house. But at this moment a depressing silence dominated the room, broken only by the rhythmic ticking of the grandfather clock. At last, Father cleared his throat and started to wrest the words one at a time from his throat. His words were like exploding shells, and left my dreams in ruins.

'I know what studying medicine means to you, and that I have promised to support you,' he said. 'But times are too uncertain for us to do what we want. Medical studies last at least five years, and no one can say what will happen in that time. This Hitler may get up to anything. We must think of our future, Ilse. You have a young mother and a little sister. I am old, and no longer very healthy. I don't know how long I can keep running the factory. I need you here. You may have to take it over very soon.'

His words resounded painfully in my ears. It was as though I suddenly had a deep hole in my tummy, and some alien force was forcing the air from my body. My medical studies had shrunk to a year's training in a bilingual commercial school in Prague that my father had chosen. Instead of medicine, I was to study bookkeeping and the basics of business management. Instead of dealing with people, I would have to handle numbers. I didn't know whether I was more shocked by my dearest dream being shattered or by Father's preparing to bow out. I couldn't stop crying.

'Ilsuschka,' said my father, almost pleading, 'you know how terribly difficult this decision has been for your mother and me. I really wanted you to have a wonderful time being a student and enjoy having freedom from worries. You are really much too young to take on these burdens. But the times we live in take no account of this. We must all take on responsibilities that aren't to our liking.'

I could only sob, and Father tried to comfort me. 'But you will still have complete freedom in Prague. You can find yourself a little apartment, and I'll give you whatever money you need. You can go the theatre, buy yourself nice clothes and enjoy life. So you'll still have a wonderful time for your year there, I'm sure.'

He was right about that at least. That year in Prague was my best year. And looking back, I am even grateful to my father for upsetting my plans. It brought me more that was valuable for my life.

It is worst for those who stay behind. Marianne especially was a bundle of misery as she helped me pack. Although our ages were so different, and we were really only half-sisters, we were bound by something more than sisterly love. Whenever I had been able, I took Marianne with me. I had taught her to ski, to swim and to row. Now I was going to learn to drive, and of course Marianne came too. Cars in those days were gawped at like rare visitors from a future world, with a mixture of disapproval and respect. My parents did not feel confident enough to learn to drive one of these hellish vehicles, but thought it would be sensible to get one. And so my father decided I should have driving lessons. I was very proud about this – after all, I was the first woman in Türmitz to pass the driving test. Hugo, the husband of my cousin Dorothea, gave me my first private lessons. He was as laid back as he was daring in all he did, crazy about anything technical and a passionate glider pilot who did not know what fear was. This caused a certain amount of head-shaking in the family. Father had bought a Praga Grand, an eight-cylinder dark blue four-door model with a white steering wheel. Under Hugo's guidance I practised wobbly turns around the factory yard. Marianne had clambered into the back, and waved excitedly out of the window. The sound of a big powerful car in those days still caused a stir. Mother wasn't at all happy seeing Marianne perched there on the rear seat. 'Get out of there, child,' she called out, adding half seriously, 'I don't want to lose both of you.'

'But Mummy,' she called back without a care, as though it was the most natural thing in the world, 'if Ilse dies, I want to die too.' She meant it seriously. Later, when it was really a matter of life and death, she uttered this sentence many times.

I think that at that time neither of us had any sense of what threatened us. Being young often provides a protection from fear.

After my initial dismay, I also had some positive feelings at the prospect of becoming to some extent independent. Leaving was made easier by the fact that I was able to move in with Traute Fehres, my old schoolmate and close friend. We went to the same commercial school in Bergmanngasse and lived as sub-tenants with a Jewish widow in a pretty art nouveau building not far from the Altstädter Ring.

Traute was my closest friend in those days. She had the mind of an intellectual, the heart of a socialist and the integrity of a politically aware young woman. With the same eagerness with which she immersed herself in books, she engaged in debates long into the night, until her face glowed and her voice croaked. I have never met anyone whose name so aptly described them. Traute, as her name suggests in German, was courageous. But for her boldness, I would never have passed my matriculation in maths. She was brilliant with numbers She sat at the desk in front of me in the exam and scratched the answers to the hardest problems on a wooden trigonometry triangle that she dropped on the floor. She had the wit to include a few little mistakes, so that I wouldn't arouse suspicion by my unwittingly brilliant performance. No one noticed, and I got a three. But it could all have gone wrong, and both of us would have been failed.

Traute regarded doing things for her friends as being as natural as standing up for her opinions. When some of my fellow pupils went out of their way to avoid me, she challenged them. 'What's the matter?' she asked. 'Are Jews suddenly not pcoplc any morc?' Four years later exclusion became a reality anyway. From the autumn of 1938 Jewish pupils were banned from the Aussig Gymnasium and the Reform Gymnasium for Girls, and all Jewish teachers were dismissed.

Traute was not Jewish. Her ancestors were from Hungary, and from them she had her creamy-white freckled skin and jet-black hair, which she wore bobbed and cut as straight as a ruler, giving her a rather severe appearance. We two complemented one another. While Traute followed her crystal-clear intellect, I was already the sort of person whose heart quickly overflows. Probably that was why we got on so very well.

After one or two months in which I got used to living in the wonderful cosmopolitan and fun-loving city of Prague, I met through a mutual friend a young man from Moravia. He came from a very poor background. His father was a postman in Olmütz. Kurt – that was his name – had been outstanding at school, and had got a scholarship to study medicine at the German University in Prague. He was my first great love. In my eyes he was not only the best-looking chap for miles around; despite not yet having overcome his humble origins, he radiated a devil-may-care attitude. His laugh was confident, and his humour had a sharp tongue. When Kurt recounted the medical lectures, embellishing every detail for my benefit, I sank my head on his lap and listened to all his knowledge. That must have been what attracted me to him so particularly. His knowledge of the important things in life. About kissing, for example. Kurt could kiss better than anyone else, of that I was absolutely sure – although my experience was not really such as to permit a statistical analysis.

Kurt and I went out a lot, to the theatre, the cinema or dancing, and I gradually realized what sparkle a large city has to offer. How happy I was! I didn't ever want to leave Prague. When I went home by train to Aussig every other weekend, Kurt sent telegrams after me. Once my father absent-mindedly opened one of these amorous messages, thinking the envelope was addressed to him. 'I love you!' was the yearning message. 'I can hardly wait to hold you in my arms again.' Father was speechless with horror, but my mother was able to calm him down. I kept to the promise that I made before leaving again for Prague: 'Kissing is OK. Everything else is taboo.' Today that is a laughable anachronism, but then it was the accepted morality.

Poor Kurt. Even though we pursued the taboo to its limits, the waiting must somehow have caused his moral sense to crumble, because during an internship in a sanatorium outside Prague, he started a relationship with his boss's wife. I couldn't really be angry with him when, contrite with shame, he confessed this to me after the inter-semester break. 'You must have suffered a lot,' I told him. But from then on our relationship was different, and more one of friendship.

My parents often visited me in Prague. Father frequently had business there, and usually took Mother with him. A business friend of my father's called Eugen Fleischner regularly invited me to his home. He was a chemist, and had developed several patented inventions with my father, but he was considerably wealthier than my parents and a man of striking generosity. He had once given my mother a valuable handbag of crocodile skin with a golden clasp, which she carried only on special occasions. Fleischner and his wife Lilly, who was a good twenty years younger, moved in elevated social circles. Dinner parties at their house had more the character of an intellectual salon, and I was always excited when they invited me.

I once sat opposite a man who I felt was constantly looking at me. His face had furrows that suggested experience of life. Deep wrinkles ran from his nose to the corners of his mouth. I judged he was in his late forties. His eyes were a kaleidoscopic mix of emotional states, now piercing and challenging, mischievous for a moment, then wise or angry. He was a great storyteller, and spoke with authority on art, literature and politics, and about journeys to countries in North Africa and the Middle East whose names I hardly knew. He was introduced to me as Oskar Kokoschka.

He had once been in Aussig, he told me later as the guests were taking coffee in the drawing room and he had sat down beside me. Kokoschka had moved from Vienna to Prague in September 1934. Since 1933 the town had been a centre for German intellectuals, for numerous journalists, artists and those in political opposition, such as the whole leadership of the Social Democratic Party. They used to meet in the Café

Continental, where there were piles of German newspapers and a German-speaking waiter called Gustav. For most of the emigrants, who no longer had any income, money soon became very tight. Oskar Kokoschka, however, who was to paint the aged President Tomas Masaryk, was almost lionized as one of the most famous guests. He had accepted a professorship at the Academy and set up a studio not far from the Charles Bridge. At that time he was not yet married to Olda.

'You have a special face,' he said to me straight out. 'I would like to paint it.' I was taken aback and at the same time flattered, and of course I would have liked to say yes straight away. But I had been strictly brought up, so I told Kokoschka I must first ask my father's permission.

'Give him a call,' said Egon Fleischner. 'He won't mind.' Households like that naturally had a telephone, so I called my father and and told him brashly I wouldn't be home that weekend because Herr Kokoschka wanted me to go to his studio. 'Are you crazy?', yelled my father into the phone. 'Just forget it. You know what painters get up to with their models. Come home straight away, or I'll come and fetch you!'

And so I have to thank my father's moral concern for the fact that the portrait by Kokoschka never came about. Some months later I was allowed to sit for Malva Schalek. The foregoing may account for a certain expression of boredom in my face in this picture. That and a feeling of melancholy, because when the picture was done, in the summer of 1935, my time in Prague was coming to an end. The days that went past in a whirl and the nights I danced through were numbered.

My father probably found it harder to impose this burden on me than I did to shoulder it, and had devised a compromise to soften the blow. Before I began in the factory, I was to take a six-month course in first aid offered by the Czech Red Cross that had been advertised in the press. Its main stress reflected the times: the treatment of war-wounded. We were taught how to deal with shot wounds and burns, apply splints to fractures, put on bandages and staunch heavy bleeding. I can't say that I thought much about wounded soldiers as we practised with healthy subjects or dolls. In my mind all that was quite remote, repressed, and overlaid by my great enthusiasm for medicine.

25

After finishing the course I worked part-time as a nurse in the Aussig regional hospital. At lunchtime I cycled to my father's factory and spent the afternoon in the office. And so my day was divided between inclination and duty; in the mornings I smelt of ether, in the afternoons of tar. At the hospital I worked in the dermatology department. I was allowed to give injections, take pulses and set up needles for infusions. In the first week or so I happened to walk into a section from which there came the sound of singing and laughter. A dozen or so pretty young women were sitting around on unmade beds, laughing, playing cards and smoking. I had not the slightest idea where I was, but started conscientiously making the beds and gathering up the dirty crockery. 'That's nice of you,' said one of the women. 'Would you mind cooking us a little something?' joked another, and the others joined in the giggling.

Suddenly a hand grabbed me, and I was dragged from the room. 'Are you crazy?' barked the sister. 'That's the closed VD ward.' I have never since been in a hospital ward where there was such zest for life.

I can't say I found this divided life disagreeable. The work in the hospital was fun, and I even took increasing pleasure in my duties at the factory. I had my family and friends around me. Sometimes, if one shut one's eyes to what was happening in the world, one could imagine that this idyllic life would outlast everything.

It was winter, and the countryside had a merciful covering of snow, which turned even ugly factory landscapes into an attractive view. I went skiing with friends in the Erzgebirge. We went by tram to Tellnitz and from there climbed with our skis over our shoulders. In those days, skiing was a rather bolder undertaking than today, as there were no ski-lifts and of course no mountain rescue service. Once I came across an injured skier lying on the ground surrounded by a few winter sports enthusiasts. He had an open fracture. The wound looked dreadful, and made me aware for the first time what it would be like actually to deal with casualties in wartime. I suppressed my feelings of nausea and, helped by a friend, tried to put the leg into a splint, using a thick branch of wood and a shirt torn in strips, so that the patient could be transported.

A few days later I visited the young man in his hospital ward. I was in the building anyway. There he lay on his covers, the leg set in plaster and raised up high on the fracture bed. As he saw me his eyes took on a glassy look. I was wondering whether it could be from the painkillers he had no doubt been given when, with reddened face, he confessed a secret. He had fallen in love with me on the spot, he revealed to me, and it was Fate that had brought us together. 'Ilse,' he said after a pause in which he screwed up all his courage, 'Would you be my wife?'

What should one say? Situations sometimes call for unusual decisiveness. In this bed-bound case his motivation was surely different from that of Otto Pospischel, who was also crazily resolved to lead me to the altar. He was not in love with me, and I had for my part seen him only as a decent friend. Otto was a good-looking, well-built fellow, always with a tan and thoughtful-looking nickel-framed spectacles that did not go with the peasant *Lederhosen* he liked to wear. He was four years older than me, and an employee in one of the Aussig factories that processed coal. We rowed and skied together and discussed politics for hours. As a convinced socialist, Otto regularly attended political meetings and often came out with gloomy forecasts of the future.

'The devil is on the loose in Germany,' said Otto. It was autumn 1935, and Hitler had passed the Nuremberg laws, which definitively and officially categorized the Jews as sub-human. Shortly before, marriage between Jews and non-Jews had been forbidden.

Otto asked to talk to my father man-to-man. 'I don't love your daughter,' he told my bewildered father, 'but I want to ask for her hand. I'm not Jewish, and our marriage would protect Ilse. We like one another, we respect one another, and we share many interests, and that is not a bad basis for a good marriage.' My father must have been deeply moved. 'I respect what you say,' he told Otto. 'Your motives are fine and noble.' He would ask me, he promised, and this he did. In his heart he must have known that I would decline. Even if romance was an inappropriate luxury in such times, for me there could only be one reason to marry: love, what else?

Kurt, my erstwhile great love, maintained a touching

devotion as a friend and visited me regularly in Aussig. He had been called up for the Czechoslovak army, which had started mobilizing. In response to the growing German threat, weapons were modernized and frontier fortifications extended. It was terribly late, though, and the gaps in defence from years of cuts and shortcomings in the army could not be put right overnight. Czech strength did not match the German, although the once derided Czechoslovak army enjoyed notably more respect than it had done, and people now responded extremely generously to calls for donations for military spending.

Kurt was proud to be a soldier. The first time he stood in front of me in his army uniform, with that unshaken winning smile in his suddenly inappropriately young face, I felt quite different. It seemed that for him it was all a game, an adventure, but in fact it had already become deadly earnest. The Czechs had started to build bunkers at various places in the Elbe valley. In autumn 1936 the people were ordered to clear junk from their attics as protection against air attacks. An office of the air defence command was set up in the old commercial school building in Aussig. The first air raid practice took place in Aussig in March 1937. The wailing of the sirens shattered the peace of the evening. We had to darken our windows, and not the tiniest slit of light was allowed to show outside.

The situation became tenser. Czechoslovakia was under increasing internal and external pressure. Inside the country the spokesman of the Sudeten Germans, Konrad Henlein, exploited the Germans' suspicions of the government in Prague. The Germans were most affected by the great economic crisis, and made up two-thirds of the unemployed. Many of the three and a half million Germans living in Czechoslovakia felt themselves increasingly cheated and marginalized by the government, which was certainly hardly willing to make any concessions. The understandable discontent came gradually to be associated, though, with a new mood of chauvinistic arrogance, which Hitler was able to promote from outside by transferring huge amounts of money to the SDP, the 'Sudeten German Party', as the Heimatfront had called itself since 1935, and financing its election campaigns. My grandfather, a long time social democrat, had seen Henlein as 'Hitler's willing instrument' from the very beginning, adding, 'And I'm afraid the Germans here at home won't hold it against him.'

Sadly, he was right. In the parliamentary elections of May 1935, two-thirds of the German seats had gone to the SdP, and the German Social Democrats lost half of their votes. The SdP had won almost 60 per cent of the votes in Aussig. Grandfather's appearance became as chalky white as his beard. He crept about like a beaten dog; all his childlike lack of concern, which had struggled against his feelings of unease, was gone. He was frightened by the breathless, ill-tempered insanity that had suddenly possessed the masses. 'The Germans are choosing their executioner,' he said.

The Sudeten German position was championed especially by the gymnastics clubs. After all, Henlein himself was a PE teacher from Asch. The gymnastics movement was well known for its anti-semitism. The German Gymnastics Association had adopted an Aryan provision in its constitution long before Hitler's takeover of power. As early as 1929 Henlein had led an anti-Semitic demonstration in Asch organized in part by the gymnastics movement. At that time he held the office of a 'Dietwart' – the name the Nazis gave to the ideological commissars responsible for promoting national socialist thinking and behaviour in the associations, and which every German sports association was obliged to appoint from 1934 onwards. However, because he feared an official ban on his party, Henlein took care not to express his hostility to the Jews openly. In July 1937 the German Gymnastics Association's 'Education Conference' took place in Aussig. 'Gymnasts' Rally' was what they called this event, where sporting competition was mixed with political propaganda. It was held at the Aussig athletics field, where there was a cinder track adjoining an open-air meeting place. There one got a foretaste of what was to come, of how boys and girls were to be brought up in a *völkisch* spirit. The sight of male and female gymnasts standing in stiffly erect rows was like that in the country next door. There was a great variety of competitive events and an exhibition called 'Gymnastics and the *Volk*'. In those days I was very keen on sport, and trained almost every day, but this kind of gymnastics movement, stoked up by a vague and confused *volk* mythology and putting 'discipline over the body' above intellectual development, I found quite grotesque. I did not realisze that this would be the last such event before the 'Anschluss'.

'Anschluss' – the word made us shudder. It occurred more and more often in Henlein's speeches. 'I just don't understand these people,' said my father from the outset. 'Why are they so set on joining this inhuman system? What do they expect from it?' But wasn't it anyway just a silly fantasy? I can still hear Aunt Olga, my father's sister, snorting in a tone of utter conviction: 'They wouldn't dare invade Czechoslovakia. And France and England wouldn't stand by and let them do it.'

How wrong she was! How dearly she – and countless thousands of others – paid for their mistaken belief. When Hitler marched into Vienna in March 1938, annexing Austria in a sudden coup, and racial hatred and terror broke over the land, it hit us like a shot in the neck. Malva Schalek left Vienna in great haste, leaving most of her pictures in her studio, and fled with Emma Richter, the mother of my Uncle Oswald, to Leitmeritz in Bohemia. In Vienna the Nazis arrested Oswald Richter, a respected social democrat, immediately after the 'Anschluss', and he had been in one of the first transports to Dachau concentration camp. Since then there had been no news of him.

In the last few weeks deep lines had come to mark worry in my parents' faces. I often heard them in conversation at night. One morning Father remained sitting longer than usual after breakfast, instead of, as he often did, setting off at first light at the same time as his workers at the factory. Dark shadows huddled under his eyes, his face looked pale and tired. Without realizing it, he screwed his hands into fists so that the bones shone white through the skin. The previous night, he had decided to turn his back on all that he had worked to build up. 'We have to get away from here,' he said, his voice so flat that it sounded as though he was speaking through a thick wall. 'We must get out as quickly as possible.' Mother tried once more to argue with him, as I am sure she had all night. 'Why should we leave a country', she said, 'to which Jews from Austria are fleeing in their thousands? This is where we are safest.'

My father shook his head, sunk in thought 'Even if we weren't threatened by a German invasion, their evil spirit is all over the country,' he said. 'It has crossed the border already, and has captured people's minds. Just look at them yelling for Hitler. They want to "go back home to the Reich". Are they out of their minds?'

It seemed so. On 1 May 1938, 70,000 people gathered in the marketplace in Aussig for the mass meeting of the Sudeten German Party. The square was black with them. They were greeted from the balcony of the Café Falk by the local SdP leader. A speaker hailed the annexation of Austria as the most important historical event of recent times, and a wave of rejoicing swept over the masses. Then Henlein came to the microphone, and applause broke out. The ethnic Germans, he yelled, have a basic right to proclaim their attachment to Germanness and to the German world outlook.

Grandfather had been that morning to the May Day rally of the social democrats, and they had joined with the communists and the Czechs of Aussig in front of the local government offices. The mayor of Aussig, Leopold Pölzl, had spoken, and called for peaceful coexistence between Czechs and Germans. Grandfather had applauded loudly but must have felt more like clasping his hands over his head in despair.

For the masses had long shouted down those who had warned or had called for moderation. In the council elections of May 1938 over 86 per cent of the Germans voted for the SdP, and the social democrats suffered their biggest defeat until then. The day before the election, a state of emergency was declared in Aussig. Czech soldiers appeared at many street corners, and the works of the 'Association for Chemical and Metallurgical Production' were occupied by members of the Czech National Guard. Gendarmes had taken up positions on the commanding high ground, on the Ferdinandshöhe and the Holomirsche. Reservists were called up, and explosive charges were placed on both the old and new bridges over the Elbe. Roadblocks and barriers were set up in the hills around.

Danger hung over our town like the sulphurous cloud from the factory chimneys. We could not go out after sunset as the Czechs feared disturbances, so we stayed within our own four walls, which had suddenly ceased to be 'home'. 'Ilse,' said my father that evening, 'I've been thinking for a long time. It makes no sense for us all to emigrate at once. I'm responsible for eighty-five employees, and I can't abandon them overnight. In any case, who knows whether your mother and I could get visas so quickly?' He took my hands and squeezed them as though to calm himself. 'You must go on ahead of us, Ilsuschka,' he said. 'An educated young woman like you should find it easier to get a work permit abroad. And when you are safe, you can help us get out.'

Marianne sobbed aloud as she heard this. Mother took her in her arms, and then me, and rocked us like small children. None of us could hold back our tears.

When pain is at its worst, one should numb body and soul with work. I still believe this today when dark thoughts assail me. I lose myself in housework or go and do the shopping. Mechanical routine is good for keeping the demons in check. At the time I speak of, once the decision was made and I had accepted it, we threw ourselves into preparing for my departure. Finding a job abroad was easier than expected. Through a friend in Dublin we put a small ad in an Irish daily paper. Although so many other young Jewish women from Germany, Austria and Czechoslovakia were seeking work abroad as housekeepers, cooks or servants to escape the Nazis, I was lucky and quickly had the offer of a job as French-speaking nanny, or 'French governess', in the home of a Jewish business woman in Dublin who was bringing up her children on her own. French I had a good command of – unlike English, which I had given up in grammar school for philosophy. At that time it wouldn't have occurred to anyone that English would one day be critical for a Jew's survival. In the final months before leaving I took weekly private lessons with the English teacher at my old school so as to have at least some basic vocabulary.

Father had meanwhile started preparing himself mentally for winding up the life he had followed until now. 'It would be best if you took our car,' he said, 'before someone else takes it away from us. You could try to sell it afterwards.' But I was afraid of a long car journey, especially as much of it would be through Nazi Germany. A young Jewish woman driving a smart Praga limousine – how far would I be likely to get?

And so we decided I should go by train. Mother got her dressmaker to come to our house every week to equip me with clothes for my new life. As a result, I was rather 'overdressed', as the English say, for a domestic servant. I had an elegant bespoke brown reversible coat padded with camel hair and a lot of fine dresses and costumes. Mother came with me to all the fashion shops in Aussig and bought handkerchiefs, light-coloured leather gloves and two of the hats that were then mandatory. Sometimes, as if from the perspective of someone not involved, I detected in all our activity something of fear and despair below the surface. Inwardly I sensed, or at least feared, that I would never see my home town again. I was being ejected from my life as it had been until then, and was trying to cram it all into a single suitcase, as though the happiness I had known and the comfort I had enjoyed could be sewn into a smart dress. My suitcase was far too small for all those things that were important to me. Kurt's love letters must go in, along with books by Kurt Tucholsky, Thomas Mann and Heinrich Heine, family photos, samples of Marianne's school handiwork and some of Grandfather's plum compôte. Basically I wanted to take them all – everything that I loved, and now had to leave them behind with no certainty when I should see them again. This uncertainty upset me more than having to leave.

On 13 August 1938 we celebrated my father's sixtieth birthday. All our relatives came: Father's brothers and his sister Olga, the parents-in-law, my mother's four siblings and their families, and of course my grandparents. It was a sad event. No one was in a mood to celebrate. Uncle Herbert, my mother's younger brother, and his wife sat side by side as though they were carved from ice. She was not Jewish, and since she sympathized openly with the Nazis, all warm feelings between them had gone. A little while later she was to divorce Uncle Herbert, and so sign his death warrant.

Aunt Olga was also married to a Catholic, although it must be said very happily. Perhaps that gave her a greater sense of security, but in any event she doubted it was the right decision, 'to send the poor child on her own to Ireland'. I would be the first in the family to leave the country. Olga's daughters, Hilde and Dorothea, seven and ten years older than me, wanted in any case to stay. By the Nazis' reckoning, they were only half Jewish, and Dorle, as Dorothea was called, was also married to a non-Jew, my driving instructor Hugo. The couple already had two young daughters, Brigitte and Renate. No, they felt no need to leave the country. 'Ilse will cope with it all bravely,' said my father, and stroked my hair. I think he was trying to give himself heart as he did this, as the time for us to say goodbye was getting close.

A week later it had come. My parents and Marianne travelled with me by train as far as the German frontier. After Bodenbach my train entered Germany. We had just a short time to say farewell on the platform. I felt quite sick with worry. Marianne cried all the time, and Mother murmured advice on every conceivable topic through her tears. I should be sure to eat enough, to write every other day, keep learning English, be really helpful to my employer and not to worry: we would all be together again very soon. Marianne clung to me. 'Ische,' she said to me – only she called me that – 'I shall count the days until I see you again. And I'm sure that will be soon.' Father was silent a long while. He rocked me in his arms and kissed me on the head, just as he had when he had told me that he was not my real father, but was a father who loved me. The guard's whistle made us jump, and as the train started forward with a jerk, my father stepped up to the lowered window of my compartment again. He had thought of something important. 'Promise me one thing, Ilse,' he panted, as he tried to keep up with the train as it gathered speed. 'Don't ever pluck your eyebrows. They are so dense, and that is a sign of intelligence. They suit your face. Do you promise?'

I promised. And I have kept the promise ever since.

3 Salo Tisch

Recently they played it again on the wireless after a long time and, in an attack of melancholy, to which I find one gets more prone with time, I turned up the sound. I still like the song 'My Heart and I'. Sometimes they broadcast it on the BBC, and most older people in England know the title. It was Fred's biggest hit here. It is almost sixty years since he wrote the words and Richard Tauber first sang it.

I often used to put on Fred's records, but I don't so much these days. For me Fred's music is like other mementos of the past. I keep them handy, carefully arranged and labelled, although being faced with them all the time would be too painful. When one of my relations from Germany, who likes Viennese songs of the 1930s, visited me recently, we dug out the well-worn LP double album, which has stood for ages in the front row next to my old record-player. To get the player going we first had to remove the books I had stacked on it and pull out the rather brittle flex. We turned it on expectantly but it hardly gave a squeak. As though it was tired with age like its owner, the turntable revolved so slowly that the sounds that came out were stretched into an unrecognizable deep murmuring. My visitor worked the few controls but the machine did not respond, as though age had long ago made it forget how to work.

Then suddenly, in a moment, the music inexplicably came back. The voices, a touch too sharp and hurried, as usual with old recordings, came bursting into the room, with the orchestra playing lively waltz, foxtrot and tango rhythms. I sat in my armchair, and my feet began to tap in time as if by remote control. I could sing along, remembering every line, and I did so – smiling while tears ran down my cheeks.

The odd thing is that, although I was never present at a performance in Vienna and I know that time only from Fred's accounts, when I hear operetta music, scenes appear before my eyes like stage sets. I see the actors there acting and singing, the conductor's baton going up and down in the orchestra pit – and I see Fred, or Salo as his real name was, sitting in one of the front rows, outwardly relaxed but inwardly, as I would surely have seen from his eyes, on the point of bursting.

He would probably have listened to the applause more than the music itself, noting whether it was restrained or wildly enthusiastic, overwhelming or polite, whether it began as a storm and ended in a dribble or surged like a mighty wave. Salo Tisch knew all the nuances of applause. And he knew every word that was sung on the stage, because it came from his pen. The young trainee lawyer preferred composing lyrics to drawing up legal documents.

Yet his prospects for a career in the courts were not bad either. He had studied law to please his mother, he told me. It seems to have been her dearest wish that her son should follow an academic career, which would show that, after years of rootlessness, they had established themselves in a foreign country. Isaak and Taube Tisch had left their home town of Tarnow in Galicia with their sons Salomon and Moishe at the start of the First World War, part of the massive migration of Jews from eastern Europe that had started at the end of the nineteenth century, in which thousands flooded to the West, especially to America, but also to Germany, Austria, France and England.

They were known as *Ostjuden*, a label that combined two things that people in the West tried to marginalize: the Jews and the East. Although Germany had brought in many of them to stimulate the war economy, they were not really welcome anywhere. These Jews were alien. They spoke Yiddish among themselves, wore caftans, beards and ringlets on their temples, and had an unwelcome air of poverty and shabbiness.

The agitation against them in the anti-Semitic press in the 1920s only anticipated what was to come years later in the gas chambers. 'Scroungers', 'rabble', 'parasites sucking the marrow of the nation' were the stereotyped clichés that were spread about the Jews from the East. The appearance of 'caftan Jews' in large numbers from Poland, Russia and Galicia even disturbed the assimilated Western, 'tie-wearing' Jews, their alien character reminding them of everything they thought they had overcome. Worlds separated them from the middle-class prosperity of the Western Jews. Many of them were dependent on the vagaries of fate, which accorded them employment, or not, as the case might be. *Luftmenschen* was what they were known as, because they had no apparent means of survival and seemed to live on air.

Unlike their assimilated brethren, the Eastern Jews adhered devoutly to their religious practices. Fred, too, had grown up in an orthodox environment. Jews had lived in Tarnow, his birthplace, since the fifteenth century. They had established their own part of the city, as the Zydowska, the Judenstrasse and Weklarska (Money Changer Street) testify to this day. The male children in the *stettl* were brought up from a young age to study scripture. Religious scholars, the *schejne leit*, enjoyed the greatest respect. Salomon's father was an orthodox Jew, devoted with iron discipline to the study of the torah and attending synagogue. Four of Salomon's uncles were rabbis, and so Salo, as everyone called him, was from infancy on deeply familiar with all the religious rites. Very much later, in advanced manhood, he was to return to this.

As a small child he had attended the *cheder*, the religious school, where boys began as young as three to study the scriptures. Afterwards he switched to a Polish boys' school. He had a 'one' in every subject, even singing and behaviour, except for drawing, in which he got only a two. His father Isaak worked as an accountant, earning a modest salary, making him better off than many of Tarnow's impoverished Jews, who had to get by as small traders, water carriers or junk dealers.

The Tischs left Tarnow not so much to escape poverty, but, like masses of Eastern Jews, to escape the dreadful pogroms that had raged since the start of the century in many Russian and Ukrainian towns, in which thousands of Jewish men, women and children had been murdered.

Isaak Tisch and his family first settled in Holešov in

Moravia, where Salo entered the German elementary school on 28 September 1914. He was put into the second class, when by age he should have been in the fourth. A year later the family moved on to Vienna. They first lived in the Leopoldstadt, the main Jewish quarter, and some time later moved to 78 Vorgartenstrasse in the twentieth district. Isaak Tisch quickly found work as an accountant with the Fanto Oil Company. His son Salo, whose school report was marked 'war refugee', first attended a general elementary school for boys, then spent two years in a Polish Gymnasium before switching in 1919 to the Josef Juranek Realgymnasium in the eighth district, where he matriculated in 1924.

The complete set of school reports that he kept show that Salo always got a 'one' for Religion and Mathematics. Even then, I think, these underpinned his life, with its pattern of constant uprooting and replanting. The logic of the intellect and the comfort of religion formed a sort of handrail that helped steady his inner life. But underlying this was an even greater passion, which he discovered early in life: his enthusiasm for writing and for the theatre.

This, he told me, he had already discovered while at school. Salo joined the theatre club *Schaubühne* in his last year, and his first stage appearance was on the cabaret stage of the Café Prueckel. The year he matriculated, he played Anatol in Arthur Schnitzler's play of that name. Salo's classmate Severin Wallach had taken on the artistic direction. What the two final-year pupils had in common, apart from their amateur status, was a great fascination for the world of the theatre. Everything else, including their final exams, was of secondary importance to them.

Some time earlier Salo had begun writing sketches and articles. He sent a handful of sample texts to the satirical journal *Die Fliegenden Blätter* in Munich, where they were published from time to time over the initials 'S.T.'.

I always admired Fred's language skills, and often wondered how someone who grew up speaking Polish and Yiddish, and had to learn Russian, Latin and French at school, could so easily master Viennese patois and later switch to hitherto alien English humour. He would probably have made a fine barrister, juggling with words, firing off rhetorical salvos or picking his way through a minefield as the situation required.

I still have a notebook of Salo's listing all the lectures he attended. They include the history of Roman and German law, civil law, the law of distraint, family, church, inheritance and international law, psychology and the history of modern philosophy. At the beginning of 1929 he passed his state law exam with merit.

A mother's pride is something I know. When my son Ian graduated in history at Oxford in the early 1980s, it was a further bond with my adopted home. There is reassurance when the next generation puts down roots in soil where their parents are never totally at home. Isaak and Taube Tisch must also have felt it marked their integration into their new world when Salo got his doctorate. At the award ceremony his mother discreetly wiped tears from the corners of her eyes, he told me. 'I always knew you would be a credit to us,' said his father, his face lit up with joy. What had been denied him, his son had achieved apparently without much difficulty.

His doctor title, Fred told me, did not mean very much to him. And yet it formed, it seems, part of an altered identity, one he decided to grace with a different first name. All his life Fred kept all his important papers in a compartmentalized leather case, which I now treat as an archive record of his life. In one compartment I found some visiting cards that he must have had printed soon after getting his doctorate. Thin and hardly half the size of a matchbox label, they recorded Salo's new identity. Above his parents' address he had had printed, black on white, the name: Dr Siegfried Tisch.

I can't ask him now why he had to choose a name that epitomized the heroes of the Germanic sagas. Considering what he suffered at the hands of the Germans, it strikes me as almost macabre. And, although he did show courage and daring in his life, I have difficulty relating it to the name he chose. For me, he was always Salo or Fred.

And so Salo started leading two lives. In the first years after getting his doctorate he worked as a trainee lawyer under his original name. He was able to appear in the commercial court and the district court, and he worked in a legal office on a variety of cases. He told me later that he had dealt with many divorce cases, and had promised himself that he would never, not even if he were very much in love, take on the ties of matrimony. 'This public washing of dirty linen strips people of the last traces of dignity and decency,' he said. In those days, Fred explained, family law allowed for divorce in cases of adultery, refusal to have children, and also irreversible breakdown of a marriage, for example through transgressions resulting from mental disturbance or disease of a repulsive nature. Because the judge's assessment of guilt decided which party would have to pay the other alimony, and how much, the mutual recriminations in the pre-hearing depositions were often totally reckless.

Fred said that he never felt this métier of discord to be his true calling, and he must have been happy that he had long before discovered another field of activity. He spent his last spare money on visiting theatres and cabarets. It was here, in the dimly lit cellars where cabaret was performed and the crystal-lit halls of the great theatres that the world of entertainment beckoned, which after the huge success of Franz Lehár's *Merry Widow* had made it respectable to visit the theatre.

Drawn as if by magic to this world, he was always to be seen in Vienna's coffee houses, frequented as they were by composers and librettists. The Café Bauer or the Imperial, the Café Museum, the Dobner and the Café Sacher near the Opernring were known as operetta exchanges, where librettists tried to market their inspirations, and composers were on the lookout for brilliant stage ideas and publishers for what might be popular successes. In these meeting places, the air thick with cigar smoke and the babble of voices, Salo, the aspiring lawyer, was becoming Siegfried the aspiring lyricist. It was here he got to know the composers Paul Mann and Egon Goldberg, who were also on the threshold of their musical careers. Salo wrote one of his first lyrics for Egon Goldberg while still studying law, in 1928. 'Kein böses Wort will ich sagen,' promised the text – 'nur duldend es tragen, was mir das Schicksal bringt durch dich!' ('I shall say no ill, but patiently bear what Fate brings me through you!') A little later, the simple plea of a song Salo wrote for Goldberg and Mann ran, '*Ich lieb dich doch!*' ('But I do love you!') The score asked the orchestra for a 'gentle blues tempo', to match the sorrows of love that spoke from the lines of the text.

You could call it beginner's luck that Richard Tauber, of all people, took a liking to Salo's song, and recorded it. In those days the celebrity tenor, who crossed the border between classical and light music with his masterly bel canto, was lionized equally in Berlin and Vienna. Tauber had breathed new life into the declining genre of operetta when, attracted by the large fee he was offered, he decided in 1922 to be unfaithful to the opera, and take a guest role in Lehár's *Frasquita* at the Theater an der Wien. This little infidelity became a lifelong affair for which the guardians of high culture never forgave him. He conquered Berlin with Franz Lehár's *Paganini* in 1926, and since then had been celebrated as 'a demigod of song' and 'the man with the golden voice'.

'Ich lieb dich doch!' went on to become one of the most played hits of the season, and from now on Siegfried stuck to matters of the heart – as the rules of the branch required. He wrote at least a dozen dance songs of this type, and they were heard all over Vienna at the time.

They were the last of a wave of pleasure seeking that had broken over the cities of Europe after the deprivations of the First World War, awakening an unprecedented craze for jazz rhythms and Latin American dances. In the evenings orchestras played in the dance halls and bars that had shot up all over Vienna, and the dance floors were crowded with couples dressed up to the nines. The men wore dinner jackets and black patent-leather shoes whose shine rivalled that of their swept-back Brylcreemed hair. The ladies had evening dresses in flowing, clinging materials, with trains and plunging backs with much visible and tangible naked skin. The chin-length hair was pressed into waves that caressed their heads; their lips shone red. They danced the shimmy, the Bummelstep, the foxtrot, the swing and the tango, they laughed and flirted, escaping for an evening from a world whose face was hardening from the pressure of post-war inflation and the worldwide economic crisis. 'The Viennese', Fred always said, 'take pleasure in repressing. No one does it better'.

Salo Tisch danced very little. He preferred to listen to the tunes and words, to see which songs the public were keen on, and which emptied the polished dance floor. He committed all this to memory and took it back to his study in his parents' home, where a growing number of musical magazines and scores lay beside his law books, and where Siegfried the poet was proving more diligent than Salo the lawyer. At nights, while his parents slept, he was forever stealing away to the glittering world of music and show business.

Even then he had an odd way of working. Later on I often teased him by saying I could tell he was Jewish by the way he wrote poetry. 'You always start at the end and work backwards.'

He always began with the final rhyming words. Of these he had a huge stock. It became his habit, whenever he happened to think of good ideas for rhymes, to record them in a small notebook he always kept with him. I still have this little volume from his time in Vienna, in which he wrote in his precise, upwardly sloping hand the rhyming couplets and triplets with a thin pencil on the finely squared paper. 'Arm – warm – Charme' is to be found there, 'Tanzlokal – Damenwahl, – jedes Mal', 'begehrt – verklaert – gewaehrt', 'Gage – Blamage', 'Mangel – Tingeltangel', 'Theater – delikater', 'Hurra – ein A!', 'Monto Carlo's – Inventar los', 'lasziv – naiv', and hundreds more like this. Only the word *Liebe* is not to be found, I expect because Siegfried already knew every conceivable rhyme for it by heart.

Starting at the end of a line, then, he would work backwards to the beginning of the verse, making up a suitable sentence as he went. At first, Fred told me, this phase was a matter of groping his way, but gradually, with more experience, the lines suddenly popped up in a stream, one after the other, verse after verse. Fred first wrote out the draft longhand, deleting and amending repeatedly until, when he was satisfied with the result, he typed it out on his small typewriter.

He wrote 'Gnädige Frau, ich darf Sie nicht lieben' in 1930 to music by Egon Goldberg, and 'In Deinem Blick liegt eine ganze Welt von Liebe' for Hans Kastner. He got to know the Hungarian composer Carlo de Fries, who alternated between Vienna and Budapest. Their collaboration soon became a close friendship, and the tango 'Nehmen wir an, Madame, dass Sie mich lieben' was published two years later in Berlin.

Most successful Viennese lyricists, such as Ludwig Herzer and Fritz Löhner-Beda, Fritz Grünbaum and Béla Jenbach, Alfred Grünwald and Victor Léon, also worked in Berlin. But Salo was almost too late to benefit from the cultural alliance between the two capitals. Only a few months after his debut in Berlin it began to crumble, soon to be wrecked completely for those Hitler declared to be vermin: the Jews.

Nobody, Fred declared, could have imagined that the prospects for Jewish artists in Berlin would change so abruptly. It did not help much that he had changed his Jewish forename to a very Germanic one. Someone called Tisch might just as well be called Rothschild. In short order the Nazis took a stiff iron brush, and made Berlin *judenrein*. Their particular targets were the liberal revues, and even more the influence of Jewish librettists and composers in the world of operetta.

Soon even Richard Tauber was made to realize this. He had contracts for guest appearances in both the Berlin State Theatre and the Vienna State Opera. In Berlin he sang Lehár operettas such as *Paganini, Zarewitsch, Friederieke* and *Land of Smiles* to full houses, while in Vienna he sang in Verdi and Mozart operas. The song 'Dein ist mein ganzes Herz' from *Land of Smiles* made him known all over the world.

He was not at all good-looking. A monocle was jammed in his right eye, the pasty face and the corpulence contained by tightly stretched waistcoats showing how much this man from Linz was devoted to the ample cuisine of old Vienna, especially its pastries. His singing, though, made one forget his visual deficiencies. He sang his way into the hearts of millions, helped by the growth of radio and numerous recordings.

Now overnight, the world star Tauber belonged to the riff-raff. His father, an actor, was a Jew. Just a few weeks after Hitler took power, a few days after the last free elections in early March, he had been prevented from appearing at the Admiralspalast in Berlin. Shortly after, he was stopped entering the Kempinski Hotel and assaulted by a group of Nazi thugs shouting, 'Get out of Berlin, Jew boy!' That night Tauber left for Vienna, not knowing that he would never see the German capital again.

Politics interested Tauber only if it interfered with his one true passion: music. So he sent a submissive letter to the Interior Ministry in Berlin stressing his understanding for the aims of the national government. The reply just announced that because of unresolved tax claims, both the Berlin villas owned by the 'Jewish half-caste Tauber' had been confiscated. For Tauber, as for so many artists, there was no way back.

In Vienna, Tauber, who had long preferred living in a hotel to a private villa, set himself up again in a suite, from where he travelled to engagements in Holland, Sweden, Czechoslovakia and France. He sang in the Vienna State Opera and continued to make records.

The same year, Salo wrote 'Die grosse Liebe gibt es nicht mehr' to music by Egon Goldberg, and Tauber bestowed his melting quality on it. It was not to be the last time that Tisch and Tauber collaborated.

Increasingly Tisch the lyricist, having abandoned law completely, was to be seen in all the right coffee houses, and his face, from whose delicate features the regular lines of youth were just beginning to disappear, was becoming known. Almost all the customers were Jewish – especially the lyricists, but also most of the composers, such as Leo Fall, Herrmann Leopoldi and Emmerich Kálmán. The famous libtrettist Victor Léon once explained why operetta, opera's bargain basement, attracted so many Jewish artists. 'Operetta audiences want to laugh and cry at the same time – and that's what we Jews have been doing since the destruction of Jerusalem 2,000 years ago.'

Many Jews had, like Tauber, to turn their backs for ever on Berlin. Germany began a boycott of Jewish businesses, doctors and lawyers in April 1933. On 1 July, the Berlin State Opera dismissed all non-Aryans. And so began the cultural haemorrhage from which Germany has still to recover. Conductors, music directors, bandleaders, professors, lecturers, actors, sopranos, tenors, orchestral players, theatre and film directors and producers fled – to Vienna, Prague, Paris, London and the USA.

Vienna still held a rich variety. The cultural and intellectual richness that had been extinguished in Berlin still existed there, and it was reflected in lively exchanges with Prague, Paris and Budapest. The spell of this cultural diversity, Fred told me, could blind one to the dehumanizing levelling down going on in neighbouring Germany. In the theatres, bars and dance halls people moved to graceful rhythms, while next door they were marching to the four-square beat of the *Horst Wessel Lied*.

The man Salo met at this time had also returned to Vienna from the cultural desecration in Berlin. They met in a coffee house. Possibly they had been introduced by a mutual friend or one of them had sat where the other was bound to see him. In any case, anyone would have noticed Hans J. Lengsfelder if he had hidden in a niche behind one of those newspapers mounted on a cane frame, because his presence filled the room. His powerful build, his quick eyes and erect bearing ensured that he could not be missed. He was two years older than Salo, a good-looking, elegantly dressed man of thirty. As the two started talking, Salo told him of the first songs he had written and the modest success he had had with them. Lengsfelder too had tried his hand at one or two texts, though with no great success. On the other hand he fairly bubbled with ideas, and knew all the producers, agents, theatre directors and composers.

Salo, who intuitively sensed the character of people he met, may well have had a feeling then that this smart jack-of-all-trades would prove the right person with whom to form a productive alliance, and a mutually beneficial relationship for the future. According to Fred, Hans had all the qualities he himself lacked. He matched Salo's modesty with an indestructible self-confidence, his shyness with a commanding presence; Salo's reluctance to haggle over fees was balanced by Hans's business skills and his ability to enthuse others with his plans. He understood how the operetta business worked, like a precursor of the modern entertainment industry, subject to market forces and popular success. 'I have the ideas and I have the contacts,' he told Salo. 'And believe me, I know what Viennese theatre-goers want to see.'

And thus the odd alliance of Lengsfelder and Tisch came into being, in accord with Alfred Grünwald's First Principle of Operetta, 'Der Starke ist am mächstigsten allein, Libretti aber schreibt man gut zu zwei'n.' ('The best writing is done alone, but librettos can do with a little help.') Many librettists at the time worked in a team. From the order of their names, one could deduce who had contributed what. The one named first was usually responsible for the plot, the second for the lyrics. So it was with the Lengsfelder–Tisch duo. Hans Lengsfelder provided ideas for the plot, Salo Tisch enriched it with punch-lines and humour and crafted the verses.

The demands of light entertainment were by no means light, Fred told me. As Franz Lehár, who had breathed new life into the genre, had pronounced long before, the success of an operetta depends above all on the quality of the libretto: 'One needs something well-constructed, an exciting and yet amusing piece of theatre, with new settings, sparkling dialogue, a mix of wit, humour, poetry, elegance, lively eroti-cism, minimal concern with deep motives, and last but not least a musical atmosphere that prompts cheerful and grace-ful and sentimental moods from voices and orchestra.'

Fred told me that in Lengsfelder he had found not only a stimulating partner but a severe critic, and that a real friend-ship had quickly sprung up. They were soon meeting every day to discuss ideas for plots and good lines for their songs.

Hans J. Lengsfelder came from a wealthy Jewish family from Reichenau, in Bohemia, who had moved to Vienna via Brno. His father had been a manufacturer, who died in 1927, leaving his wife Elfriede and his three grown-up children a house in Lannerstrasse in the nineteenth district. Although born in Vienna, Hans had a Czechoslovak passport, the value of which was to become evident much later on.

Lengsfelder grew up with operetta. When he was learning to walk, Lehár's *Merry Widow* and Oscar Straus's *Waltz Dream* were playing all over the country and abroad. These works heralded the 'silver age' of operetta, and Vienna had an unprecedented four dozen competing new productions a year. After the First World War and the collapse of the monar-chy, this frenzy had noticeably abated.

Now the Vienna theatres were in severe financial trouble. Mass unemployment, economic recession and new competi-tion from the cinemas threatened their existence. The newspapers reported on the crisis in the theatre almost daily. Debts, insolvency and excessive cost levels burdened the private theatres, many of which had to close their doors, at least for the time being.

But Lengsfelder refused to be discouraged. Hadn't he seen how enthusiastically Lehár's operettas had been received shortly before the Nazis took over in Berlin? And hadn't the old master himself shown in January 1934 what pulling power this supposedly moribund genre still had, even in Vienna?

On 20 January 1934 Franz Lehár opened with *Giudita* on the sacred ground of the Vienna State Opera. The first night was a sensation. The event was broadcast by 120 radio stations, and tickets sold for huge sums on the black market. Lehár, quietly relishing his admittance to the halls of high culture, conducted the Vienna Philharmonic, and Tauber sang some numbers three times, to an enthusiastic audience. Takings exceeded all expectations, and the following forty-two performances were sold out. The libretto for this box-office triumph was by Paul Knepler and Fritz Löhner-Beda, both later to cross Salo's path, each in his own particular way.

Lengsfelder and Tisch got tickets for *Giudita*, and saw how the audience couldn't get enough of what – as a concession to the distinguished venue – the programme announced as a 'Spieloper', though in reality it was only an operetta. As they descended the steps of the State Opera, the shrine to high culture radiant with the light of a mass of chandeliers, Lengsfelder dug his hands in his pockets, as he tended to when his thoughts wandered. They made for a bar, and Hans, who had been humming Tauber's tunes over and over, ordered two glasses of champagne. 'To our future!' he grinned at a surprised Salo. 'Tonight we heard where it is. We must write an operetta, I tell you, and not just short dance numbers.' After a pause he added emphatically, 'And we'll write one.' Scepticism mingled with respect, Salo clinked glasses with his friend. Neither supposed that Fate would first give them another chance.

And that of all things in a medium which, with its great technical finesse, had come to compete with the simple world of the stage: the sound film. Many composers and songwriters worked for the new entertainment form, writing film music and songs for the soundtracks. Films and music were very tied up with one another at that time. A hit could make a film a success – and vice versa. If a film failed to find favour with the public, it usually sealed the music's fate, and it was instantly forgotten.

Scope for work in sound films was limited, especially for Jews, Fred told me, and was becoming more so. To keep its place in the German market, the Austrian film industry was forced to make concessions in its casting to German anti-Semitic cultural policy. As early as 1933/34, four Austrian films were blocked by the German authorities. The German State Film Guild had suggested that Austrian film producers submit their manuscripts and cast lists for the perusal of official German literary managers. Only if they agreed the content and casting could a film hope to avoid problems of access and censorship. The Austrian authorities had accepted this, and so sanctioned a *de facto* ban on employing Jews and other unacceptable elements in the film industry.

But Lengsfelder was not one to be troubled by such problems, to the amazement of his partner, who had perhaps acquired a certain regard for the law from his study of it. Hans, Fred told me, had more chuzpah than he had, and he envied him for it. One day Lengsfelder rang Salo at his parents' very early in great excitement. 'Guess who was sitting at the next table in the Heurigen in Sievering yesterday,' he yelled into the phone. Salo of course had no idea. 'Peter Kreuder and Willy Forst,' said Lengsfelder breathlessly. Kreuder was then a successful composer, and Forst had made a name as an actor and director. "The whole evening they talked about the music for the film *Burgtheater*, and they kept singing this tune …' Lengsfelder hummed it over the phone, a tune so catchy that you couldn't forget it. Kreuder had altered a Johann Strauss polka so that you couldn't get it out of your head. As yet it had no words.

Lengsfelder smelled a great opportunity. Naturally, as a Jew, he had no chance of being engaged by a German film company to write the text, but he knew someone whose name would not be suspect, a distant relation by the name of Harry Hilm. He got this straw man to call Peter Kreuder in the Rosenhügel studios the very next day and offer to write words to the film melody.

The political situation in Germany, where the 'elimination of all Jewish elements' from cultural life was being pursued, left no choice. In March 1934 Joseph Goebbels had decreed that to appear in public, performing artists must belong to an association controlled by the state music or theatre guild. This required Aryan credentials.

Jewish influence was to be removed from music. To this end, the Nazis did not hesitate to adapt the words of Bach's and Handel's cantatas and oratorios to conform to their new view of the world, revising the original texts and deleting Hebrew content or words like 'Sion' or 'Jahve'. Handel's *Judas Maccabeus* became a patriotic song of struggle and triumph, and was later entitled *The Warlord*. Even the Mozart opera libretti of da Ponte fell victim to this 'cleansing' operation. Mozart's oratorio *La Betulia liberata*, a piece about Judith, was germanized and given the title *Ildiko und Etzel*, and recounted a story about Ildiko, a woman from Burgundy. The revisionist writers in Germany included lesser-known music directors but also some well-known professors of music. But then – apart from the worship of false gods – there was the matter of considerable fees, because the oratorios were frequently played.

The horrors of the aryanizing of Jewish property are familiar, but little is said of the injustice of dispossessing Jews of their intellectual and cultural property. This was no less damaging, and for this there has to my knowledge been hardly any gesture of restitution or even apology.

Salo may stand as an example of this injustice, which he experienced in many and grotesque forms. Not only did he and Lengsfelder have to conceal their authorship. The perpetrators also had to perform elaborate contortions to get around the embarrassing fact that in the case of most of the successful pieces, some Jew or other was involved, whether as composer, director or librettist. Later on they did not even hesitate to aryanize a Tisch and Lengsfelder hit. If it had not been so inhuman, one could have described it all as theatre of the absurd.

First, though, Lengsfelder and Tisch used the trick with the straw man to get around the work ban in Germany. In the film industry, using a pseudonym donor in this way was not unusual, for the use of foreign-sounding cover names had been banned by the Reichsmusikkammer in 1934 and a year later it brought in a notification requirement for works of émigrés among publishers and dealers. A number of Jewish scriptwriters now sought a pseudonym donor, under whose name they could go on working. Sometimes the donor was a friend, and sometimes money changed hands.

In Lengsfelder's case the dodge worked. Kreuder in fact agreed to look at a text draft from Hilm, and asked him to produce one quickly.

I don't know how long Salo and Hans sat that night and the following nights, nor how many screwed-up sheets of paper landed in the waste-paper basket before they struck the right note. Finally, anyway, a line came into existence that would go around the world and at the same time be a sort of tag-line for their lives: 'Sag beim Abschied leise Servus'.

4 Siegfried Conquers Vienna

It is quiet in my house, especially during the day when I am alone and the radio and television are not on. But inside me it is never quiet. There are always songs and tunes that come from somewhere or other unbidden and keep me company for a while. They lodge in my ear, often for a whole day at a time, and set me humming quietly to myself. When I feel low, music, whether from outside or in, sets me to rights again.

Music is something essential for me. It is more dependable than people, who can move away or leave us for ever. In its way, it is immortal. Fred has gone, but he has left me his music: the operettas, the popular hits, the ballads and chansons. I have many of them on record, although I don't need to play them because they are so vivid in my mind. Now and then the tune of Sag beim Abschied leise Servus steals into my day and stays with me until I go to sleep.

> 'Sag beim Abschied leise 'Servus'
> Nicht 'Lebwohl' und nicht 'Adieu'
> Diese Worte tun nur weh!
> Doch das kleine Wörtl 'Servus'
> Ist ein lieber letzter Gruss,
> Wenn man Abschied nehmen muss.
> 'S gibt jahraus, jahrein an neuen Wein
> Und neue Liebelei'n.
> Sag zum Abschied leise 'Servus'
> Denn gibt's auch kein Wiedersehen,
> Einmal war es doch schön.*

---

*Say 'Servus' quietly as we part / Not 'Lebwohl' and not 'adieu' / These words just cause pain! / But the little word 'Servus' / Is a sweet last greeting, / When one has to part. / Every day and all the time there are new wines / And new loves / Say 'Servus' quietly as we part / For, if we never meet again, / It was once so sweet.

It took some time, Fred told me, until the lines were as we know them today. Several times the composer, Peter Kreuder, wanted words altered. Hilm, the straw man, who arrived at the studio with the drafts, was in extreme difficulty because Kreuder asked him to make the changes there and then. He was surprised that Hilm always refused, saying he could work properly only at home. In fact, of course, he called Lengsfelder and had him dictate the changes over the phone, reappearing in the studio with the revised version some time later. And so the fraud remained undiscovered.

No one could then imagine that a worldwide hit was in the making. When *Burgtheater* reached the cinemas in November 1936, 'Sag beim Abschied leise Servus' sung by Hans Moser was to become one of the best-known songs of the inter-war years, and was translated into twenty-six languages. Only three people knew that the libretto was not by Harry Hilm, as the film posters and sheet music announced, but by Hans J. Lengsfelder and Siegfried Tisch.

To this day there exists no written proof of Salo's role in this worldwide triumph – only his own account. Soon after we met he told me about this song, as though it was a seal of approval of his former work, later withdrawn. Yet for Fred it was never a real triumph that he had snatched from the Nazis, but was marked by bitterness from knowing that nobody would ever link his name to the world-famous Viennese song. To this extent, clever ruses notwithstanding, the aims of the aryanization policy had been realized. But for a single one-off payment, Salo received no money for his work. Nor did he seek any later. He did not accept money as a currency of atonement, as later became clear on several occasions.

In summer 1935 Hans Lengsfelder arranged a contact with Fritz Spielmann. Spielmann came from the world of cabaret, and was also starting his career. In 1931, aged twenty-five, he made his debut as a pianist and interpreter of his own works at a Richard Tauber evening of song at the Vienna Konzerthaus. At the same time he gave the first five programmes as resident composer and pianist in the *Liebe Augustin* cabaret in the cellar of the Café Prückel, moving later to the Fiaker nightclub. About the same time as Lengsfelder and Tisch, Spielmann met the composer and lyricist Stephan Weiss, who was already successful in the popular music world. From then on, the two worked together – on the same principle of shared labour as the librettists, and with a similar division of roles. Weiss had a special feel for the business side, Spielmann a many-sided musical talent. Fred said he honestly admired Spielmann's huge gifts, and that he showed the same ability as a composer as he did as a pianist, singer and lyrics writer. He was just a year younger than Tisch.

Spielmann, Weiss, Tisch and Lengsfelder planned to mount together a burlesque operetta about the origins of the talking film. It was to be their first work for the stage, and Fred said that he had hardly been able to sleep at first for excitement. He had little opportunity in any case. He spent whole nights in Lengsfelder's apartment in Lannerstrasse crafting lines, scrapping them, writing new ones and constantly honing them. Lengsfelder's mother was an excellent cook, and kept the two supplied with goulash and dumplings and pastries – and if it was late, she took a glass of wine or strong coffee into them. Often in the early light of the next day the clacking of a small portable typewriter could be heard from that room in Lannerstrasse.

On 24 January 1936 *Achtung … Grossaufnahme!* had its première in the Kammerspiele in Rotenturmstrasse, the small sister stage of the famous theatre in the Josefstadt led by Max Reinhardt. Lengsfelder and Tisch invited all their friends and acquaintances. And of course Salo's parents and Elfriede Lengsfelder, their misgivings about their sons' prospects now replaced by approving respect.

Many of Salo's student friends had spread themselves around in the dress and upper circles. His one-time classmate and fellow theatre buff Severin Wallach was also there, with his cousin Jakob Wallach. Both shared Salo's passion for the theatre, and they applauded enthusiastically. Jakob especially had a masterly way of suddenly starting to clap, almost like the crack of a whip, a fraction of a second before the rest of the audience. Although it was not his real calling, Jakob had all the skill of the professional claqueur. They were widely used in the theatre at the time. Many great artists even had their own personal claqueurs, who deliberately, even before the last note had died away, set off loud applause as though starting an avalanche.

On this occasion, though, nothing of the kind was needed. The audience received the 'sound-film report in two sections', as the programme note called it, with enthusiasm. 'Bravo!' and 'Encore!' they called, and they especially wanted repeats of the popular 'Mickey Mouse' number. Tisch and Lengsfelder, who were sitting in the first row, were called up on stage and bowed low to a warm shower of applause. I wonder what Salo felt as he looked from the lighted stage into the darkened auditorium at the movement of hundreds of clapping hands blurring the lines of the seated rows. I never asked him, but as I knew him later, he celebrated moments of triumph or pride, alone, on a tiny stage inside himself, and hardly allowed anything to permeate to the outside.

Apart from the catchy tunes and the cheeky text, the public had been taken with all sorts of technical refinements in the show, such as having the audience filmed at the start of the first act and shown on the screen just before the end. A little novelty for theatre-goers, and a great moment in Salo's life. With *Achtung ... Grossaufnahme!* he and his partner had achieved what the billboards now hailed as a 'runaway hit'.

The following months, Fred once admitted, were the most exciting of his life. He was overwhelmed by the sudden success, which had catapulted him into that glamorous world that was the favourite subject of the theatre itself in those days, the world of show business. Suddenly he and Lengsfelder were invited to all the first-night parties and got to know famous composers, singers and actors. Hans, who was always succumbing to the charms of the delightful girls of Vienna, made the most of his good fortune, and Fred admitted that he too had enjoyed *la dolce vita* to the full. Both had what the Viennese call a *'Hetz'* – a whale of a time.

The most productive year for the pair was to be 1936. Only a few months after their stage debut, the comedy *Happy* had its première in the Theater in der Josefstadt, and they provided words for the musical numbers. Immediately after this, on 5 June, *Hochzeitsreise* had its first night there. The operetta's music was by Salo's friend Carlo de Fries, and Lengsfelder and Tisch reworked the Hungarian original for the German-speaking stage, twice travelling to see the production in Budapest. The main roles in Vienna were taken by the famous actors Hans Thimig, Gusti Huber and Christl Mardayn. There were eighty performances. Fred said that he saw it more than a dozen times. He must have quietly enjoyed the 'din of applause at the end of every act' noted by the *Neues Wiener Tagblatt*.

Through Stefan Weiss, their companion-in-arms in *Achtung … Grossaufnahme!*, Salo and Hans got to know the young composer Leonard K. Märker. Only insiders knew that K. stood for Kuh, because Märker's name was really Kuhmärker, but what chance had a composer with a name like that? Märker was only twenty-five, and had huge talent. The famous Viennese opera composer Hans Gál had given Kuhmärker free lessons from the age of fifteen, and sharpened his sense for what Gál once referred to as 'real, genuinely felt, creative, inspired music that sings'. For four more years, Märker studied harmony with Alban Berg, the composer of *Wozzeck* and *Lulu*.

Sometimes Märker sang them, over the telephone, tunes he had just written and Salo and Hans worked all night long to find suitable words, scanning, declaiming and revising, and reading the results back over the telephone next morning. In this way two operettas came into being after weeks of work: *Der schiefe Hut* and the musical comedy *Warum lügst du, Chérie?* Lengsfelder managed to find theatres in Vienna to mount these operettas, both based on foreign models.

Suddenly, Fred told me, things took off. *Burgtheater* opened in the cinemas in November 1936, and everyone was singing 'Sag beim Abschied leise Servus'. Only two weeks later the operetta *Der schiefe Hut* opened at the Theater in der Josefstadt. The leads were taken by Jane Tilden and Fritz Schulz, the public's current darlings, accompanied at the piano by Leonard K. Märker.

In the operetta the two sing the duet 'Erinnerst Du Dich?' It too is on my LP, and when I hear it I can't help laughing and crying at the same time. Perhaps it affects me so much because it was a presentiment of my first meeting with Fred, which – although without the song's dog Bulli and his obsession with trousers – was disastrous and painful, comical and touching.

It certainly wasn't romantic.

> Es war ein Vorfall, der harmlos aussah,
> Der zueinander uns geführt
> Weil damals keiner von uns voraussah,
> Dass sich das Schicksal oft maskiert...
> Ich muss noch heute darüber lachen,
> Wenn ich dran denk, was uns geschah,
> Wie es teils komisch war, und teils auch peinlich war,
> Als ich zum erstenmal Dich sah:
> Erinnerst Du Dich?
> Es was ein Dienstag im Juli, im Monat der Rosen,
> Erinnerst Du Dich?
> Da gingst Du vorbei
> Und Dein entzückender Bulli zerriss mir die Hosen,
> Erinnerst Du Dich?
> Wir gingen dann ins Kaffeehaus, dort goss ich den Tee aus
> Auf Dein neues Kleid, das tat mir leid,
> Erinnerst Du Dich?*

Der schiefe Hut had excellent reviews. *Der Wiener Tag* praised its 'well-crafted punchlines, visual wit, inventive refrains, and stirring numbers with catchy words'. The *Neue Freie Presse* judged that Hans J. Lengsfelder and Siegfried Tisch had written 'an absolutely contemporary text of uninhibited topicality'.

Just a few weeks later, on Christmas Eve, the fourth operetta from Lengsfelder and Tisch in a year had its première. It was to be the most spectacular. Hans Lengsfelder had persuaded his old friend Adolf Tersch to finance it. The private theatres were under severe financial constraint, and no longer willing to carry alone the costs of production and the risk of failure, and so less well-known authors and

---

* *It was a seemingly harmless incident / That brought us together / Because at the time neither of us realized, / That Fate often comes in disguise ... / Today I have to laugh / When I think what happened to us, / Because it was partly funny, and partly embarrassing too, / As I saw you for the first time: / Do you remember?*

It was a Tuesday in July, when the roses bloomed, / Do you remember? / You were passing by / And your charming bull terrier tore my trousers, / Do you remember? / We went to a coffee house, where I poured tea / On your new dress, I was so sorry, / Do you remember?

composers especially – as with films – had first to find wealthy backers to stage their projects. Tersch was a benefactor and an admirer of the theatre in equal measure.

Tisch and Lengsfelder had given him the script of *Warum lügst du, Cherie?* to read, and Tersch, a man of quick decision, had agreed to finance it. 'The piece has charm,' he found, 'And I think it is just right for Vienna.'

The setting is a country house in Fontainebleau, not far from Paris. This 'musical comedy in three acts' used the old Cinderella theme that made *My Fair Lady* one of the most successful musicals ever over a decade later: a famous playwright who, as author of a number of successful plays – including *Warum lügst du, Chérie?* – has risen into the aristocracy of money, meets a street girl who tries to burgle his house, and falls in love with her.

The urchin girl's role was taken by the blonde Friedl Czepa, who had appeared with Hans Moser and Jan Kiepura in sound films, and, as Salo apparently found out later, had good contacts with Joseph Goebbels. The *bon viveur* Gaston was acted by Hans Schott-Schoebinger. The Christmas première was a success. The *Neues Wiener Tagblatt* praised Tisch and Lengsfelder as 'authors who didn't just fill an evening, but crammed it to bursting'. The piece attained 'the gigantic stature of the monumental operettas of the golden age'. The hit songs, 'charming and attractive', felt familiar to the audience even on first hearing.

Salo, it seemed, had made it. As he was called on to the stage once more, he noticed his parents in the front row, applauding with raised hands. Isaak nodded in acknowledgement and Taube's eyes again glistened with tears. 'I am proud of you, my son,' said his father later at the first-night party. 'You know, if anyone had told me twenty years ago that I, a Jew from a Galician ghetto, would be applauding my son on the stage of a theatre in Vienna, I'd have said he was completely *meschugge*.'

What a good thing, Fred said later, that his father, as he banged his son time and again on the shoulder, drunk with joy and fatherly pride, had no sense of the dark future that awaited them all. In any case, though, he would scarcely have believed it.

Salo himself could hardly believe how Fate had suddenly raised him up and held out the prospect of a lightness of being that had something unreal about it. Could he, a Jewish war refugee from Galicia, really have found recognition in a city where anti-Semitism was being expressed more and more openly? Wasn't he always, for all his success, an alien twice over, a Galician among Viennese and a Jew among Gentiles? Liberal attitudes predominated in the theatre world, it was true, but even here effects of the pact between Germany and Austria, who had come to a 'normalization and friendship agreement' in July 1936, were being felt more and more. German newspapers, some of which were allowed to appear in Vienna again, warned of German culture being 'overwhelmed by Jewish influence'. The works of Nazi writers were sometimes also staged in the Burgtheater. Through casting agreements, national socialist aims were implemented in films and theatre, mostly against Jewish artists.

But on that evening all this was forgotten, and Salo bathed in congratulations, shook hands and had his cheeks made red with kisses from the female members of the cast. *Warum lügst du, Chérie?* was a great success, and was performed well over a hundred times in Vienna. One day, as Salo learned years later, this cheerful piece was to find favour with Goebbels himself, and he was to think up a way of cheating its Jewish creators and staging it in Nazi Germany.

In Vienna it was the theme tune of *Warum lügst du, Chérie?* especially that became a hit, and was taken up by all the dance orchestras. Its swinging tune is still in my ears.

Countless dance halls sought out Lengsfelder and Tisch. Salo, starting to ape his partner's cheek, had the chuzpah to claim tax relief on his visits to them. I know this because he kept his tax returns for the years 1936 and 1937, probably because later, under the Nazis, the so-called taxation regularity declaration could mean life or death.

Enquiries came from theatres everywhere that wanted *Warum lügst du, Chérie?* in their programme – from Prague, Hamburg, Karlsbad, Olmütz, Franzensbad, Bratislava, Paris, Bucharest, Copenhagen, Oslo, Budapest, Salzburg, Graz, Linz, Innsbruck and many other cities. In all, there were over 5,000 performances.

In Vienna it ran more than 150 times. The well-known actor Otto Wallburg played the distinguished valet Horatio Cromwell to great applause. Arthur Hellmer, the new director of the Theater an der Wien, wanted to engage him after the run in the film operetta *Katinka*. But Wallburg was a Jew, and moreover had left Germany in 1934. Under the new laws, Jews from Nazi Germany working in the theatre must be members of the 'Circle of Austrian Stage Artists' – or of the affiliated Czech, Swiss or German professional association. It was forbidden for Jews to belong to the German Reichstheaterkammer, and the Austrian Ring did not accept them as foreigners, and Wallburg could get permission to play only in a single production. Hellmer tried to get an extension, but this popular comedian was merely allowed a further seven days. The première of *Katinka* took place without him.

To get around such bans, many theatrical artistes and authors who had fled from Germany tried to hide their identity, just as Salo and Hans had successfully done with the film *Burgtheater*. For example, the successful Berlin writer Hans José Rehfisch, who had emigrated to Vienna, concealed his identity and some of his plays were even produced in Germany under various American and British aliases.

Probably the most sensational concealment was by the actor Leo Reuss, a Viennese Jew, who had returned from Berlin in 1935 and been unable to get work. Reuss suddenly disappeared in spring 1936, to return half a year later as a thickly bearded character from the mountains called Kaspar Altenberger and audition at the Josefstadt Theatre. He was engaged on the spot for the role of the bourgeois in the Schnitzler novella *Fräulein Else,* and the newspapers pounced on the improbable case of a mountain peasant with a calling for the stage. The *Reichspost* praised this natural-born talent as proof of the genuine artistic genius of untutored members of the Germanic race. Shortly before the first performance of *Warum lügst du, Chérie?* however, the deception was revealed, and the German press now found confirmation of Jewish slyness and the spread of Jewish influence in the Viennese theatre.

Perhaps because the concealment of their role in *Burgtheater* had stayed undiscovered, Salo and Hans still felt in control of their fate. They were already working on a new piece with an eminent artist Salo was to meet again in grimmer circumstances. The Jew Fritz Grünbaum was an institution in Vienna. He had written the lyrics for Kálmán's *Zigeunerprimas* and Leo Fall's *Dollarprinzessin*, but was especially noted as a compère and raconteur. With his scowling face, and mischievous look scarcely contained by his thick metal-rimmed glasses, Grünbaum exposed the foibles of the world in general and of the Viennese in particular. Together with Karl Farkas, he had developed a double act where the two fed each other funny lines.

Grünbaum had taken one of the leading roles in *Happy*. Fred said he had never stopped learning from him. After more than thirty years on the stage, he was a past master in verbal wit, political allusion and funny tag-lines. But the true greatness of Grünbaum as a man was something Salo was to experience later.

On 16 April 1937 *Sie Johann* ... opened at the Volksoper. 'Ja, das koennt' in Wien nicht passier'n' is the title of a song which made fun of Viennese conditions, Austrian bureaucracy, radio censorship and the dire state of the telephone system. As such references were forbidden by the censor, Grünbaum, Tisch and Lengsfelder simply transferred their snide comments to Brno. The ironic refrain left no doubt, though, which city was meant. The critics were well disposed, and praised especially Grünbaum's acting range, but it was not a great success, and was taken off after a month.

In summer 1937 Salo Tisch and his companion Hans J. Lengsfelder travelled to Paris. It was the first time Salo had been there, and he told me the big-city atmosphere, the wide avenues and boulevards and the stone emblems of Napoleonic grandeur had an overwhelming impact. Above all, Paris was pervaded by a different, freer spirit than the chicken-livered moral cowardice taking over the Vienna of Austro-fascism. Hans and Salo were twelve days in Paris, and hardly had time to see the main sights.

They negotiated over the French production of *Chérie*, and met, as Salo later announced on his tax return, 'the well-known director Reinhold Schünzel'. Schünzel was then a great and especially courageous film-maker – or had been, because the Germans had expelled him in June 1937 Until shortly before he had been under the personal protection of the Führer, who had elevated him, a half-Jew, to an honorary Aryan because of his outstanding services to the German film. After all, Schünzel had made a great star of the actress Renate Müller, who was said to have a special relationship with Hitler. He had made the successful musical comedies *Saison in Kairo* and *Viktor und Viktoria* for Ufa. *Amphitryon* had been made in 1934, an elaborate comedy about the gods of antiquity, for which Hitler, after visiting the Babelsberg studios, had provided 200 SS men from his bodyguard as extras. But Schünzel, playing a double game, had made, instead of the expected propaganda film, an irreverent send-up of dictatorships. It was to be the last time that Schünzel cocked a snook at those in power in Germany. In his next film, *Land der Liebe*, which also turned out to be a satire, all the critical passages were edited out before showing. Even before the première Schünzel had slipped out of Berlin by night.

And now he was about to leave for Hollywood, whither MGM had enticed him with an undreamed-of salary. I do not know – and no one can ever find out now – how Schünzel learned about *Warum lügst du, Chérie?*, and how the contact with Tisch and Lengsfelder came about. But as he was expert at filming musical comedies, the piece was certainly in good hands. The project came to nothing, though – like countless other fragments of ideas and identities of artists left behind on the way into exile.

Paris was worth the journey, though, and provided the setting for the next comedy with music by Leonard K. Märker. *Das Ministerium ist beleidigt* was again to have a Christmas première, opening on 22 December 1937 in the Wiener Komödie, the theatre in the Kärntnerstrasse. Both main actors from the successful *Chérie*, Friedl Czepa and Hans Schott-Schöbinger, appeared in the key roles.

The action takes place in the French Ministry of Finance, which is in turmoil because pictures of the minister's daughter appear on billboards advertising ladies' underwear. The librettists sugared the political allusions with an air of sweet naïveté to get past the censor. And yet there peeked out from under the witty cream confection on the surface, cold fear about a world out of joint, fear of politicians whose stupidity was exceeded only by their corruptibility, fear about an 'institution' in Geneva that looks on when submarines attack ships, about a Spanish Legion in which nobody speaks Spanish, and about the Kafkaesque bureaucracy.

The *Wiener Tag* praised the 'charming satire, not without deeper reference'. There were many encores, endless curtain calls and storms of applause, reported the *Neues Wiener Tagblatt*. The 'reliable libretto firm' of Hans J. Lengsfelder and Siegfried Tisch were serving up 'sharp and piquant humour', thought the *Kleines Volksblatt*.

As Salo again enjoyed the warm glow of recognition and nestled in friendly laughter on this eve of the Festival of Peace, preparations were in train elsewhere for war and the cold blast to come.

Perhaps, Fred sometimes brooded, it was this particular piece, laced as it was with political meaning, that was his undoing as his city fell into a foul morass and laughter died. Even the wildest satire could never have anticipated what was to happen in Vienna just a few weeks later.

5 Rain

The rain is beating against my window. It is not the striped showery rain that often hangs like a mourning ribbon over London. Cloudbursts have been unloading water over these islands for days now. In some counties the water is many feet deep. On my patio, the drops were hammering on my garden table. Earlier on I folded it up. The clatter was suddenly too much for me to bear.

Whenever it rained, Fred was transformed into a cowering nervous wreck. When the asphalt-grey clouds scudded over one another, shadows passed over his face too. We had known one another about six months when I first learned how the drumming of the raindrops would drag him back into the past. Just as one often associates the smell of a perfume with particular scenes or people, for him the sound of rain always evoked experiences that he did not wish to remember. He curled up in an armchair, a blanket pulled around him, drew his knees up under his chin and put his fingers in his ears. So it was every time. Often his whole body shook, and sometimes, when he thought nobody saw, he cried quietly to himself in a monotone.

At first I didn't know how to react. I stroked his face, held his hand and spoke comfortingly to him. Usually I made him a pot of tea and put some briquettes in the stove – to stop him trembling. Of course, he was not freezing outwardly. What it was that made him shudder inwardly I learned in the course of months and years. It emerged bit by bit, with many repetitions, sometimes only after much hesitation, gradually building up a picture.

I sometimes think he could still have got away. Why didn't he leave immediately like the others who packed their cases that very day and took the train across the frontier? But Salo, alias Siegfried, aka Fred, was not a man to act on impulse. He was someone who planned things, someone who valued order, who took one step at a time, and didn't rush to conclusions. When the Nazis entered Austria on 12 March 1938 and the Viennese rabble, bawling and drunk with national pride, showed their true nature, marching through the streets and at last daring to spit openly at the Jews and beat them up, when the whole city lost its mind in a frenzy of hate and *folie de grandeur*, Salo decided to prepare quickly for another life. It would certainly be in another country, with another language. But how would he earn a living? Not from his knowledge of Austrian jurisprudence, which interested no one beyond the border! Not as a writer of German songs and libretti, which no one understood! *Nebbich*, he would have to find something new. On 15 March, the day Adolf Hitler yelled his 'Sieg Heil!' on the Heldenplatz in Vienna and the unchained masses rejoiced with arms stiffly outstretched, on that day Salo Tisch broke with his native country for ever.

As soon as the Germans invaded Austria, Jewish bankers and businessmen were arrested by the SS and SA. The offices of Zionist associations were smashed up and closed. That evening, armed SA marched through the streets of Vienna plundering the synagogues. On 18 March the head office of the Jewish religious community was occupied without warning. Adolf Eichmann, whom Hitler had sent from Berlin to deal with the 'Jewish question', took part in the raid.

To escape these arbitrary attacks, many non-Jews quickly pinned on little swastikas, and foreigners wore their national colours in their buttonholes. This meant the Jews were even easier to recognize. A few days after the invasion, Salo Tisch, lawyer and librettist, enrolled for a six-week course in 'Viennese speciality confectionary' at the Albert Kofranek Cookery School at 3 Schottengasse. 'What else should I have taken from Vienna?' he asked me later, because I was amused at the idea of him making sponge mixtures and marzipan flowers. 'The only thing the Viennese didn't have to be ashamed of at that time was their cakes.' Later he showed me a certificate stating that he had followed the course 'with great interest'. He also trained as a barman, in the hope that knowing how to mix drinks would prove useful in a hotel or on an ocean liner somewhere in the world.

It didn't come to that. Although he acted in his typically pragmatic way, events overtook him with a speed that still amazes me. Suddenly the easy-going Viennese couldn't bring in anti-Jewish measures fast enough. New decrees and laws were issued in weeks. Vienna's bureaucrats, renowned for their leisurely and sloppy ways, suddenly showed an energetic, painstaking enthusiasm that resembled the Prussian.

While the changes came in slowly in my native Bohemia, the Viennese adopted the evil new ways in one fell swoop. Overnight they trampled with their highly polished black boots all over a flourishing Viennese cultural life. Denunciations were rife. Innkeepers who played songs by Jewish composers were anonymously reported, and Jews were pointed out to the police. 'Anti-Semitism', said Fred, 'fell on fruitful ground in Vienna. The soil had been prepared for years.'

Jewish children were forced to paint the word 'Jew' and insults on the front of their parents' shops. The favourite sport of the mobs was to round up Jews for 'scrubbing parties'. Jewish men and women were forced to scrub the pavements and streets on their knees with a strong bleach. The solution they knelt in burned their skin, and some needed medical attention. SS men were to be seen driving around in stolen cars belonging to Jews, on which they had painted SS insignia. Every day SA and SS hauled Jews from their homes and made them wash their own 'requisitioned', i.e. stolen, cars or clean the floor and the toilets where they were billeted. Even Adolf Tersch, Tisch and Lengsfelder's wealthy friend who had underwritten *Warum lügst du, Chérie?* was ordered to a floor scrubbing at some Nazi office. Fred told me that he entered the office with head held high, and asked, 'Why don't you give these people a hand? Don't you realize they can't even keep their own places clean?' The SA thugs sent him away. People who did not deign to be humiliated – and there were some in the early weeks – did not make satisfactory victims.

'You need chutzpah,' Adolf urged his friends. (He dropped his unfortunate name when he went into exile.) 'And you must keep a straight back.' Just like his young wife Edith, who a few days after Hitler entered Vienna met her neighbour on the stairs, wearing his light-brown SA uniform. Clicking his heels, he stretched out his arm and bawled 'Heil Hitler' at her. She looked him up and down with contempt, from his neat parting to his polished sole, and just said, 'Aren't you ashamed of yourself?' For a moment the man was at a loss.

But many Viennese, Fred told me, were not in the least ashamed, and rejoiced in an orgy of envy, ill will and wild, blind revenge. Looting and blackmail were daily occurrences. Sometimes the confiscations were 'legitimized' by the NSDAP, sometimes the robbery was on private initiative. National Socialists and fellow travellers broke into the homes of Jewish bankers, into department stores on the Mariahilferstrasse and the little shops in the Leopoldstadt, stealing jewellery and money, clothing, furs, carpets, works of art and furniture. Many Jews had stickers put on their doors ordering them to evacuate their homes by such and such a date or were threatened with being ransacked. After being forcibly cleared, the homes were taken over by Viennese Gentiles or party members or officials from Germany.

Every few hours some horrifying new report made the rounds in the Leopoldstadt. 'We must get what little we have to safety,' said Salo's father. In this dire situation it happened that a doctor from Oslo had fallen in love with Salo's cousin, and travelled to Vienna as often as he could to see the lady of his heart. Whether because his love gave him extra courage or simply because he was a decent person, he regularly smuggled out the Tisch family's valuables. So jewellery, furs, family silver and religious objects landed up in Norway. Happily this minor traffic over the border remained undetected. Although it was only material objects that reached safety, they later took on significance as the only links with lives that had been extinguished.

Salo was no longer earning. Overnight, all sources of royalties had dried up. On the theatre and cabaret stages, in the opera houses and elsewhere, a cultural life that had shone beyond the borders of Austria was snuffed out. Fred said that those who had seen how the Germans had pursued a campaign at home against Jewish artists sensed what now threatened Austria. Many of the giants of Viennese cultural life had long been on the index in Germany. In the *Handbuch der Judenfrage* it was said that there was a duty to act ceaselessly to remove Jewish influence from music. It named Paul Knepler, Alfred Grünwald, Ludwig Herzer, Béla Jenbach and Fritz Löhner-Beda.

Löhner-Beda, Franz Lehár's regular librettist and author of 'Dein ist mein ganzes Herz' and 'Ich hab' mein Herz in Heidelberg verloren,' was one of the first to suffer. The day the Nazis marched in, this father of a family was arrested by armed troops in his flat in Langegasse and taken to the prison on the Elisabethpromenade. The man who had enchanted all of Vienna with his lyrics was now a public enemy. His name was on the list of 'notables' – in company with opposition politicians, industrialists, trades unionists, judges and Jewish artists.

The blacklists, that universal tool of Nazi violence, had been compiled months before by Austrian Nazis. They were the lubricant in the mechanism of tyranny. Only two weeks after the 'Anschluss', on the morning of 1 April 1938, 150 notable Viennese citizens were taken from the police prison on the Elisabethpromenade to the Westbahnhof. Löhner-Beda was among them, as were the mayor of Vienna, Richard Schmitz, the vice-president of the Vienna district court, Alois Osio, the president of the trades union federation, Johann Staud, and the writers Viktor Matejka and Rudolf Kalmar. Among the prisoners in the so-called 'transport of notables' was Oswald Richter, the well-known social democrat and lawyer, and my mother's cousin.

That very day, Oswald Richter and the others were taken to the concentration camp in Dachau. They were handed over to SS staff from Dachau at Vienna's Westbahnhof. I later read Rudolf Kalmar's account of what happened to them on the train. They were kicked with hobnail boots and struck in the ribs with rifle butts and in the face with clenched fists. They were forced to gaze for minutes at a time at the electric light without blinking or to do hundreds of knee-bends, to hit the person sitting opposite or spit in their faces. The feeling of inescapable loneliness, of being completely shut off from everything that was human, wrote Kalmar, was worse than any physical pain.

Salo had no presentiment of a similar fate awaiting him. His beloved Vienna, he told me, was unrecognizable. Suddenly this city, so delightful, worldly, pleasure-loving and witty, was a place of fear and arbitrary terror. Jewish social life had been goose-stepped into oblivion. Everywhere, in the theatres and cinemas, the cafés, inns and dance halls, there were likely to be raids. Landlords were not keen to have Jews among their guests, and he himself had no great desire, he said, to go into a coffee house. And so the plan to marginalize the Jews took effect even before curfew decrees came in. Hardly anyone still dared to be seen around for fear of ending the evening in prison. In the same group as they had previously gone out together, to the theatres and bars, Salo, Hans, the Terschs and various female friends now met in private.

They missed little by way of artistic life. The Viennese cabaret stages, the Liebe Augustin, the Literatur on the Naschmarkt and the Simpl on the Wollzeile, had closed. Shortly before, Karl Farkas and Fritz Grünbaum did the their last double-act at the Simpl, Farkas, as a tourist guide, explaining the new political situation to Grünbaum, who had just come from the provinces. Soon afterwards, reality went far beyond any such sketch. On 10 March Fritz Grünbaum stood on the totally dark stage. 'I can't see anything,' he said. 'Nothing at all. This must be the Nazi cultural scene.'

Two days later, it was said in theatre circles, Grünbaum and his wife Lilly tried to cross into Czechoslovakia. In Bratislava they were taken off the train and sent back. For a time they hid in friends' houses and sought help from a lawyer, whom they paid a large sum for visas for Belgium – in vain, it soon turned out. A short time later, Fritz Grünbaum was taken off to Dachau. More and more Jews were disappearing.

Hans announced at a bridge evening of their private circle that he would leave the country at the first opportunity. 'Let's face it,' he said, looking over his cards, 'in Vienna our future is behind us.' Edith Tersch looked down at her very personal future in the shape of an enlarged tummy under her dress. 'Just as soon as the baby is here,' said her husband, as though following her thoughts, 'we'll pack our cases too.'

What was Salo to say? He had never in his life had as much money as Adolf, who had made a fortune early on as an estate agent. He did not have the blessing of ancestry like his friend Hans Lengsfelder, whose Czechoslovak passport would let him pass without hindrance. Like thousands of others, Salo would have to queue at the consulates. Since Hitler's invasion they had stood like grapes on the vine, in their hundreds and thousands, hoping to get the papers allowing them to flee the country. Some stuck it out all night, and it often happened that people exhausted from their long wait on the street were attacked by uniformed men, who abused them and chased them through the alleyways. Many, especially the sick and the weak, lost their place in the queue in which they had been standing all night.

The bolder ones tried to leave illegally, on their own initiative like Grünbaum or with paid guides. Early on, many Viennese Jews fled to Switzerland, which did not have a visa requirement for Austrians. This chance, which again Salo did not use, was soon lost. Switzerland brought in the requirement at the end of March.

We were often asked why did we not flee immediately. There are many answers, none of them really satisfactory. Whether in Vienna or in Aussig or elsewhere, we clung to our roots. We had our families there, our friends and those we loved, we had our work and our traditions, our language and our way of life; it was where we were happy. Many found out too late that they must give up their life in order to save it.

Hans J. Lengsfelder prepared his exit without delay. One afternoon Salo brought him the carefully compiled documentation of their mutual success. Their modest fame filled a whole suitcase. There were many pieces of sheet music, shellac records with recordings of operettas, volumes of songs, large posters, text drafts and a folder with critical reviews of their work. 'I can't take all that with me,' said Hans. 'I'll have to leave some here.' The proposal he then made was typical of him. For a long time they both searched the house where he lived with his mother, looking for a safe hiding place. There could be a house search any day, usually as an excuse to loot Jewish property. 'I know where', cried Lengsfelder suddenly, and dragged Salo to the toilet, where he pointed out a small light shaft behind the overhead cistern. 'No one will find it there', he said, and, standing on the toilet lid, pushed the things into the gap.

Fred returned home with very mixed feelings, he told me later. He was relieved the documents were safe, but what a pass things had come to when music that had entertained thousands ended up in a toilet light shaft, suddenly worth no more than the paper it was written on, a pile of nostalgia nobody wanted, or was allowed, to hear.

The same day Salo wrote out a power of attorney for his old partner. I still have it. It gives Lengsfelder 'irrevocably and bindingly the right to dispose of their joint work at his absolute discretion, to conclude agreements, to collect all proceeds, to initiate and terminate legal action and to do all that he judges right in our common interest'. Thus Siegfried Tisch handed over responsibility for everything he had written to his friend. Lengsfelder never abused this trust.

Soon afterwards Salo accompanied his friend to the departure hall at the airport, with its swirling mass of people hoping to leave that mad city, and pressed into his hands a farewell gift of a box of hand-made pralines, in accord with his belief, perhaps, that confectionery was the only sweet thing that Vienna had to offer. Fred said that for once Lengsfelder, that extrovert charmer with his imperturbable 'it'll-be-all-right' air, was speechless. He pressed him close for a long time and let go only hesitatingly. He waved to Hans as he went towards the plane but Hans did not look back.

Baron Rothschild, one of the wealthiest Jews of Vienna, had tried to leave from the same airport. The Nazis caught him before take-off and put him in prison. Nobody knew what had happened to him there, but he was released on condition he made his whole fortune over to the Nazis. The Gestapo confiscated the Palais Rothschild on the Prinz-Eugen-Strasse, calling it the Central Office for Jewish Emigration. It was here that decisions were made about emigrating or staying, and thus about life and death.

Salo had no luck with visa applications for himself and his parents. For Isaak and Taube, both over sixty, he could not get work permits abroad. And the Tischs did not have enough money to buy their freedom, as many wealthier Jews were forced to by the Central Office. They now put their hopes in Fred's brother Moishe, who had gone to London in 1936, less, it must be said, for political reasons, than encouraged by a friend who had emigrated previously and had reported that there was no shortage of work or pretty women. Since then, Mundy, as he was called in London, had lived in a small apartment in Swiss Cottage and sent cheerful letters home. Being capable and a good businessman, he had quickly worked himself up to business manager in a factory making labels for fashion firms.

When Hitler entered Vienna, the tone of the correspondence with Mundy had changed suddenly, concentrating on the critical question of how to escape. Britain, which Mundy now knew, seemed an island of hope. But emigration was subject to many conditions. To leave their homes and buy their freedom, refugees had to leave almost all their wealth and possessions behind. Securities and bonds, of which Salo's father had a modest amount, could not be taken abroad, and insurance arrangements could not be transferred. Receipts had to be produced for anything recently bought that one wanted to take, and a 100 per cent supplement paid. An inventory had to be drawn up of all items to be exported, and multiple copies supplied to the exchange bureau.

The chicanery did not end there. Before being able to leave, would-be refugees had to run a bureaucratic gauntlet, and many of them stumbled and some, caught up in the tangle of conditions, did not complete the course. Much of what Fred told me was familiar from the despairing letters that my parents sent me from Prague.

The Nazis required a 'confirmation of tax regularity', and this took weeks to obtain. One had to produce papers from many different government offices, and of course these were only open at certain times and always beleaguered by long queues. Many Jews who had sold their possessions in a panic at give-away prices no longer had the money to pay the exit taxes demanded by the Nazis. The 'Tax for Fleeing from the Reich', the 'Expiatory Contribution' and the mandatory payment to the 'Emigration Fund' together sometimes took more than half of what people had. Because prices under conditions of forced sale were often way below the Nazis' official estimates, the bottom line often showed a negative amount, and meant that one could not leave.

The cunning of this system was that, before letting Jews go, the Nazis robbed them by confiscating their property in various ways, hoping also thereby to export anti-Semitism on the reckoning that no country would want to take in impoverished refugees who brought social problems with them. Britain also hindered immigration at this time by raising numerous barriers. Granting of permanent right of stay was mainly limited to those thought likely to benefit the country, such as eminent scientists and industrialists, who brought material or intellectual wealth. Those not so endowed had to prove that they would not be a burden to the welfare services and show that they had a job or that a British citizen would stand guarantor for them.

And so Mundy, the playboy who had gone to London, had the fate of his parents and brother in his hands – an unimaginable burden for someone who has not had to bear it. Mundy set about getting private guarantees for his family. He telephoned friends and business associates, wrote to acquaintances and spoke to colleagues. At the same time he tried to find a job for his brother, although he did not know English and, apart from his now useless knowledge of Austrian law and his writing, had no relevant qualifications – apart, that is, from his probably miserable skills as a confectioner.

It was easier for young women to get work in the United Kingdom. Thousands of Viennese Jewish women applied to the British consulate for employment as house-maids in England. Salo, however, found nothing, even though his brother wrote and telephoned until his fingers were sore. He must have felt as though he was on a leaking ship with the lifeboats long cast off and no lifejackets left. Friends and acquaintances were now disappearing without having time to say goodbye. Hans had left; so had the Terschs and thousands of others. Yet Salo was still there.

One morning in June there was a ring at the door on the second floor of the house at 78 Vorgartenstrasse, and before Isaak could open the door, fists hammered on it. Two SA men had come to arrest Dr Salo Tisch, the legal assessor. They weren't especially unpleasant, said Fred, and gave him a few moments to say goodbye to his parents. Taube, now that her fears of the last few weeks had become reality, just stood in front of him, paralysed with horror. 'We'll get you out again,' said Isaak hoarsely.

Salo spent several days in the prison on the Elisabethpromenade. Many of the nearly 70,000 people arrested in the first few weeks were initially locked up in barracks. On 22 June, on a Wednesday, Salo, together with other prisoners, was taken to Dachau. It was a very hot day. In the compartments on the train six prisoners sat on each side, crammed into places meant for four. They were made to look at the ceiling light all the time, and anyone who didn't was beaten. The journey took twenty-six hours, and nobody was allowed to go to the toilet the whole time. Fred said that he must have got rid of body fluid through sweating, not from the heat but from fear. No one knew where they were being taken. In Munich the prisoners were transferred to a cattle truck. They had to move at the double. Anyone who stumbled or had difficulty climbing on to the high floor of the truck was beaten repeatedly. Some broke their legs. The trucks were sealed for the final few miles to Dachau.

On arrival, they had to pass a double column of SS men firing rifles in the air to intimidate the new arrivals, some of whom were grazed by bullets and collapsed. They had to undress completely and were taken to the shower room. The guards' violence was completely random, Fred said. Some people were hit because they used soap to wash, and hit again when they washed themselves without it. After showering, their heads were shaved. Salo was given camp clothes and an appropriate prisoner label. He was registered as a Jew in protective custody with the number 16886.

The camp commandant addressed the prisoners, saying that nothing would happen to those who behaved properly, but that those who broke the rules would be severely punished. The prisoners lived in barracks, with one part for eating and another, with bunk beds, for sleeping. There were sixty prisoners in Salo's barracks. They were woken at five a.m. and had to jump out of bed within seconds to avoid being reported to the SS guards. Fred said making the beds in the morning was a special harassment. The blankets had to be drawn completely smooth as if with a ruler, with no trace of a crease, or one was again threatened with being on report. Salo's habit, which he never lost, of stroking flat folds in a tablecloth or blanket, no doubt dated from this time.

After making their beds, the prisoners marched off to get coffee. There were weekly rations for bread. The rest of the food, Fred said, was tolerable and there was enough to keep one alive. At six a.m. they paraded and numbered off on the Appellplatz. Once the individual sections had been reported by their *Kapos*, the prisoners marched off to work. Fred described how, because he was not at all used to heavy physical work, all his muscles burned with pain for the first week. When there was nothing better to do, prisoners were made to carry stones to a pile and then carry them back, even when it was pouring with rain. Others were detailed for lighter work such as keeping records, peeling potatoes and darning socks. It was usually taken for granted that Austrians who managed to get on these details tried to have their compatriots join them.

The Austrians, who were deported to Dachau in hundreds immediately after the 'Anschluss', were something new in the German camp, Fred told me. Not by Nazi reckoning but according to their own feelings, they belonged to another nation, and attempts to beat this out of them welded them closer together. 'What are you?', they were often asked in the first weeks. On no account were they supposed to say, 'Austrian', or they would be kicked and beaten or made to run with a wheelbarrow full of stones. The Nazi word *Ostmärker* was one most of them did not want to use. Like many others, Salo would say he was 'Viennese'. Years later he couldn't bring himself to say this. As far as he was concerned, his Vienna no longer existed.

He soon got letters from a soulless Vienna. Worn down after days of waiting to hear, his parents had finally found out where their son was. Dachau was a name feared in Vienna, one that was whispered, as though just saying it aloud could bring disaster. The first urns from the concentration camp had reached Vienna in the meantime. Without warning or explanation, relatives had received the ashes of their loved ones, along with a bill for the costs of carriage.

Isaak sent his son money in the camp, as though this would influence fate – which in many cases it actually did. Ten to thirty marks from things the parents went without. The money was handled via an account in the camp. It allowed

Salo small privileges, such as buying a few potatoes, apples or onions in the canteen. As often as possible he bought himself bread spread with butter, on which he put thick layers of raw onion rings. Onions give the stomach the feeling of being full, even if it is only with air.

The worst forms of selfishness, based on pure survival instinct, that later developed in the death camps, were not yet evident in Dachau, according to Fred. In his barracks everything was shared. Those who could buy a few things gave some to those who had not received money.

In his letters Salo's father struggled to be brave. He was fine, he told his son, neglecting to say that his mother cried every day and had almost lost the will to live. Little that was good had happened since Salo's arrest. Isaak and Taube had been rounded up for a 'scrubbing party'. They had been given toothbrushes and a bucket of bleach and made to clean the cobbles while kneeling in the dirt. His father did not write that he had stood at the washbasin that day and tried to scrub the filth from his trouser legs, as though it could brush away the humiliation. He did not admit that even he, a devout Jew, now sometimes doubted the omnipotence of God.

Only a week after Salo's deportation Isaak lost his job. After over twenty years as an accountant at Fanto Oil, he was sacked without notice. He had had to give a statement of means by 30 June, as had all Jews in annexed Austria. Under occupation, he had put 'dismissed employee'. With the conscientiousness of a book keeper, he listed his few securities and estimated his modest pension for the next nine years. He had no idea he would not see the third year of his enforced retirement.

Isaak Tisch kept doing all he could to get his son out of the camp. At least Mundy had managed to find a guarantor, who had written to the British Foreign Office saying that he wanted to invite his cousin Dr Salo Tisch from Vienna to visit him for an indefinite time. Mr Jaffe, an acquaintance of Mundy's, who was of course not even distantly related to the Tisch family, stressed that he would provide the wherewithal for his guest's keep. He therefore asked that the British consulate in Vienna be directed to issue the requisite visa. Now all that was needed was a passport. Isaak Tisch had approached a Dutchman, Frank van Gheel Gildemeester, whose office was near St Stephen's Cathedral, in a connecting house in the Wollzeile. Gildemeester was an ambiguous figure. He had good contacts with the Nazis because he had represented imprisoned Austrian National Socialists before 1938. Now he had started to assist emigrants, using part of the money extracted from the wealthy to enable Jews without means to emigrate. Well-off emigrants lost their fortune, which was 'aryanized' or made over to the German Reich. Ten per cent went into a fund to cover the costs of Jews without means. This action took place with the agreement of the Nazis, who still wished to expel as many Jews as possible whom they had previously dispossessed.

Gildemeester was a final straw for Isaak Tisch to clutch at, and to hang on to, as the Dutchman was said to be especially concerned with the release of prisoners from the concentration camps and was always sending petitions to the Gestapo about it.

Isaak Tisch, as I know now from his declaration of means in 1938 that a relative came across, had almost completely used up the modest amount he possessed. He had paid four lawyers for consultations about his son's emigration. He had settled his son's tax bill and paid for his sister Jette Pridles's funeral. He had supported Jette's widower with 100 Reichsmarks a month, a tidy sum if one thinks that an unskilled labourer earned forty-five pfennigs an hour. His brother-in-law Pridles was out of work, and very quickly fell into poverty, like many of Vienna's Jews at the time.

Isaak had paid Gildemeester fifty marks for a passport, which he had received. It is only now that I have discovered – from documents in the archives of the Austrian resistance – that Salo was supposed to be released in October 1938. There is a 'list of Jews in Dachau whose exit papers are ready and completely in order. Deposited by Herr Gildemeester' on 11 October 1938, along with the order that 'the Jews on the attached list are to be released within three to five days and allowed to leave the country'.

I am looking at a copy from the archive, and against Salo is written, 'Emigrating to England'. I believe Salo was unaware to his dying day how close he had been to freedom then. He would have been spared much suffering if he had not been taken to Buchenwald. I am sure he would have been a different, less damaged person. But the release papers came just three weeks too late, when Salo was no longer in Dachau.

In the middle of September 1938 there was suddenly unusual activity in the camp, for reasons Salo was later to discover. On 15 September 1938 Chamberlain and Hitler met in Berchtesgaden. Hitler had demanded the annexation of the Sudeten areas and clearly signalled that Germany was prepared to go to war. Since July, troops had been massing on the frontier with Czechoslovakia. At the same time, the Nazis were preparing to suppress Czechoslovak resistance, and began emptying the concentration camp in Dachau, where they planned to lock up Czech opponents.

On 23 September, just three weeks before his release papers came, Salo was taken from Dachau to Buchenwald, just one of 1,200 Jews transferred that day. There were many Austrian intellectuals in the mass transport: doctors, lawyers, politicians and artists. Uncle Oswald Richter, the courageous social democrat, was among them, as were the young poet Jura Soyfer, the cabaret artist Paul Morgan and the librettist Fritz Löhner-Beda. All were loaded on to a train and taken via Weimar to Buchenwald. For the last stretch from the station, they were taken in buses guarded by armed SS.

The camp was not prepared for the sudden influx, and the arrivals from Dachau were squeezed into crowded barracks where there was a shortage of tables, chairs and beds. Each double-bunk bed had three occupants, and dozens slept on the floor.

Henceforth they were deprived of everything that made up their identity. They had all been made to look alike, their heads were shaved, their bodies given numbers, and they were classified by type of prisoner and condemned to an endless round of hunger, beatings, murder and forced labour. I sometimes wonder how long it takes to extinguish a human personality. How long can the spirit hold out against being dehumanized? Fractions of a second or days? And why did they keep him there at all when he would have been freed from Dachau? Nobody will ever be able to answer these questions for me, just like other gaps in Salo's life that can never be filled again.

Fred did not tell me by any means all that he saw there. He did not want to subject himself to pictures of what happened, and above all he wanted to protect me. 'You wouldn't have survived the third day,' he said to me. 'Someone with your fellow feeling would have been broken.' In order to survive, one had to be able not to look and not to listen. One had to turn oneself to stone to cope with it all.

Salo was given a worn-out blue-grey striped camp uniform. On the left side of the patched jacket was sewn a triangle in red material with a yellow triangle below it, so that the two formed the outline of a Star of David. Given the dreary uniformity of the prisoners' appearance, these 'angles', as these triangular bits of material were called in the camp, were all that distinguished the prisoners. Red denoted political prisoners, green ones those with previous convictions, black the work-shy, violet the Jehovah's Witnesses, blue the emigrants, pink the homosexuals. Yellow was for Jews. The yellow 'angle', as Salo was to learn, relegated Jews to the lowest rung in the camp hierarchy, and made them the preferred targets of SS terror.

'Jedem das Seine' ('To each his own') stood at the gate of the camp. All the new transports, which arrived on Mondays and Thursdays in Buchenwald, had to be present at a punishment ceremony in the parade yard, at which prisoners strapped to a punishment block were lashed with a leather whip. The dull insensibility into which many of the new arrivals had retreated even when in Dachau, the hardening of inner feeling, hardly sufficed to enable them to bear the cries and groans of those being tortured. Nothing they had so far seen prepared them for what they had to adjust themselves to here. 'Compared with Buchenwald,' said Fred, 'Dachau was paradise.'

Salo was sent to a workplace that was regarded as hell in the camp: the stone quarry. Most of the prisoners, especially the Jews, had to survive their first weeks here. There was no form of mechanical assistance, and no proper work clothes. The cutting and breaking up of the limestone, loading the trucks and pulling them out of the floor of the cutting, carrying the stones and transporting them to the camp, all this depended solely on the bodily strength of the prisoners.

Severe injury and maiming were unavoidable, and anyone who tried to dodge the danger was beaten or punished by the SS, *Kapos* and foremen. One of the most feared punishments was being suspended from a tree, Fred told me once, haltingly and with tears in his eyes. The victim was hung with his hands bound behind his back, and dangled in the air until the ball joints sprang out of the shoulder sockets. The sight of the figures hanging on the beech trees crying with pain, for hours until they lost consciousness, haunted Fred repeatedly in his dreams. In the same way, he was pursued by the picture of prisoners harnessed to the carts who were known in the camp as the 'singing horses' because they were forced to sing as they dragged their loads of many tons.

The systematic organization of life in the concentration camp served just one purpose, said Fred: to inflict the greatest possible torment. Men who spoke the same language as their victims, and had the same lullabies sung to them by their mothers as children, had devised a vision of hell that no one could have begun to imagine. Of all the torments they invented, water deprivation was one of the worst.

According to Fred, after hours of heaving around stones, many so heavy that an athlete would have staggered under the weight, his throat began to burn. Swallowing a mouthful of water before, during or at the end of what was often thirteen hours' work was a punishable offence. Each prisoner got only a quarter of a litre of water a day to drink. There was none for keeping clean. The camp commandant Koch had fixed the daily ration at four bucketfuls per hut, four buckets for more then a hundred men.

Fred said that on the few occasions he could have a cursory body wash, he had deliberately avoided looking at his body, which had become emaciated within a few days. The daily ration was barely a pound of bread, a litre of thin cabbage soup, some margarine and a sausage or cheese. The food would not have been enough for someone doing normal work, and it condemned the forced labourers to constant hunger.

The parade ground, above all, with a gallows standing in a socket and a few isolated beech trees scattered around as a cynical reference to a vanished world, must have been for Salo

the place of ultimate damnation. Mental pictures of the humil-
iations suffered there always overcame him when it rained
heavily. The hammering of raindrops reminded him of the
sound of rain beating on the roofs of the wooden huts.

It rained a lot in Buchenwald, said Fred. The damp cold
was more bearable when they were working in the day than
at evening roll call, which often went on for hours. The
prisoners stood in wooden shoes, torn boots or with their feet
bound in rags in mud often reaching above the ankles. They
had to stand at attention all the time, whip the caps off their
heads when ordered, sing marching songs or witness punishment being administered on the whipping block. If any
prisoners were missing, the terror often lasted for hours. After
two had escaped on one occasion, they had to stand in the
open all night in the icy cold. Some prisoners died from
exhaustion in the following days.

One can get used even to the constant presence of death.
To many it seemed a deliverance. *Muselmann* was the name
given to prisoners who had given up all will to live and
wavered with vacant eyes between the worlds of life and
death before they left the worse of the two, ending as so-
called 'wrens', and throwing themselves on the electric fence.
But there were also many who kept their humanity, defending it against the horror around them with dignity and
civilized values.

The Austrian artists had not forgotten how to laugh
through the tears. Fritz Grünbaum, the cabaret artiste from
the Simpl, Paul Morgan and the young poet Jura Soyfer dared
to go into the huts of their fellow prisoners and perform
sketches there. They even went into the huts of non-Jews,
which was strictly forbidden. A table was pressed into service
as a stage, and Grünbaum improvised cabaret turns for his
fellow sufferers. Fred said that for half an hour he took them
out of their misery, and that for a short while merriment
entered the huts, borne on that spirit and deep humanity that
was so far removed from the world they moved in the rest of
the day.

The Viennese cabaret artiste Paul Morgan had a good
chance of getting out of this hell. He had all the papers he
needed to emigrate to Holland and Yugoslavia, and was about

to be released when his block was put on a punishment detail because the block leader had found food in the beds. Again it was raining, and an icy wind was blowing on the parade ground. Paul Morgan signalled to the block leader, tore the cap from his head, and stammered, 'I'm ill, Blockführer, I have a fever.' He was forced back into the ranks. When a whistle finally sounded to signal the end of the punishment, Paul Morgan had to be carried to the sick bay on a stretcher, where he died that night, 10 December 1938. By special permission of the commandant's office, Hermann Leopoldi and Fritz Grünbaum carried their dead friend from the sick bay to the camp gate. His fellow prisoners hummed 'Wer wird denn weinen, wenn man auseinander geht?' ('Who shall cry when we part?'). It was his favourite song.

Fred said that there were two kinds of music in the camp. One was the music that accompanied the horror, the other helped one bear it. Every morning the blocks of prisoners marched on parade to the sound of the camp orchestra and afterwards off to their places of work. The twelve-man band also had to play when punishments were being carried out, for example when prisoners were being tied to the whipping block. The worst abuse of music was camp commander Rödl's habit of forcing the prisoners, as they returned dead-tired from work, to sing children's songs. At the end of 1938, Rödl had the idea of a competition to write a camp song. The prisoners were to devise a suitable march, and he promised a ten-mark prize to the winner.

Fred said that he tried writing words, but he clammed up inside. How could words express what there were no words for? Finally it was Löhner-Beda who wrote what was in essence a revolutionary text, and Hermann Leopoldi wrote the tune.

It was given out that the author of the text was a Gentile – even in the concentration camp the Nazis insisted on 'music free of Jewish influence'. The trusty in the sub-post office submitted the song, and the camp commander liked the Buchenwald March. On Christmas Eve 1938, Salo Tisch, prisoner from Block 9, stood with thousands of other sad figures on the parade ground in Buchenwald and sang:

Salo's Song

Wenn der Tag erwacht, eh die Sonne lacht,
Die Kolonnen ziehn zu des Tages Muehn
Hinein in den grauenden Morgen
Und der Wald ist schwarz und der Himmel rot,
Und wir tragen im Brotsack ein Stückchen Brot
Und im Herzen, im Herzen die Sorgen.

Oh Buchenwald, ich kann dich nicht vergessen,
weil du mein Schicksal bist.
Wer dich verliess, der kann es erst ermessen,
Wie wundervoll die Freiheit ist!
Oh Buchenwald, wir jammern nicht und klagen,
Und was auch unser Schicksal sei,
Wir wollen trotzdem ja zum Leben sagen,
Denn einmal kommt der Tag: dann sind wir frei!

Und die Nacht ist kurz, und der Tag ist so lang,
Doch ein Lied erklingt, das die Heimat sang:
Wir lassen den Mut uns nicht rauben!
Halte Schritt, Kamerad, und verlier nicht den Mut,
Denn wir tragen den Willen zum Leben im Blut
Und im Herzen, im Herzen den Glauben.*

Although it must have been the last thing the commandant intended in commissioning the song, said Fred, it gave heart to thousands of prisoners. It became the anthem of the uprooted. When they marched out in the mornings and back in the evenings, they put all their hatred and hope into it. Rödl, the commandant, seemed too stupid to grasp this, but liked to dance to the tune as the band played on one side of the parade ground and people were being flogged on the other.

---

* When the day awakes ere the sun smiles, / The columns march on their daily toils / Off into the grey morning / And the woods are dark and the heavens red, / and we bear in our rucksacks a piece of bread / And in our hearts, in our hearts we carry our cares. /
Oh Buchenwald, I can never forget you / For you are the fate I am bound to. / Only those who leave can measure,/ How wonderful freedom is! / Oh Buchenwald, we'll never complain, / Whatever fate has in store, / We'll always say yes to Life, / For the day will come when we're free!
Though the night is short and the day is long, / A song shall be heard of our home: / We shall never give up on our courage! / Stay in step, Kamerad, and keep faith, / For we have in our blood the will to live on, / And in our hearts the belief that we shall.

Salo's parents of course learned nothing of all this. Twice a month the prisoners were allowed to write to their families – saying that they were fine, as ordered to. This at a time when his wasted body was showing the first signs of a possibly fatal illness. Without his knowing it, his time had started to run out.

In Vienna, Isaak Tisch still struggled desperately to rescue his son. The city was in turmoil. In October some synagogues had had windows smashed, torah rolls had been violated and places of prayer destroyed. The big synagogue in the second District had been set on fire, and on Yom Kippur, the most important Jewish holy day, hundreds of Jews had their house keys confiscated and were told to assemble at the Ostbahnhof for deportation. Only the following afternoon did the families get their keys back.

The dams of civilization had already been undermined, and it did not take much to release a torrent of malice over the city. The pogroms in November, which the Nazis called 'Kristallnacht' because of the smashed glass with its glistening reflection of the fires they had laid, extinguished Jewish life in Vienna. More than forty synagogues and places of prayer were burned. The violent, looting mob took over the city. The community offices were stormed and several hundreds of their employees arrested. People were beaten to death, thousands were arrested and many deported to Dachau.

Almost 10,000 Jews were also taken to Buchenwald between 10 and 14 November. A special pogrom camp had been erected to the west of the parade ground, with five improvised barn-like barracks divided from the other blocks by barbed wire. There was no sanitation, no heating, no windows, not even any foundations. To sleep, the prisoners were crammed together on wooden shelves without blankets or straw.

Isaak Tisch did not mention in his letters to his son that his home had been wiped out too. Much of what the parents had built up through years of hard work was lost. They had got an order from the housing office expelling them from 78 Vorgartenstrasse, where they had lived for a quarter of a century, and directing them to flat 26 at 21a Taborstrasse, which had been a shopping street with mostly Jewish shops.

The house they moved to was a fine art nouveau building near the Karmeliterplatz. It is still there. I went to see it once. Thick stucco garlands line the entrance hall, and light enters through bevelled glass windows. Flat 26 lies behind a gleaming oak door. It has a room for a servant, a kitchen, and high double doors connect four rooms en suite. A lovely flat for a small family, but they had not chosen to live there, and they had to share it with several other families. Probably, like most families, they had no more than a single room for themselves. Halfway through the year, the Nazis had started herding the Jewish population together like cattle in certain parts of town. Landlords were forced to give notice to Jewish tenants, and Jewish tenants to take Jewish sub-tenants. Jews could live only in designated Jewish houses, of which 21a Taborstrasse was one. Immediately after the *Anschluss* it became subject to official control.

Even those who had hesitated to leave the country now tried to flee. At the end of 1938 the first large transports of children left the city. Many children could only say goodbye to their mothers because their fathers were in concentration camps. Escape was no easier after the pogroms in November because everyone now wanted to leave. The emigration section of the community offices in Vienna was hopelessly overrun.

But the unbridled brutality of the Nazis had finally alarmed other countries. Britain and the USA relaxed their immigration requirements. The persecutions in November had opened even the most reluctant eyes, and destroyed once and for all the hope to which many had clung, that the old, the women and the children would be spared the horror. I do not know whether Salo's parents devoted as much effort to their own escape as they did to getting him freed. Because an exit permit lapsed after three months, Isaak Tisch had to start all over again to try to get a visa for his son.

Although they had lost almost all they had, he went on sending Salo thirty marks every month to Buchenwald, which was the most prisoners were allowed to receive. The money often meant survival, Fred told me, not only because it meant one could buy things in the canteen, but because one could 'contribute' it to the SS or to trusty prisoners in the hope of being slightly less badly treated.

Salo must have become infected around Christmas. No one realized that a deadly disease had broken out in the camp. At some stage he must have had a fever, felt constantly washed out, had severe headaches and fits of shaking and shivering. At about that time the order for his release from 'protective custody,' must have been issued because Mundy had managed to get him a visa for the Dominican Republic.

Even as Salo Tisch left Buchenwald concentration camp on 19 January 1939, and, shaking and covered in cold sweat, signed the release declaration in which he undertook never to speak of his experiences, he must have had the small red abdominal rash symptomatic of typhus. He still wore his prisoner's clothes. He was far too thin to withstand the cold. Salo shivered, and moisture ran down his temples.

When he later found out the reason for his fever, he was convinced the deadly disease had saved his life, and that he had been released for fear of a typhus epidemic in the camp. He also told me that he was picked up outside the camp gates by Jewish helpers, and I have since learned that people from the local Jewish community met people released from Buchenwald at Weimar station and took care of them. Salo was medically examined, and given food and warm clothing and a train ticket. His parents in Vienna were informed, and asked to take him to a hospital immediately on arrival. He was given money for his journey and urged to burn his clothes in Vienna, and not, as was usual, to send them back to the aid committee.

For the first time in ages he wore the same sort of clothes as other people, although no doubt his head, which had been completely shaved shortly before, and his emaciated body marked him out clearly enough as someone who had been in a concentration camp. I wonder how he felt, seeing a world which seemed to have forgotten where he came from. I wonder what he thought when he saw women, children and other travellers walking upright without fear, or when people exchanged friendly words with him. Salo must have passed the journey back to Vienna in a daze, one less to do with his illness than with hardly being able to believe that he had escaped from the rain in Buchenwald.

I know today that, deep inside him, it had never really stopped raining.

6 Mrs Laver

Last night I was up until way after midnight. The lights in the other rooms were off, and my lodger had been asleep for hours. She is a doctor (it is reassuring to have a doctor in the house), and has to get up early. I sat at my desk for a long while and typed a letter to a relative of mine in Chicago. The clatter of keys broke the silence of the night. I like the sound. It gives me an inner peace and muffles the restless sounds of the day like a thick woollen cloth. Thoughts somehow become clearer, and seem to have space to spread out. I can't count the nights I have spent at my typewriter. Even now hardly a day goes by without my writing a letter on it. My fingers don't fly over the keyboard as they used to, but they are agile enough to keep up with my thoughts.

I always set the minimum line spacing – a tiresome habit from the war, when one often had only a single sheet of paper and crammed the words into the last bit of space, words about everything that had been going on, the good and bad news, anxieties, hopes, joys and despair. Often, to get around the censor, the true message was hidden between the lines.

Before I left for Ireland, my parents and I had agreed code words to conceal things or people in our letters. A Dr Kind was disguised as 'Mr Babyson'. 'Cruiser' was the synonym for bad news, 'buttons' the secret name for money, I still recall. A rather appropriate one, admittedly, and probably the censors found it amusing. All the same, buttons meant life and survival to us – as the letters themselves did, because they kept alive the confidence that we could have a future together.

After I arrived in Dublin I wrote home every week, and there was never enough paper to describe all the things that were new to me. Fate had brought me into a house in which

Jewish traditions were much more alive than at home in Bohemia. It was really in Dublin that I first encountered the Jewish way of life.

Although not given to unworldly piety, the lady of the house followed Jewish practices. Mrs Sally Citron and her sister Rosy Wine owned one of Dublin's most expensive fashion salons. Every month they travelled together to London to buy material at Liberty's, from which their seamstresses made one-off 'creations' based on their own or other designs. Mrs Citron's marriage had been dissolved under Jewish law (there was then no civil divorce in Ireland), and she had a five-year-old son, Sammy, and a seven-year-old daughter Keila, whom I was to look after. I spoke French to the children, which was then much easier for me than English. Keila had been a cripple from birth. Her legs and arms were thin and deformed, and she had a large hump on her little back. I felt sorry for her, and tried to be especially careful with her. But it made her angry, and she sometimes told her mother that I had hit her. 'Of course,' said Mrs Citron, 'I know my daughter is lying. She did it with your predecessors. It takes a long time for Keila to let anyone near her. Please be patient with her.'

In the mornings I drove Sammy and Keila to school in the family car. At four I collected them again, and we spent the rest of the afternoon together. We sometimes went to the seaside to bathe and have a picnic. Beyond the dunes I had discovered a deserted beach. It was sandy and the water was shallow, and the children could play safely in the waves. I loved this spot with its uninterrupted view to the horizon. Here, far from the restricted views of the Elbe valley at home, I first experienced the boundlessness of the ocean. It gave me an expansive feeling inside, and I returned from the beach with my confidence raised that I should soon be sitting there with my parents and Marianne staring into the waves.

In the mornings, when the children were at school, I tidied their rooms and washed their things. In accordance with orthodox tradition, Sammy wore a little *tallit*, or prayer shawl, a rectangular piece of white material with an opening for the head, and tassles, called *tzitzit*, at each corner. Its original white had long given way to grey grime, so I put it in the wash to give it a thorough cleaning. Mrs Citron, who came home about eight o'clock, when I had got the children to bed and read them a good-night story, was horrified to see the gleaming white shawl. 'What have you done?' she asked aghast. 'I've only washed it,' I said. 'But don't you know it's sacrilege to wash a *tzitzit*? They're a reminder of religious obligations. They help guard against sin. They must never be washed.' No, of course I didn't know. There was much I didn't know. I had no idea about kosher food, and didn't know a word of Hebrew.

In time I began to find my way into this new world. On Sundays we often visited my employer's parents. Sometimes when Mrs Citron was in London on business, I went there on my own with the children. Their grandfather, old Mr Solomon, and his wife lived in a large, elegant house in Dublin. A plump, warm man, with sympathetic eyes, he must have seen me as a lost sheep. After a kosher lunch, he always told me Old Testament stories and taught me a few words and letters of Hebrew.

'If you like,' said Nora, whom Sally Citron employed as her cook, 'I'll teach you to cook kosher. And you should really learn the main Irish and English dishes. You never know, you may need them one day.' She was right. Many Jewish women from the Continent were now working in the British Isles. I knew only Czech cooking, and that only from watching. In the final weeks before leaving home, I had looked over our cook's shoulder and been told how to make dough for dumplings, *Tafelspitz* and apple strudel. I had packed Mother's *Prague Cookbook* in my case and some of her handwritten recipes. But I wondered whether people in Britain would be enthusiastic about pastries and *Wiener Schnitzel*.

No one knew about my cooking lessons with Nora. It was our secret. So that I could watch, Nora began cooking supper for Mrs Cotton at lunchtime when the children were at school. I mixed and tasted and helped prepare food as best I could, and wrote all the recipes in a notebook. I recorded such basic things as how long to boil potatoes, and how to make plum pudding or *gefillte* fish or Irish soda bread. I liked these hours in the mornings when we cut ourselves off in a little world,

concealed from the outside behind a screen of misty conden-
sation on the windows caused by steam from our cooking.
Cooking is still something of a contemplative activity for me,
although it now takes me longer because I often can't concen-
trate so well.

Rosy, my employer's sister, lived not far from us in the same
area. She also had a young Jewish girl from the Continent
working for her. Bina Wallach, who was from Vienna, was a
year younger than me. She had left home in the summer of
1937, and was now hoping she could get her brother Jakob to
join her in Ireland. We quickly became friends. Exiles instinc-
tively gather around them people with similar experiences. It
welds them together. Even today, most of my friends are
people who came as Jewish refugees, and Bina is one of the
closest. We mostly speak English to one another now, of
course, but at the time being able to talk to her in my mother
tongue brought me a bit of home. We spent almost all our free
days together, going to the cinema or the theatre, and Bina,
who already spoke fluent English, whispered the translation to
me when I didn't understand. At first, I usually worked out
what was going on in terms of a vague idea, and that only
thanks to the pictures. I grasped only small fragments of the
accompanying dialogue, often spoken as it was with an accent,
which meant it might as well have been in code.

I admired Bina's learning. She was from a strict Jewish
home with social democratic sympathies, had been a member
of a Zionist youth club in Vienna and had managed to become
amazingly well-read. She now read English books: Oscar
Wilde, Charles Dickens and Galsworthy. In many ways she
reminded me of my friend Traute Fehres. Her unshakeable
honesty could be demanding. She was not one to hide her
opinions, and she sometimes found it hard to forgive shortcomings in others. Once on the way home from the cinema, I
took the liberty of picking a rose that hung over a stranger's
fence to add a bit of colour to my plain room. 'Are you mad?'
Bina shouted at me. 'That's stealing! What do you think
people will say if they catch Jewish girls stealing flowers?' I
was so overcome with bad conscience that I guiltily pushed
the rose back into the ground, as though the deed could be
undone and the rose go on growing.

When she arrived from the Continent, Bina had not had a friendly reception at all. Before going to Dublin, she had been a nanny in the family of an English Jewish dentist in London, and although she was Jewish too, they had treated her in the most degrading way. She got starvation wages of only ten shillings a week. She was not allowed to go into the dining room because they thought she would damage the wooden floor, and before the family took her with them on their holiday to the seaside, the wife went through her wardrobe, and sorted out the smart dresses, so that nobody could possibly mistake the nanny for the lady of the house. Bina was told she mustn't swim in the sea, and in the evenings they locked her in a room with their little daughter. But all that wasn't as bad, said Bina, as their forbidding her to mention her mother and brother in Vienna. On the return from the holiday, Bina gave notice, and took the job in Dublin. For the first time she felt genuinely appreciated.

While Bina concerned herself with my moral values, I concentrated on external matters, suggesting what colours and shapes best suited her when I went shopping for clothes with her or encouraging her to try a new hairstyle. In theory, because of our employers' business, we should both have been very much *à la mode*, but as a rule little from their studio came our way. And, truth to tell, I had more to worry about than being the height of fashion.

My homeland was being destroyed. It was being battered and trampled by barbarians, and sacrificed to false beliefs to satisfy the power lust of a paranoiac. Only three weeks after I left, Hitler made a speech promising the Sudeten Germans his 'protection'. In Aussig, where the speech was relayed on the radio, thousands gathered in spontaneous demonstrations in the market square. Many Jews packed immediately and fled to the interior of Czechoslovakia as exiles in their own country.

Every day the front pages of the British papers reported on the Czechoslovak powder keg and the 'Sudeten crisis'. On 15 September 1938 Chamberlain travelled to Berchtesgaden to negotiate with Hitler over the future of the Sudeten Germans. I could hardly sleep at this time. Nobody in their right mind could, at a such time of fear for the world's future. In London gas masks were distributed, and trenches dug in Hyde Park. In the best parts of town the wealthy were clearing their valuable possessions from their big town houses and transfering them to the safety of their places in the country. One English newspaper set the three and a half million Sudeten Germans against the potential ten million dead of another world war, with the implicit question: is it worth it? But it was much more than a matter of deciding between war and peace. It was one of resisting a man who was seeking to subject the whole world to his will.

Instead, he was given a free hand. I still remember the picture in the paper showing Chamberlain getting out of his plane in London after signing the Munich Agreement that determined the annexation of the Sudeten areas by Hitler's Reich. The British breathed a sigh of relief, but for me it was a moment of shame and betrayal. Neville Chamberlain proudly waved the copy of the treaty and announced – at the cost of the Sudetenland – it was now 'peace in our time'. I wanted desperately to be there and to force him to say why he had abandoned us and sacrificed us to a reign of terror. It was the policy of 'appeasement', he would probably have said, and Czechoslovakia is a faraway country of which the English know little.

That night, on 29 September, my family left their home town for ever. The father of a schoolfriend of Marianne's rang at my parents' door late at night. He was a worker and a leading social democrat, and had listened secretly to the radio, although some days earlier the Czechs had ordered the confiscation of all receivers in Aussig. He had heard what was decided in Munich, and set off in his van to warn my parents. 'Get away,' he begged my father as he opened the door. 'German troops will march into the Sudetenland on 1 October. You must get out, or something will happen to you.'

My father did not hesitate for a moment. He woke my mother, Marianne and the maid and told them to pack all their important possessions as quickly as they could. The sudden threat forced them to decide in a matter of hours the relative importance of all the many things they had acquired in the course of a lifetime, and to part with some for ever. A pain that must be familiar to all émigrés is the knowledge that many plants that are wrenched from their native earth at such times never take root again.

My parents spent hours packing that night. They rolled up the valuable carpets and put Malva Schalek's pictures between covers. They packed up the Meissen and Rosenthal china, the silver, the Bohemian glass and the valuable damask tablecloths, the bedclothes and jewellery. They put some of the furniture in the storeroom of the house of Hugo, my old driving instructor. Father fetched the details of his chemical discoveries and the patents from the safe in his office, and stuffed this foundation of his material existence into a leather briefcase. Marianne hugged her favourite doll as they rumbled through the dark and fog towards Prague.

I first learned of all this when they rang Mrs Citron's house from Prague, where they had found shelter in a friend's house. Father's voice sounded cracked, but it might have been the poor line. 'Everything is upside down here,' he said. 'Every day we hear something new, often the opposite of what we heard the day before. Refugees are coming from the Sudetenland every day, and we don't know how long the Czechs will put up with us in Prague.' I heard the anxiety in his words. 'I am trying absolutely everything,' I assured him. 'But it's still hard for me to find the way around here. The language is strange to me, and I don't know anybody.' If I had spoken for longer, I am sure I would have been overcome with self-pity. Homesickness, fear, the strange surroundings and loneliness built up in me, ready to burst into a torrent of tears at any moment. But the long-distance call was too expensive to allow for crying. And Father broke in. 'That will be all right, Ilse,' he comforted me. 'You have so much ability with languages; in a few weeks you'll probably be dreaming in English. And someone like you isn't alone for long. You'll soon find friends. Don't give up so quickly. Perhaps it will help us if you mention my chemical inventions. You've got copies of my patents. Just try to show them in the right place.'

I tried. It must have been boldness born of anxiety that gave me the courage to go to the highest level, to the Irish foreign ministry. I got an appointment the following week with a member of staff there, a Mr Ford. I was given ten minutes; ten minutes to save my family. I hardly shut my eyes for nights before. Bina helped me prepare my plea, which I learned word for word. My key argument was that my father's knowledge could help the 'war effort', because Fritz Lönhardt had developed a patent for manufacturing diesel oil from coal. I went over my speech again and again, and practised with Bina answers to possible questions and sharpened up my phrasing.

The day finally came. The appointment was on a Tuesday morning, and Mrs Citron gave me time off. Mr Ford was very friendly. He met me with a firm handshake and asked his secretary to get a cup of coffee. I think the copies of my father's patents, which I was clutching, shook in my wet hands, and I'm sure I stuttered a bit as I made my speech. I didn't get very far. 'Miss Lönhardt,' interrupted Mr Ford very soon, 'I know what hopes you have set on this meeting, and believe me, if I could do anything for you, I would. But my hands are tied. Ireland can't take any more Jewish refugees at the moment. We have reached our quota, and we are a poor country. If I can give you some advice, take the next boat to England and try to get work there. There are a lot of Jewish organizations in London which can help you, and England can take more Jewish immigrants than we can.'

One eventually gets used to setbacks. You just shake the water off like a dog, time and again, each time with a little less hope. But after this first failure I felt like a dry branch that had been trodden on and broken in two. It took a long time for me to realize that people who had had a secure life at home, and contributed to the culture and the life of their country for generations, were suddenly dead wood that no one really wanted. It never stops torturing me, knowing that many thousands more could have been saved if other countries had just taken more.

On 5 October 1938 the president of Czechoslovakia, Edvard Beneš, resigned. On 9 October, Aussig was occupied by German troops. Far beyond Pockau, a small suburb of the town, masses formed up like a guard of honour to greet the Wehrmacht troops coming from the Erzgebirge. Swastika flags and brushwood bundles of fascist insignia decorated the buildings, and above the crowd a forest of outstretched arms gave the Nazi salute as the soldiers passed by. In the evening

the people of Aussig gathered at the sports arena for the 'liber
ation rally', and the masses sang in chorus, 'Wir danken
unserm Führer'.

As usual, the Nazis didn't hang around. Two days later, the
remaining Jews had to declare all their possessions. Their
houses were confiscated, the owners expelled or arrested.
Jewish shops, some of whose window displays had been
smashed by the Nazis earlier, were expropriated. Aussig, once
a proud and sophisticated city, was now in the hands of the
lawless.

A friend told me later that they picked up Fritz Hutterer at
this time. Hutterer, a Jew, was now very old, and was one of
the best-loved actors in Aussig, a man of the theatre through
and through, and a gifted comic. The town had paid for a
celebration of the fiftieth anniversary of his stage debut, and
he was regarded as an institution. Now the Nazis dragged
him from his house, put him on a handcart, and drove him
out of town. Nothing was ever heard of him again – nor of
any attempt to stop him being taken away. The Aussig opera
had for years been a refuge for many Jewish artists driven
from Hitler's Germany, who had made the cultural life of this
small city comparable with that of a metropolitan centre. The
conductor Franz Allers had been in charge of the opera, and
had staged *Carmen* and *Fidelio* and the complete *Ring* cycle.
Fred Destal had emigrated there after being thrown out of the
Berlin opera, and was a distinguished Wotan, Hagen and
Rigoletto.

But Aussig was no longer a place of refuge. Jewish pupils
and teachers were thrown out of the German schools. The
director of our Girls Reform Realgymnasium, Hugo
Lebenhart, also had to leave because he was a Jew. All Jewish,
Marxist and liberal books disappeared from the municipal
library, and the memorial tablet in the entry hall, commemo-
rating its Jewish benefactor, Eduard Jakob Weinmann, was
removed.

My grandmother, Oma Hedwig, sent me from Türmitz a
number of written sheets of hand-made paper, which she
thought could be turned into money. They were autograph
letters written to her by Johann Strauss when she was a young
girl. They were indeed very valuable, as an auction house in

Dublin confirmed to me. Grandmother sent only one letter at a time from fear that they might go missing on the way. She encouraged me to sell them. I could certainly make better use of the money than she could, and perhaps it could even help speed up my parents' exit from Prague.

Meanwhile, numerous private aid organizations from England had begun work, among them the Quakers, a 'Save the Children' fund and an aid fund of the Labour Party. At first they were concerned less with emigration than giving aid on the spot. The British Foreign Office, the English papers said, was trying to limit the number of Czechoslovak refugees coming to Great Britain. Jewish refugees were low on the scale of priorities. It was known that the British ambassador in Prague, Mr Newton, was advising that the refugee problem be handled in a restrictive way.

Father wrote to me that, given his serious position, he had even asked Ferdinand Rauter for help. Rauter, an Austrian, was the son of the head of the school for the blind in Aussig, and was himself a pianist who was much in demand, and hence widely travelled. He toured all over the world with the Icelandic singer Engel Lund, and had appeared in almost every major European city. They had made understanding between peoples, just as the world was turning away from it, the core of their programme, and presented folk songs from all over the world. I had heard them several times in Aussig. Engel was no heavenly beauty, but her voice was like a gift of God. She performed songs in seventeen languages, and Ferdinand accompanied her on the piano. When Engel sang, she hardly moved, and her face was almost expressionless. It was as though everything was concentrated in her voice, and her singing left almost no listener unmoved. Engel sang 'Maria durch den Dornwald ging in German, Arum di lichtelach' in Yiddish and 'De tolv hellige Ting' in Danish. The duo had often appeared in Germany. One day before Hitler came to power, they gave a concert in Hamburg, and decided not to take four Yiddish songs out of the programme. Afterwards an SS officer came to the green room and expressed his surprise that such a miserable people could write such beautiful music. When the Reichskulturkammer later invited Ferdinand Rauter and Engel Lund to present a

Nordic recital in Dresden, Ferry wrote back that they were
otherwise engaged until the end of the Third Reich.

Both had moved to Britain. Father was happy to have a
good friend there, and asked Rauter to contact me. Many
years later Ferdinand gave me my father's letters, which were
always wavering between distress and a disciplined reminder
to keep one's head, and I am very moved when I read them
today. On 7 November 1938 my father wrote to 'Dear Ferry'
that he probably knew meanwhile from his parents that 'great
misfortune has overtaken us'. It was widely claimed, wrote
my father, that 'non-Aryans' had a right of option, and would
be given time and opportunity to wind up their assets. This
had not happened. Returning to their old home was impossible; in fact, people who had stayed behind were now all
gradually coming to Prague. One didn't know how long the
Czechs would tolerate them there, and what was important
now was to find a new home. Almost all countries were
barred, and transfer of money was difficult, said my father.
But one mustn't lose heart. A number of members of the
Schlaraffia masonic lodge planned to emigrate together with
their families. Any country would be welcome, my father
stressed, and they were not afraid of any kind of work. He
never forgot, at the end of his letters, to send warm greetings
and hand kisses to Fräulein Lund.

Ferdinand, bless him, did not fail us. He set off for Dublin
and one day, there he was at the door, and all because my
mother had written that I felt lonely in my new surroundings.
I was so delighted to see him! We drove to the beach, to my
favourite spot, and went for a walk. Ferdinand told me about
his concerts in London. A few months before he had given a
private recital at 20 Maresfield Gardens, in Hampstead, the
home of Sigmund Freud, who had invited his friends to an
evening of music. Engel and Ferdinand had presented their
programme 'Folk Songs of Many Lands'. 'The guests enjoyed
it,' said Ferdi. And even Sigmund Freud, who was known not
to be unduly fond of music – except for the Mozart operas –
applauded for a long time. His views were much valued in
musical circles. After all, he had known many composers
personally, including Brahms and Schönberg. He had been
consulted by Gustav Mahler in Vienna, and by Richard

Tauber. Ferdinand Rauter's and Engel Lund's appearance was the only recital that ever took place at Freud's home in exile. Freud died there in September 1939.

'You should try to get to London,' said Ferdinand. 'You won't be so lonely there; London is teeming, especially with German-speaking Jews. And the Jewish Committee is working in Bloomsbury House day and night to help Jews emigrate. They will be able to do more for you and your parents than anyone in Ireland.' I told Ferdi of my failure with the foreign ministry. 'I'm now clear that I must go London,' I said. 'But first I have to find a job there, or they won't let me into the country.'

Rauter promised to keep his ears open. I wasn't to worry. When he was leaving that evening, I didn't want to let him go, because all that he brought that was comforting and familiar would go with him. Ferdi smiled at me through his round spectacles and held me tight. 'I'll write to you just as soon as I find something,' he said. 'Don't give up, Ilse. You'll see, you'll be sitting in the front row at our next recital in London.'

Father had also told Ferdi of his fears for Marianne. He thought that at fourteen, she was too young to work abroad, and too old to go to a boarding school. Marianne was learning sewing and hairdressing in Prague, her high-flown dreams of being a painter reduced to the bare need to survive. She was their greatest worry, my parents admitted.

So that afternoon Ferdi and I also took time to visit a Catholic convent school called Loretto Abbey near Dublin, of which Ferdi had had positive reports, especially as they also took young girls from the Continent. The fees were not especially high, and the school itself had an air about it that was friendly, if a little strict. When my parents heard of this chance, they must have felt immense relief. They wrote to Ferdinand 'with heartfelt thanks' that he had freed them of what was at present their greatest worry. 'If there is a God, he will reward you,' said my father. A sentence in one of his letters moves me in particular. 'In future, you can be more of a father to Marianne than I can,' it says, as though he had already begun to fear the worst.

Anxious months passed before Marianne arrived. In their letters my mother and father told of the horrendous things happening at home. All non-Aryans would be arrested and released only if they undertook to emigrate. 'Now the poor people must leave without a sou,' wrote father. 'Even those over seventy are being arrested and made to sweep the streets.' Herbert, my mother's younger brother, had been taken to prison in the castle at Königstein in Saxony. His 'Aryan' wife had left him.

My parents spent all day doing the rounds of government offices, queueing, writing letters, submitting requests, getting confirmations and fighting their way through the jungle of changing announcements and official decrees. When, at the end of October, it became known that Great Britain was issuing some visas, the British passport office in Prague was besieged. My father spent days there but was eventually sent away. Then it was back to the refugee committees, to be registered on a list. Nobody could say when they would know anything because the British aid organizations, the refugee committees and the British passport office were constantly at odds over who should have the last word in deciding case priorities. And so it was the fate of many people to have their name entered on a list and never subsequently acted upon.

Father and Mother lived from the money that my father had been able to rescue. He had transferred the firm to his non-Jewish partner and was waiting for a pension that had been arranged for when he would retire. As usual, money was the lubricant in the works of the Kafkaesque bureaucracy. For a long time it was said that the Czechs allowed emigrants to take 100,000 crowns abroad, but they would have to leave 14,000 behind, said my father. There had previously been a rumour that the German Jews would not be allowed to stay in Prague. My parents wrote that the Prague authorities were acting 'cold-bloodedly' on directives of the erstwhile enemy, and it was feared the same games would be played in the capital as in the Sudetenland.

The Munich *diktat* cut off Czechoslovakia's most important limbs and incorporated them into the German Reich. The country had lost a third of its population, almost the same proportion of territory, the greater part of its heavy industry, two-thirds of its coal deposits and 40 per cent of its domestic product. What remained was an amputated trunk that had ceased to be a democracy, and submitted itself like a vassal to Berlin's hegemonic claims. After passing an enabling law on the German model, the new government in Prague suspended the constitution and introduced a one-party system. Opposition was banned, and concentration camps were built for political enemies. Although the League of Nations High Commissioner vetoed it, the Czech government began sending thousands of Sudeten German refugees back to their previous homes, including even social democrats who had opposed Henlein. Particularly for those who had been politically committed, this meant prison and concentration camps, if not certain death. Some took their own lives out of despair.

My parents' letters from a dehumanized world always caused me inner turmoil. Worse still was what Bina heard about Kristallnacht in Vienna. What no one thought possible had now happened. The worst of it was having to look on at the destruction that was taking place without being able to do anything. This powerlessness clung to us, cold and clammy, like wet clothes to our bodies, and whenever we thought to have overcome it by plunging into all kinds of frenzied activity, and warmed ourselves with a shimmer of hope, it came up on us again and blew a cold draught over us.

On 1 December 1938 Joseph Goebbels spoke in the hippodrome in Aussig. There was an election meeting for the 'special supplementary election' in the Sudetenland, which was to be three days later. The town was bedecked with thousands of flags, and the shops had pictures of Hitler and Henlein in the windows. In the evenings SA and SS held torchlight marches through the town. On the Sunday, 99 per cent of the electors voted for the new government – according to the Nazis' official figures, anyway. Four weeks later, on New Year's Eve, the Aussig synagogue burned down.

Father begged my mother to leave with Marianne. It would be easier for her to find work as he was already sixty. 'I keep telling her to,' he wrote, 'So at least she and the children will be safe.' She was quite determined not to leave him, and took no notice. 'Leaving,' he said, 'is not as easy as people in England think. It is very difficult. They want to get rid of us, but put obstacles in our way.' The plane was fully booked three to four weeks in advance. It was even harder to get to America, he complained. Even people with affidavits, an entry permit for the USA, had to reckon with a delay of at least one to one and a half years, he wrote. In his letter, my father, formerly an entrepreneur, offered his services for any work, even the most menial. He would go with his Grete as a servant anywhere in the world, though one must bear in mind his limited knowledge of foreign languages. In Prague he tried to learn Czech, but his old head, he complained, had a block. Like many refugees from Bohemia and Moravia, he had applied for Czech citizenship, and hoped to get it. Then, he believed, he and Grete would be safe for the moment. He was to be proved wrong.

My friend Susie wrote from London. She had fled with her family from Aussig some months earlier. Susie's and my parents were close friends, her father was a Schlaraffia member like mine, and we girls had also become friendly. Susie went to the same gymnasium as I did, but three classes lower. Her parents owned several coal mines in Aussig, and the prosperity of the Meyer household had always slightly unsettled me. At meals, which were brought in by girls with white bonnets and lace-trimmed aprons, several different silver knives and forks were laid out either side of the china plates, and I never really knew whether I used the cutlery in the right order.

Now such demanding conveniences were of no account and, like so many Jewish refugees, Susie, the girl from a good family, was now working herself as a domestic servant. She was a governess in a family in London and said she was well treated. 'The cook has given notice,' she said, 'and my employer, Mrs Laver, is looking for a new one. I have told her that you are a fantastic cook. She is very interested. Oh, Ilse, it would be so lovely if we could work under the same roof, don't you think?'

I certainly did. I wanted at all costs to get to London, especially because of the Jewish aid organizations, but also because more and more friends from Aussig and Türmitz were arriving there. Bina had also now found a position with a Jewish family in London, and she had left Dublin in the meantime. I followed her on 24 December.

It suited me well to spend my first Christmas without my family on board a ferry rocking about on storm-tossed waves in the Irish Sea en route to England. The dining room was deserted because all the passengers were feeling seasick and crawled away to their cabins or were hanging with green faces over the rail like washing left to dry.

'Well, young lady, you still have a healthy colour,' one of the sailors said to me in the dining room. 'Fortunately, I am never seasick,' I replied. 'Then you meet all requirements for joining us,' he joked. 'Would you like to keep us company this evening? We are celebrating Christmas with a little dinner.'

Actually I didn't feel so much like celebrating, but it surely would do no harm to calm my thoughts down through some diversion, as they were hardly less wild than the sea. In the rolling toilet, I slipped into a nicer dress and pinched some redness into my cheeks. For the wild body of men that greeted me with 'Hoho' and suppressed whistles I proved to be a tad too elegant. The whole evening the seamen were concerned to convince me of the legendary Irish capacity for alcohol, drinking Guinness like fish and singing at the tops of their voices. Their faces glowing red like Christmas tree decorations, they bawled out Gaelic carols and Irish drinking songs and repeatedly encouraged me to sing along with them. Many of them were still rolling about as though still in stormy seas as the ferry slipped through quieter coastal waters towards the Welsh harbour of Holyhead.

I was also a bit weak at the knees, but for other reasons. Susie had praised me to the skies to her employer, and I trembled at the thought of having to live up to the expectations she had created. What did I know about cooking? On the train to London visions swam before my eyes of food burned to a cinder, stone-hard roasts and runny custard. I would totally disgrace myself. And my mother would be ashamed of me.

I have never in my life been inclined to pessimism, but that day after Christmas I was a crumpled wreck of timidity and anxiety. Nevertheless I then experienced what happens to pessimists more frequently than to those like me who assume the best: I was positively surprised.

I liked Mrs Laver from the start. She greeted me in a quite un-English way with an embrace, after Susie, with tears in her eyes, had practically squeezed the air out of me at the joy of seeing me again. 'I have heard lots of good things about you,' said Mrs Laver, beaming. 'And I am excited at what you will cook for us.' My stomach sank, and I shot a questioning glance at Susie, who grinned back. Tomorrow for sure they would throw me out of the house. A pity, because it was a beautiful house the Lavers had, an elegant, grand Regency house overlooking Wellington Square in Chelsea. Mrs Laver showed me my prospective domain in the basement. In front of the ochre-coloured walls of the kitchen hung copper saucepans from open wooden shelves. In the middle stood a large table with scratches and burn marks. Next door there was a cellar where coal and wine were stored and a maid's room, with a table and chair, a wardrobe and bed. 'Do you know English cooking?' Mrs Laver asked. 'A little, but I know more about Czech,' I said. 'To be honest, I don't have much idea what that's like,' she said. 'We only know a little about French cooking from our travels on the Continent. We found that excellent.'

I explained that there was a world of culinary difference between France and Bohemia. 'Why don't you simply cook us a sample meal and surprise us,' she suggested. 'Because it will end in disaster,' I wanted to say, but of course I agreed.

I had put together a menu in the past few days, and I practically knew Mama's *Prague Cookbook* by heart. Susie went with me to the market and showed me where to buy the ingredients. I spent the whole afternoon in the kitchen, trying to remember everything that Mother and Nora had told me. The windows were misty from hot steam, and I was quite steamed up myself with anxiety.

In the evening, the food was eventually carried up to the dining room in a lift and served from there by the maid, Kathlyn. I cleared up the kitchen and went nervously to bed. Next morning Mrs Laver came into the kitchen full of praise. 'The supper was splendid, Ilse,' she announced, 'really splendid! Tell me what all these strange dishes are called, and how you do them.' I was only too happy to explain that the little balls in the soup are called *Markklösschen*, the *schnitzel* is dipped in egg, flour and breadcrumbs the Viennese way, and the roast potatoes owe their strong flavour, so different from bland English mashed potatoes, to lots of onions and parsley.

I had passed muster, and so began a job that was to be one of the most agreeable I had. I didn't earn much – a pound a week – but it was enough to live on. I soon developed a close relationship with the Lavers' children, Patrick and Bridget. Actually they were not supposed to talk to the junior staff or go into the kitchen basement but Mrs Laver knew from Susie that I was more educated than most cooks, as I had matriculated and knew four languages. Every morning she came down the steep steps to inspect the kitchen and discuss the day's menu. In the afternoons, after school, the children burst in, picked at the dumpling dough and left finger marks in the cream – all of which was strictly forbidden.

The Laver household upheld Victorian traditions. At five p.m., Patrick and Bridget changed their clothes and their hair was combed and brushed. They then spent an hour with their parents in the drawing room. Once Mr Laver came crashing into the kitchen with the children, just as I was beating out the pastry for a strudel. 'Tell us, Ilse,' he burst out. 'We have been betting where Albania is. Can you tell us?'

With my finger I drew the boot of Italy and the eastern Mediterranean in the dough. 'There,' I said, 'Albania is northwest of Greece.' 'You're a good girl, Ilse,' said Mr Laver, banging the table with the flat of his hand, and throwing up a cloud of flour. 'Children,' he said to Patrick and Bridget, 'it seems your old father has lost the bet.'

At six the children had their evening meal, or 'high tea', without their parents, in the company of Susie, who then put them to bed. The parents ate alone two hours later in the dining room. Mr Laver always wore a dinner jacket, and Mrs Laver an evening dress whose silk rustled across the floor. Heavy jewellery adorned her décolletage.

It was a strange picture, and in its way very British. With the world falling apart all around, they clung to external formalities, as though this would keep the chaos at bay. In the meantime, though, many Britons had realized that events on the Continent could no longer be handled with the kid gloves of appeasement. Since the beginning of December, transports with Jewish children had been arriving in Britain from Germany, Austria and Czechoslovakia. In the coming months, no other country would take as many children as the United Kingdom, almost 10,000 in total. Jewish organizations and many private individuals gave £50 per child for the required guarantee, and Marks & Spencer provided food and clothing.

The newspapers printed pictures of these arrivals from a brutalized world. They wore thick overcoats and caps and had labels with their names around their necks. How I wished Marianne could be among them. The arrangements for her leaving had dragged on for almost three months. She had long had the official acceptance from the convent at Loretto Abbey, but there were always more papers that were required.

Every Wednesday afternoon I met Bina, and we went by underground to Bloomsbury House. The great building had been a hotel. Here and there the stucco was breaking away and there were cracks in the walls. No one worried about these signs of decay because it housed our future hopes. Most of the refugee organizations in England worked from here. On the ground and second floors was the largest, the Jewish Refugees Committee, with whom most of those who had fled from Hitler were registered. The Movement for the Care of Children had its office on the first floor, and above them were the various religious and professionally based associations, like the Quakers, the Catholic, Protestant and Anglican aid committees and organizations that found jobs for Jews from the Continent. Only a few refugees were fortunate enough to be able to resume their own occupations. Most, including doctors and lawyers, had to be content with work as farm labourers or domestic servants.

Bina and I took numbers and joined the large queue besieging the offices. The faces of many of those stranded here in the waiting hall of bureaucracy reflected the misery of exile, which, except for their mere existence, had deprived them of everything that had once given them pleasure and a place in life. For the mercy of mere physical survival, they were dispossessed, humiliated and uprooted. It often took hours until we were admitted to a large office and approached one of the dozen or so desks there. The assistants, of whom there were sometimes 600 working in Bloomsbury

House, were without exception friendly, and made an effort to encourage us.

As a result of the pogroms in November and criticism from many refugee committees and private individuals who had asserted Britain's moral responsibility, the government began to treat the immigrants more generously. At the end of January, Britain and France agreed with the Czech government to make £4 million available to assist emigration. A visa system was introduced whereby visas were issued not only to those who could show they had work or a maintenance guarantee, but also to people in transit via Great Britain. Children up to the age of seventeen could enter without a visa. Marianne's chances were good. All that was now needed was a guarantee that she would have means of support.

My employers the Lavers – and for this I shall be grateful to them all my life – declared they were willing to stand guarantee for Marianne. With my meagre wages I would never have been able to find the £50. In Dublin the solicitor of my previous employer, a Mr Collins, offered to pay Marianne's fees at the convent. I had become friends with Mr Collins during my stay in Ireland, and he had repeatedly stressed how happy he would be if he could help me and my sister in any way. Like countless other refugees, Marianne owed her rescue to generous people like these.

At last came long-awaited news from Prague. Every Friday evening, when Kathlyn, the maid, had time off, the Lavers let me call my parents. I was unhappy about their telephone bill, and tried to cram all the news into a few minutes' conversation. 'Don't worry about the money, Ilse,' Mrs Laver often said. 'These minutes are the most important in the week for you, and they won't bankrupt us.' Sometimes, when my eyes were full of tears after these calls, she would take me in her arms and try to comfort me. In her great goodness she often reminded me painfully of my mother.

It was the middle of January when Father was able to give the exact details of Marianne's arrival. She would come by train like the Kindertransports, but on her own. Like me a few months earlier, she would have to cross Germany and then travel on to England via Belgium. But travelling conditions had become worse in this short time, and Marianne was only fourteen I was very worried about her.

Few pictures have etched themselves into my mind like the one I have of my sister, standing in floods of tears on the platform at Victoria station. Her wet face glistened, her pageboy hair was in disarray. Around her neck was a large label with her name. I still can't forgive myself that I arrived ten minutes late, perhaps more. My bus had not arrived and I had run with a stitch to the underground and then up the steps to the mainline platforms. There she stood, like a statue, in a restlessly surging mass of people coming and going, as though she was afraid that any further step she took would result in her being caught up in this human torrent and consumed. How abandoned she must have felt in the eternity of the wait. 'There you are at last, Ische', she sniffed. 'I'm so sorry, little one,' I said. 'My bus didn't come.' For the long moment of our embrace all the bustle around us dissolved, and I heard only Marianne's sobbing and felt her trembling in my arms. I couldn't keep back my tears either. I had my little sister again. I had her, at least.

Marianne stayed with me for the next few days. Mrs Laver had bought a wardrobe and bed for her and put them in my room. But the first few nights we snuggled up together in one bed, as we often had in the room we shared at home. Late in the evenings, when we settled down after all the bustle of the day and lay in the dark, the shadows started to lift. Marianne often cried. I held her in my arms and stroked her soft hair. 'I miss Mummy and Daddy so much,' she said. 'Do you think we'll ever go back home, Ilse, when all this is over?' I tried to banish any trace of doubt or fear in my voice. 'Yes,' I said, 'I'm sure we shall. And we must never give up hope.'

'Can I stay with you, then?' Marianne asked for the hundredth time. 'I don't want to go to Ireland, to a school with nuns, where I don't understand anyone. I want to go to school here.'

'I've told you over and over why that's not possible,' I said wearily. 'I must work to have money for the two of us, so I can't look after you. And London is too dangerous. Everywhere they're digging trenches and building bunkers. If there is a war, the big cities will be hit first.'

'But you're here, and if you die, I want to die too,' said Marianne stubbornly. 'I don't want to live without you.' I stroked her for a long time, until she dropped off on my arm, which had gone to sleep long before. Fortunately, she had not noticed my tears.

Mrs Laver kept back part of my wages for Marianne's cost and lodging – a token part only, as Marianne had the lively appetite of a growing child. 'You seem to have learned some cooking, Ische,' she said, as she sat with me at lunchtime in the kitchen and devoured the fourth dumpling with meat sauce. 'Mummy would be proud of you.' To be honest, I had sometimes had the same thought as I took off my apron late in the evening and fell exhausted into bed. My parents would have been proud of me if they had been able to see how well I coped with this unfamiliar way of life. My nights were short. I had to get up at 4.30 a.m. to rake out the fires in the house. Sometimes I thought that I would have felt it degrading, as an entrepreneur's daughter, always surrounded herself by servants, to be a servant girl if my father hadn't always brought me up to be modest. He always used to say, 'You children must be prepared for difficult times. In bad times, believe me, spoiled children don't survive.' Father insisted that we wash our own underwear, because that was not a job for a laundress. Marianne and I had to keep our room clean, too. Sweets were like medals that had to be earned through good behaviour; they didn't just fly through the window. Although I sometimes suffered from my father's strictness, and Marianne probably more so, I was grateful to him later. I didn't regard my work for the Lavers as degrading, but as a chance to prove myself. Sometimes it amused me that I had smarter clothes hanging in my wardrobe than those my boss wore. Many Jewish girls from the Continent were better dressed in their time off than their employers.

I knew how difficult it was for girls from privileged backgrounds to work as domestic servants. At home they had learned to converse in French and play the piano with the aim of making a wealthy marriage. Even apart from many who had not so much as held a broom or cooking spoon and lacked domestic skills, some were treated degradingly by their employers. Acquiring the rudiments of cooking shortly before coming here was certainly not enough to help them deal with the inner pain that their changed status brought. I heard of two Jewish girls from Aussig who later took their own lives.

My colleague Susie, for whom prosperity was also a thing of the past, adjusted to her new life with a shoulder-shrugging composure for which many envied her. She had one big worry fewer than I did: her parents were already in London, and had even been able to salvage some money. Enough, in fact, at that time to live in a hotel. Her family planned to emigrate soon to America, and Susie saved as much as she could for this. As a nanny, she got a pound more per week than I did. All of us tried to put aside a little of what we earned. Actually I was supposed to cook every lunchtime for Susie, Kathlyn and myself. But we decided to forgo this luxury and be paid the money for the food instead. And so we sat chatting at the long table in my kitchen, disposing of the leftovers from dinner the evening before or eating bread and butter. Mrs Laver suggested to us, 'It makes little sense if we throw away the food from the previous day, and Ilse cooks again every lunchtime. If you don't mind eating leftovers, we'll add the food money to your wages, so you have a little more.'

It sometimes seemed to me that she felt guilty that her country had failed for so long to take Hitler seriously, and that she tried to appease her discomfort by her generosity. Soon after Marianne left for Dublin, Mrs Laver came to the kitchen as usual to discuss the evening menu, to find me dejectedly cleaning vegetables for a soup. I had meanwhile cooked my way to a certain status in Wellington Square. Mrs Laver invited guests almost every week, she said, so she could boast about her Czech cook. My cooking was met with what was, for the British, wild enthusiasm. Expressions of emotion – and all my life I have worn my heart on my sleeve! – the English view with a mixture of awed fascination and sheer horror. I have never really been able to get used to this coolness.

In contravention of the British commandment to keep a 'stiff upper lip', Mrs Laver really showed her feelings. Perhaps this was because she was an actress, a respected member of the Royal Shakespeare Company, and was used to expressing her own emotions and not regarding other people's as an imposition. 'You miss Marianne, don't you?' I nodded silently. 'You know, Ilse, I've been thinking,' she went on. 'It's not good that you have so little contact with other people here. You have your friends Bina and Susie, but that's not many when you're here for a long time. What do you think about inviting your friends from Aussig here for supper once a week?'

She gave me no time to answer, but came out with all the ideas that she must have been thinking about for days. 'Friday evening would be a good time,' she said. 'That's when the Jews have their Sabbath meal, and I'm sure some of your friends are practising Jews. And it's Kathlyn's evening off, and Mr Laver and I usually go out, so that would be the perfect time. You can cook a full meal, so everyone can eat all they want once a week. You can have a completely free hand in what to buy; just get the shops to put it on the account as usual, and we'll pay for it at the end of the month. And if there's anything over, let your friends take it home.'

'Mrs Laver,' I stammered – and as always, when I was deeply moved my English began to falter – 'all I can say is thank you. A thousand thanks. You don't know how happy you've made me.'

'How many friends do you have here from Aussig, then?' she asked. 'It's thirty-six now,' I replied, and saw how her eyes widened with surprise. 'That many?' Now she was at a loss. 'Well then, in that case you must just invite a different six every week, so that each of them has their turn every six weeks.'

The Sabbath meal became a wonderful custom. Every Friday evening I played host to some of those from home. I usually cooked the Czech way. I didn't know too much about kosher cooking, and anyway the Lavers' kitchen was not run on kosher lines. I spread a white tablecloth over the worn kitchen table, put out the everyday china and set up candles, which are traditionally lit at the start of Sabbath. I always cooked three courses: first a wholesome soup, a meat or fish main course and a pudding.

These suppers soon became an institution. The guests included a lot of young men from my Aussig rowing club and my circle of friends. Unlike the female refugees, of whom many were domestic staff and had enough to eat, the men often lived just on fish and chips. Most, like me, had had to leave their parents behind in provincial Bohemia or in Prague, and we told one another of our various attempts to get the rest of our family out. Despite this, the mood was never depressed, and the unalloyed joy of being able to see one another again ensured that we obeyed the Jewish injunction not to remind people on the Sabbath of misery and suffering. The evening almost invariably ended with us telling one another Jewish jokes. Paul Friedländer, a rowing companion, who now lived in London, always had the latest refugee jokes, which mostly turned on the inadequate English of the émigrés. 'Do you know the one about the two Jewish refugees on a bus to Wembley?' he asked. 'One asks the other, "Is this Wembley?" – "No, it's Thursday", says the other. – "So am I. Let's get off and have a drink!," Sometimes my stomach ached from laughing and tears ran down my cheeks. Maybe this mixture of laughter and tears is very Jewish, but perhaps it's also a matter of how one approaches life. Thank God, I have never lost it.

Before Kathlyn came home at ten, I gave the leftovers of the supper to everyone in screw-top jars to take with them. For many of my guests, it was the only proper meal of the week. Several times Hans Fürth was one of my guests, the Hans from Halle who twenty years earlier had been delivered by the same midwife as my sister Marianne.

He had obtained my address from his mother in Germany, and got in touch with me. At our first meeting he immediately asked about Marianne, whose development he had followed with approving attention from when she was very young whenever he and his mother visited us in Aussig. Hans, who like most refugees had acquired a new name and now called himself Anthony Firth, had moved to London as early as 1936. His father, a chemist like mine, had died very young two years before, and the powerful industrialist Franz Petschek, who owned coal mines in Aussig and in Halle, had adopted him out of long-standing friendship. 'The boy must get out,' he said to his mother in 1936, after the situation of the Jews in Germany became drastically worse. Petschek got him a place to study automotive engineering in Chelsea. Now Tony had finished his studies and was looking for a job because if he didn't have one he risked losing his residence permit. But it wasn't in Tony's nature to worry about such things. He was resolved under no circumstances to go back to Germany.

In the middle of 1938, along with two friends, he had founded a cosmetics firm making liquid lipstick – an invention of Tony's. I laughed when he told me about it. Even if the world was collapsing all around, you could be sure Tony would fall back on one of life's indispensable trivialities and meet adversity with the gambler's *belle indifférence*. Because of problems with the supply of raw materials, he planned a two-day trip to Prague of all places in February 1939, to a city where the Jews were set on nothing more than trying to get out. He had already booked the flight, and he asked me for my parents' address, as he was keen to visit them.

His announcement unsettled me very much. It gave me a strange feeling of powerlessness to think he was visiting them and would be sitting at the table here with me in a week's time – without them, and at best with a letter from them. And so it turned out. Tony came back with his usually undaunted manner visibly shaken. He had met my parents in a café. They had been very pleased to see him, and given him letters and photographs for Marianne and me. And Father had pressed his Omega gold watch into his hand in case his daughters ever needed money. 'They are fine, and they are looking well,' Tony assured me. And yet it had not escaped him that the noose was slowly tightening around the city. A number of people had offered Tony a fortune for his return ticket to London. At this time Oskar Kokoschka had left Prague with a ticket his wife Olda had got him for one of the last flights to London.

An undertone of uncertainty permeated the town, threatening like some monster that could strike a fatal blow at any time. At the end of January the Czech foreign minister was allowed an audience with Hitler after being refused several times. He wanted to know what Berlin expected, and gave assurances his government would submit to German wishes on all matters of dispute between them. The Slovaks, struggling for their own state, could not be restrained, and played straight into the hands of Hitler, who was determined to resolve the tiresome Czechoslovak question to his advantage.

On 16 March I was scrubbing the old wooden table in my kitchen when Mrs Laver appeared suddenly in the doorway, a waxen pallor on her pretty face. 'Ilse,' she said, 'I was on my way to a rehearsal and I came back because I didn't feel well. I'll stay at home today and have a little lie-down. When you've finished here, wake me up. I'd like to come shopping with you to find out how you manage things so well.'

It was an unusual suggestion. Mrs Laver had never taken it into her head before to go shopping with me. But I thought nothing of it, and half an hour or so later I knocked at her door. She was already dressed, so we set off, each carrying a shopping basket.

At the corner of the street there was a newsagent, with a little board on the pavement outside with the day's headlines. It carried four words in thick letters, which struck me like an arrow: 'Nazis move into Prague.' The letters swam before my eyes, and I dropped my empty basket. I felt my legs giving way, and Mrs Laver's arm around me as I staggered. She held me tight, and at that moment I knew that her supposed sickness was no more than a pretext not to let me face alone this news that was to change my whole life. I cried as she held me tight and squeezed my hand. And then she said something that I have kept in my memory to this day. 'I will be a mother to you now,' she said.

7 War

My trip to the supermarket is always a minor expedition. It takes me more than half an hour to walk there, pushing a little four-wheeled trolley to put my shopping in. It also gives me some support, and without it I'm sure I would sometimes be in danger of falling. I need a lot of supports in my life – handles to hold on to in the bath, an extra rail on the left of the stairs, a walking stick.

Old age calls for a new sort of courage, a kind one never thought one would need. It is true that decay mercifully creeps up slowly over the years, but its progress is unremitting. At the same time, one remains young inside, and body and soul retain the memory of what they have experienced and done.

When I shut my eyes I can feel the wooden tiller in my hands, and the way my tummy muscles hardened up every time I leaned back and pulled the oars through the water of the Elbe. I can recall how it felt to ski down the slopes of the Erzgebirge and the sound of skate blades scraping on a frozen lake. Perhaps being able to remember the strength one once possessed helps cope with its loss. Apart from that, there is only self-control and dignity.

It is etched into my memory how concerned Fred was to create an impeccable impression when we met for the first time, and how his struggle to be dignified only underscored his disability. It wasn't just the crutches he held that made him look a broken man; he had that air.

Bina telephoned me on that Wednesday morning, 24 May 1939, at the Lavers'. As usual, we had arranged to meet on our next afternoon off. For once we were not going to Bloomsbury House, but to a hairdresser in Tottenham Court Road who Bina had discovered charged nothing if you let him try new styles. It was all we could afford.

But we didn't get our hair cut. That morning Bina had been called by her brother Jakob. He had been in London since March, and she was happy to have got him out of Vienna. It was still early when the phone went. Jakob's words burst from the receiver. 'You remember Salo Tisch, the songwriter from Vienna?' he had asked excitedly.

Of course she remembered him. Shortly before leaving, she had seen the production of *Warum lügst du, Chérie?* with Jakob at the Scala in Vienna. Jakob had clapped wildly and yelled, 'Bravo!' Afterwards they had all gone to a bar to celebrate. Salo had drunk more than his delicate body could handle, but it had been a wonderful evening, and life was looking good for him.

Bina remembered the words of her brother, who was eleven years older, when he arrived from Vienna two months before. 'Salo is going to die,' he had said. 'I saw him in hospital before I left, and he has death in his face.'

Jakob was the faithful companion who had enthusiastically applauded so many of Salo's performances, who had proudly followed his rise from obscurity to fame, had consoled his anxious parents when their son was dragged off to a concentration camp while secretly fearing for him just as they did – and Jakob's joy had known no bounds when he learned in January that Salo was alive and back in Vienna. He had gone immediately to the Rothschild Hospital, the Jewish hospital where Salo was. The other hospitals no longer took Jews. Jakob had been sent away again because the patient was too weak and couldn't have visitors for a long time.

Salo was wrestling with death in the isolation ward, cut off from the outer world. Typhoid fever had taken over his whole body. There were rashes all over his trunk and limbs, those soft pale red marks that denote camp fever. Sometimes the fever made him delirious, and apparently drunk. They tried to reduce this state by cold bandages around the body and gave him oats and barley gruel and boiled water. But he could keep hardly anything down and lost weight day by day. In Salo's case, the fever, which usually abates after the fourth week along with the measles-like rash, persisted, and that is almost always a sure sign that the end is near.

Salo had two relapses, and when Jakob was able to see him shortly before leaving Vienna, he was horrified by the face that looked at him through tearful eyes screwed up against the light through the glass wall that separated the victims of infectious disease from the world of the healthy. It was not the thirty-three-year-old Salo Jakob saw lying there, not the man he had cheered on the stage and done the round of the bars with at night. Jakob saw death in the emaciated face of an old man.

Bina recalled all this as she heard her brother on the phone in a voice that was clearly carried away with emotion. 'Bina, you won't believe it,' he splutttered into the phone. 'Salo is here! He's here in London! He came the day before yesterday. Can you believe it? He's right outside! This afternoon we're going to meet him and his brother in Hyde Park. It would be lovely if you and Ilse could come too.'

We naturally cancelled the appointments with the hairdresser. We got to the park first, and lay in a couple of deckchairs. With your eyes closed and the warm rays of the May sunshine stroking your face, you could imagine being part of a peaceful idyll. The sound of children laughing floated through the air, the birds twittered, and from deckchairs around came the sound of clanking knitting needles. How good it would have been to be able to forget for a moment that air raid shelters were being dug in all London's open spaces and gas masks given out too, that the fear of a war was stalking the land, that Hitler had announced that if there was a war, 'the Jewish race would be wiped out in Europe', that the concentration camps in Germany were overflowing, and that my mother and Bina's were trapped – along with many thousands of others.

I sensed a shadow across my eyelids and opened my eyes. Three of them stood there: Jakob and his friend Moishe, whom I knew slightly, and who called himself Mundy in England. Between them a man who looked very old, and whom they introduced as Mundy's brother Salo. For a moment I almost shut my eyes, the sight was so dreadful.

Death still lurked in Salo's face. The skin stretched like parchment over his hollow cheeks. His eyes had a dull, vacant gaze. I thought I also saw something akin to pride flare up there, but perhaps I imagined it. Salo looked at me a long time, and I quickly held out my hand in greeting to distract his gaze, which struck me as too intense for a stranger's.

116

1 Malva Chalek's pastel drawing of the young Ilse Lönhardt in 1935

2 Mother's joy: on 2 February 1915 Grete Schnitzer gave birth to her daughter Ilse

3 The family: Fritz Lönhardt (third from left), his daughter Marianne (sixth from left) with Ilse and their mother on her left

4 The last picture together: Ilse (left) with her mother and Marianne in spring 1938

5 Siegfried Tisch and Hans Lengsfelder in 1935

6 Scene from 'Hochzeitsreise' with Hans Thimig and Christl Mardayn (1936)

7 Music from the operetta 'Warum lügst du, Chérie?'

8 The newly married Fred and Ilse Tisch

9 Ilse Tisch in London, 1950

10 Passport photograph of the young Salo Tisch

11 Wedding day, 24 August 1947

12 Ilse Tisch, autumn 2001

He bent down carefully as far as his crutches would let him to kiss my hand. I could have cried. Not just because the gesture reminded me of the customs of my home country, but because a dreadful feeling welled up in me as I saw this bent, emaciated man in front of me. The feeling that it was all true. Everything the newspapers reported about what was happening in Nazi Germany and was rumoured and surmised about the travails of the Jews – it must all be true. Here stood this wrecked man, who had got out of a concentration camp several months before, and was living proof of the suffering of a people. So that's what men can do to one another, I thought. I would never have believed it.

Pictures of my parents raced through my head, sentences from my father's letters. 'Try not to worry,' he had written from Prague shortly before. But that was no longer possible. Looking at Salo shattered every illusion. If I didn't succeed in getting my parents out of occupied Czechoslovakia, they were lost.

I stood up as if to shake off these leaden thoughts. 'Won't you sit down?' I asked. 'Oh, thank you very much,' he said, smiling. As Jakob held him, he sat down carefully on the chair, and it was even more striking how thin he was. Under the suit his brother must have lent him his hip bones and knees stuck out like dead branches.

'Believe me, I hardly recognize him,' Mundy whispered to me. 'He weighs only forty-two kilos. I wonder what he has lived through. He won't speak about it.'

It was to take years before Salo found words to describe it.

'How did you manage for him to leave?' I asked Mundy. It was one of the first questions that refugees asked each other in exile if they had relatives at home.

'We got him a transit visa for Shanghai,' said Mundy. 'He can stay here only three months, then he must leave England.'

Shanghai was on my list of places of exile for my parents. Several thousand Jews from Germany, Austria and Czechoslovakia had found refuge in this great trading centre. You could enter without normal visa restrictions, but had to show you had a passage booked on a ship in order to get a transit visa, and this made things very much harder. The ships were all booked, horrendous prices were being asked for

117

tickets, and it was said that in Shanghai itself, European Jews did not face a rosy future. The prospects for freelance businesses in this port city, with its four million Chinese inhabitants, were very meagre. Most of the Jews had to live in the run-down suburb of Hongkew, which was controlled by the Japanese. All the same, they were alive.

And now Salo too had a passage to freedom. Mundy had got him the boat ticket to Shanghai because the visa for the Dominican Republic had expired while Salo had been ill in hospital. In the passport he showed Jakob was a resplendent visa stamp in red ink – a seal of survival hardly anyone would have thought possible. No one who has not had the feeling of being totally at the mercy of events can know what it means to have such a stamp. I would have given anything for my parents to have one at last.

Mundy tore me away from my thoughts. 'Let's go to the Cumberland,' he suggested. 'I fancy a coffee, even if you can hardly tell it from tea there.' The huge grey-white building, near Hyde Park and behind Marble Arch, was only five years old, but it had become a sort of institution for Jewish refugees. From early to late a babble of tongues filled its art deco lobby, which was thick with smoke. German, Yiddish and Viennese dialect predominated, but since the number of immigrants from other countries was growing, increasingly Czech and Polish. Over a watery coffee that you could take as long over as you wanted, you had a sense of your identity from meeting people like yourself, and being able to speak your own language.

This was forbidden in public places. On arrival, all Jewish refugees were given a little blue book with rules on how to behave in Britain. Ours told us (in German) that we must not speak German, read German newspapers or criticize British customs or regulations. One should avoid attracting attention through manners, loud speech or the clothes one wore because the English disliked people 'making an exhibition of themselves'. One was not to join any political organization, but to comply with social customs and retain the 'best Jewish qualities'.

We made honest efforts to fulfil these 'obligations', and everyone learned English as fast as they could. I took more and more to keeping quiet in public. My faltering English and foreign accent would have made me instantly recognizable as a foreigner, and I wasn't very keen on that.

'Do you speak English?' I asked Salo as our group pushed its way into the foyer. 'Maybe a dozen words,' he answered, wrinkling his forehead, as I noticed he tended to, especially when he was embarrassed. 'But I don't find languages too difficult,' he said. 'I've always learned them quickly.'

'You can learn the English menu by heart in three minutes,' said Bina. 'There's not much choice. Shall I get you a sandwich? They're quite reasonable.'

Salo nodded submissively. He seemed overwhelmed by everything. Like a puppet whose strings have been cut, he sank into a huge leather armchair, which almost swallowed him up. He smiled politely, and every time I looked I caught him looking at me. Everything else about the new world around him seemed to pass him by. His eyes were directed at me, and his look was not devout or rigid or insistent, but rested on me like a warm hand. My embarrassment slowly subsided, and I began to talk.

I told him about my work, my parents and my sister. I told him too about my nice employer, Mrs Laver, who had recently given me the job of whitewashing the outside steps to the basement. Because I couldn't tell doorways in England from one another as they all looked the same to me, I had with great care whitened and polished the steps to the neighbour's basement. They shone as never before, so I was very indignant when Mrs Laver told me off for not doing what she had asked. The neighbour, on the other hand, was highly delighted at my mistake.

Bina and the others laughed at my misfortune and for the first time a smirk at last appeared on Salo's face. It was a weak smile, as if he had forgotten how to express what prompted it.

'You look tired, Salo,' said Mundy. 'Let's go home. You need sleep.' Salo rose from his armchair with difficulty. As we said goodbye, he said – so quietly that the others couldn't hear – 'Fräulein, I must see you again.' It sounded almost like a plea.

'When you've got your strength back, you are very welcome to one of my dinners,' I said. 'We meet every Friday at half-past seven. Your brother has my address.'

'I look forward to it very much,' said Salo, and again kissed my hand to say goodbye.

I went back on my own on the underground to Chelsea. On the way everything suddenly burst out. All at once I felt a horror and fear that I had never known before. It wasn't like the sort of panic that sometimes overtakes one and sets the heart racing. Instead, every impulse and every movement seemed to be slowed down by a cold shock. It was in the middle of May, and I was stiff with cold.

Sleep eluded me that night. I cried a lot, and couldn't get the picture of Salo out of my head. I kept seeing his eyes in front of me. They were silent, and yet they were shouting something that no one could understand.

My state did not escape Mrs Laver. 'Ilse, you're worried, aren't you?' she said next morning. She must have known from my face that I had been crying. I was happy that I could tell her everything – that the day before I had met someone who had been in a concentration camp, that I had not slept a wink all night, that his look haunted me and I feared dreadfully for my parents and grandparents, Uncle Herbert, Aunt Hilde and Aunt Trude, and all those trapped at home.

'Calm down, Ilse,' said Mrs Laver softly. 'Look what you've done already. It won't be long before your parents can leave Prague. The world has woken up, and everyone knows the danger to the Jews from that monster in Germany. Don't give up now.'

Did the whole world really know the threat to the Jews in Nazi Germany? Sometimes I wondered. I had hoped that after the Germans entered Prague it would be clear to everyone how dangerous that madman was – and not only to the Jews – and that a policy of appeasement would not stop him. But the opposite was true. The setting up of the Protectorate of Bohemia and Moravia encouraged the restriction of immigration in Europe and elsewhere. On 15 March Switzerland introduced a visa requirement for holders of Czechoslovak passports. And in April 1939, after a period of relaxation, even Great Britain again restricted Jewish immigration. Canada closed its borders on the grounds that the immigrants came from territory now occupied by a hostile country. It had certainly not become any easier to escape.

Early in the morning of 15 March 1939 more than 450 Sudeten German refugees passed through Mährisch-Ostrau, which was already occupied by German troops, and left the Protectorate heading for the Polish Baltic port of Gdynia. With them some of the staff from the Prague office of the British Committee for Refugees from Czechoslovakia transferred to Poland to organize emigration to Great Britain from there. The emigration section of the Prague Institute for the Care of Refugees ceased to function on 15 March 1939, and its link with the British organizations was broken.

The shock of the German occupation triggered a flood of refugees. Many left on their own initiative, crossing the frontier illegally. Some got to Poland hidden in coal trucks, others escaped through underground mine workings that stretched across the frontier or swam across the border rivers. By such means several hundred had reached Poland by mid-April – mostly without travel documents. Almost all were Jews.

My parents remained trapped. Father thought that heading for Poland without having the assurance of a visa was too great a risk. We all thought it made more sense to use the fact that I was already in Britain, and wait until I could do something.

But the refugee organizations were short of money because the increased reluctance of other countries to take them meant that emigrants were now staying in England longer than two or three months. The British Refugee Committee had asked for more financial assistance for evacuating them, but the government in London had refused.

At the time I couldn't understand what my father wrote. He said he had often stood all day, and when it was at last his turn, he had been sent back to the end of the queue and told to wait. It probably had to do, he surmised, with his looking so Jewish.

He may well have been right. I know now that in the spring of 1939 government departments like the Treasury and the Foreign Office agreed on a 'prioritizing' of Czechoslovak refugees. The highest priority was given to political refugees, and the Jewish asylum seekers were mostly classed as 'economic refugees' – as though they had no more to lose than their possessions, which in any case most had lost already.

And so there was a form of selection, over whose precise operation the British refugee committees were deeply divided. On the whole, the prospects were better for non-Jews than Jews, although the latter made up most of the asylum seekers and the majority of the émigrés. One repeatedly heard that Jews trying to reach Britain who had fled in thousands to Kattowice and Cracow were returned to the Protectorate by the Polish authorities, and sometimes handed over directly to the Gestapo.

There wasn't a day I did not rack my brains for something I might still do. Sometimes I was quite faint from all my broodings, which lay over everything like sticky threads. I was glad to have things I had to do. Work helped cut through the tangle of thoughts.

On Friday I did the shopping for the Sabbath supper. 'Cook something special,' Mrs Laver had said. 'It will help you think of something else.' As before, the Lavers paid for my supper evenings. As a starter there was to be a thick Czech potato soup, for the main course a *schnitzel*, and for the kosher guests fried herring, with fresh peas and carrots. For dessert, I wanted to make *Powideldatschgerl*, a sort of plum ravioli. At 6.30 there was a ring at the door, an hour before my guests were expected. My kitchen looked like a battlefield, and I opened the door with my apron splattered with flour.

In front of me stood a thin figure, almost hidden by the huge bunch of roses he held in his hand. It was Salo. He looked a bit better than he had two days before. His hair shone with hair cream, and he was again wearing the borrowed suit. He still held the crutches, and I wondered how he had managed to get the roses all the way to Chelsea from Swiss Cottage, where he lived with his brother.

I must have looked surprised. I had supposed I would see him again in no less than two months' time, assuming he was still in London and not on a boat to Shanghai.

'Excuse me, I know I am far too early,' he hastened to say. 'But I didn't know how long it would take me, and so I set off this afternoon. Perhaps I can give you a hand.'

The son of a Jewish mother, and on crutches, wanting to help in the kitchen. There was an offer I couldn't refuse! I invited him to sit down at the kitchen table, where I had set an extra place for an unexpected guest, and offered him a glass of water (there was never alcohol on Friday evenings).

As I rolled out the potato dough for the *Powideldatschgerl* on the flour-covered work surface scattered with flour and stamped out little circles, in the middle of which I put a dab of puréed plum, I again felt Salo's gaze following my movements. Leaning on the table he told me of his mother's wonderful cooking and her fabulous chicken soup, whose numerous ingredients he had never been able to work out fully.

When Salo arrived home in Vienna after his release from Buchenwald, his mother had at first offered him kosher chicken soup, but he had not tried so much as a spoonful. Taube Tisch had been almost offended. 'Was the food in the camp so good that you turn your nose up at my soup?' she had asked, until she realiszed that her son was too weak to eat it, and they had then taken him to the hospital.

'How are your parents getting on now?' I asked. Salo shrugged his shoulders. 'Terribly, like all the Jews in Vienna,' he said. Every day, there were new decrees restricting the Jews even more and discriminating against them. In November, Jewish students had had their matriculation qualifications nullified and Jewish bookshops had been closed. It was forbidden for Jews to visit libraries, theatres and cinemas, and even curfews could be arbitrarily imposed. They were no longer allowed to own motor vehicles, and Jewish doctors and chemists could treat only Jewish patients. Thousands of Jewish firms in Vienna were 'aryanized', and those Jews not already under arrest were paid derisory sums for them. The Max Pfeffer Verlag, which had published many of Salo's songs, was confiscated.

In February the Jews had to deposit all gold, platinum and silver objects, and valuable jewellery, at public purchase points, and again received only a fraction of their material value. This quite apart from any sentimental value the items may have had.

Isaak and Taube Tisch had also had to give up the few valuables that they still had.

Many were thus reduced to poverty, and had to rely on support from Jewish care agencies that gave out several thousand rations of soup to the needy every day. Jewish men and women had to add the name 'Israel' or 'Sara' to their own names. Soon after, just before Salo left, rent protection for Jews was abolished, as a first step towards a sort of ghetto-ization. By then almost 100,000 Jews had left this city of terror. 'I must get my parents out,'said Salo. I knew what anxiety lay behind those words.

Later, as the other supper guests arrived, Salo kept these things to himself, as though something inside held him back. He mostly followed the conversation in silence, answering only when he was directly spoken to, and then usually with a bare 'yes' or 'no'. Whenever I looked at him, I met his brown, strangely immobile eyes directed at me.

At ten o'clock people started to leave, as it was about the time that the Lavers usually came home. Salo remained seated, and waited until they had all gone. 'It's late, Salo,' I said eventually, after we had talked for a while. 'You have a long way to go, and I must be up early in the morning.'

I went with him to the steps outside leading up to the street. Salo said goodbye in the old-fashioned way by kissing my hand, and set off towards the tube station. As he went, I watched his small, shadowy silhouette outlined against the greenish light of the streetlamps. All over London they had this new ghostly-green street lighting that made things look unreal. Salo, too, as he slowly got further away, bent slightly forward, shoulders raised, teetering along with his crutches out at an angle, now looked like a creature from another world. Only two years before, this man had filled theatres and attracted wildly enthusiastic audiences. How little had been left of him.

To his dying day he never knew that that very evening, 26 May 1939, as he was hobbling along to catch the tube in London, an operetta called *Lüg nicht, Baby!* was having its first night at the Kleines Theater in Berlin. It was stolen goods, an unsuccessful plagiarized version of the successful original *Warum lügst du, Chérie?* Salo and Lengsfelder's greatest stage hit had simply been 'aryanised'.

I know this now only because I have the score of the plagiarized version in front of me. It was even published by the came – in the meantime 'aryanized' – Max Pfeffer Verlag as the original. The action and characters are almost identical, although *Lüg nicht, Baby!* is set in a country house in Scotland rather than in Fontainebleau, and the piece was adjusted to fit Nazi ideology. For example, the German lyricist Berndt Werner changed a song in which Tisch and Lengsfelder praised a young bachelor's life for one extolling marriage with a 'racially pure' woman. The music was by Hans Carste, then an ambitious thirty-year-old composer of film music who had his own dance band in Berlin. Carste, I have learned, later composed the title tune for the news programme 'Tagesschau' on West German television, which must have been more profitable than the flop *Lüg nicht, Baby!* At the end of the 1950s, Carste became chairman of the board of the German Copyright Society GEMA. I wonder whether he knew the writers of *Warum lügst du, Chérie?* were Jews whose copyright had been infringed?

It would only have upset Salo to know this. I still recall how worked up he got when, a few weeks after he came to London, he had a letter from the actress Friedl Czepa, telling him she had sung Goebbels (whom she called 'Pepperl') songs from *Warum lügst du, Chérie?*, and he had been delighted, and that it was now being performed under the title *Lüg nicht, Baby!* in Berlin. Salo didn't respond. What was the point?

I recall that on that evening of 26 May, I remained myself in a state of strange inner turmoil that did not subside even as I did the routine chores of clearing up the kitchen or later as I went to bed. My thoughts centred on Salo with his sad eyes. In the first place I felt sympathy for him, and an almost motherly desire to build him up with good food. But mixed with this was something else, though I couldn't say what it was.

Some days later a letter came from my father that made me laugh and cry at the same time. He had at last got a visa for Great Britain. He owed it not least to guarantees that Franz Kind from Manchester had signed, the man whose identity we concealed in our letters as 'Babyson'. He was a chemistry PhD, the son of a former employee of my father's, and was now general manager of one of the largest oil refineries in Manchester. He undertook to stand guarantor for both my parents, so my father was confident that my mother too would soon get a visa. Dr Kind said he would also keep his ears open for work for them, although he knew none of us personally.

Difficult times show people in their true light. Some show courage and integrity, and there are the others. One meets both kinds.

Fear of a war, which had declined after Munich, now spread in London, and was more tangible by the day. Since Hitler had occupied Rump-Czechoslovakia it had dawned even on those who had supported appeasement that Hitler would stop at nothing. Munich had just been a pause for breath, and now a time bomb was ticking. With its population of eight million, London, then the largest city in the world, would be the main target of German attack. It was the heart and brain of the country, its greatest strength and also its most vulnerable point.

I was happy to know that Marianne was safe. She wrote regularly from her convent school in Dublin. She didn't seem very happy there. The language was difficult for her, the food grim, and the nuns strict, insisting the girls wore a shift, even in the bath. Besides, she missed me, and was counting the days till the summer holidays.

Tony, the friend from Halle, often asked when my little sister, who was slowly growing up, was coming to London again. Tony's beauty business, with the fine-sounding name Adèle Maurice, was not doing so well. The fantastic contract agreed in Prague in the spring could now be used as toilet paper, he complained. Besides the liquid lipstick, Tony now offered home visits by cosmetic advisers who dolled up society ladies for parties. For a while this had gone well, but demand was lessening perceptibly.

People had other problems. Some hoarded staple foodstuffs and bought first-aid products in the chemists. Everyone living in London received official flyers, which warned them of the danger of a German gas attack and gave advice in case of an air raid. Everybody was issued with a gas mask, and children had Mickey Mouse masks, which didn't greatly contribute to the general merriment.

Countless trenches scarred the face of the city. For hundreds of miles they cut their zigzag courses through the parks and public squares so beloved of Londoners. Hundreds of thousands took up the government's offer to subsidize the construction of a small shelter, the so-called Anderson shelter, in their gardens. They were simple to build, and held six adults. They were to be seen everywhere, the earth-covered roof often planted with lettuces or flowers. For the royal family a gas-proof room and a shelter were installed in the basement of Buckingham Palace.

The Lavers had no garden, and so no room for an Anderson shelter. So Mr Laver inspected the coal cellar next to my kitchen, and shook his head slowly. 'It would be all right at first,' he said, 'but it definitely isn't a permanent solution.'

But what would be a permanent solution? In official circles, like the ARP (Air Raid Precautions), there was debate over whether it would be sensible to convert public parking places into shelters for 30,000 people, and whether underground air raid shelters would withstand a 1,000lb bomb or become a mass grave. Nobody knew how deadly the German weapons would be.

After nights of discussion, the Lavers decided they would leave London if and when war broke out. Many Londoners – at least those in a position to do so – made the same decision. The evacuation of children from the city had begun months earlier.

The Lavers had a place in Wales, and wanted to move there with another couple with whom they were friendly. I understood their decision only too well, but I was shocked when they told me that I would lose my job because they wouldn't be able to take me.

'But we have found something else for you,' said Mrs Laver consolingly. 'The delightful Piggotts would be only too pleased to take you as maid and cook.' The 'delightful' Piggotts were friends of the Lavers, and, as luck would have it, Lady Piggott, who was very keen on music, was friendly with Ferdinand Rauter and Engel Lund. I had even been invited several times to tea parties there with Ferry and Engel. Henry Piggott, whom I was told I should address as 'Sir Henry', was an MP, and worked in the Ministry of Transport. Despite his position and standing, there was nothing of the snob about him. He was a warm-hearted man with his feet on the ground. His wife, slim and willowy in the fashion of the upper classes of the time, had sharply chiselled features and was quite the opposite. To me, though, she was always expressly friendly, and never failed to praise my cooking. 'If ever you get fed up with earning your bread here,' she would often joke, 'you can start with us tomorrow.'

Once again world events took decisions out of my hands. If war started, I too would leave London with the Piggotts and move to Reading, where the Ministry of Transport would be relocated. I would work for them, running their household. Much as I myself disliked the thought, there was one person who was especially happy: Salo. He would be glad to know I was safe, he said, and that I would have to take care of myself, if only for the sake of my little sister, who had spent the whole of her summer holidays with me in London shortly before.

Salo now came to supper every Friday, a bunch of red roses in his hand. Instead of six, I now had seven guests. Salo thought this was only right, as seven is a Jewish lucky number. The Sabbath supper seemed to agree with him in every way. His hollow cheeks slowly began to fill out, and his bony arms peeking out of his short-sleeved shirts were showing more flesh. He was wearing his own suits again, too.

He now tucked in and helped himself at table, and was no longer reticent at joining in the conversation. I was struck by his knowledge, not only about music and law: he knew about politics, philosophy and literature, and had always read enough on a subject to form an opinion, which he did not try hard to conceal. I enjoyed listening to him and asking him questions. There were so many things to which I didn't know the answer. Salo almost always had one, and that gave me a strange sense of security and of being in good hands. I thought I had left this feeling at home, but now I had it again.

Salo carried a small dictionary, and was always looking up English words. He told me that he had already been to the cinema a lot, and always took a little torch with him to write down new words in a notebook. It was amazing how quickly Salo got to grips with the new language. Every time we met he knew many more words.

We had now changed from the formal second person

plural of '*Sie*' to the more familiar '*Du*,' though without any
silly initiation by drinking to fraternity, which would have
been inappropriate at a time like this. Salo revealed to me that
from now on he would call himself Fred S. Tysh, and have this
entered in his passport, because he wouldn't get anywhere in
England with a Jewish or German name. It would be Salo's
(alias Siegfried's) third identity.

As though following some inner impulse, our relationship
became closer and more trusting at each meeting. Now that
Fred was gradually starting to look like a human being, I saw
him more and more as a man. He often came to visit me in the
evenings, helped me with my work or sat with me at the
kitchen table. Once he stayed so long that he missed the last
tube and had to walk for hours all the way from Chelsea to
Swiss Cottage. At least he didn't need his crutches any more.

We talked a lot about his religion, and Fred wanted to
know my views on faith. I told him that I had not had much
to do with it – unlike him. As they said goodbye at Vienna
airport, his father had urged him to 'stay a pious Jew'. He was
keeping this promise, and not just from filial piety.

One evening, Fred told me how in exile he had returned to
the Jewish faith. His words moved me very much. Thirty years
later I heard this story again when Fred was made *Chatan
Bereschit* in his synagogue. *Chatan* is the Hebrew for bridegroom.
On *Simchat Thora*, the festive day of the faith, the *Chatan Bereschit*
initiates the annual cycle of readings from the torah. It is the day
the torah rolls are carried seven times around the lectern, the
faithful sing, and there are feasts to celebrate the torah.

At the evening celebration, Fred gave a small address to the
members of our Jewish congregation. He was very moved at
the honour bestowed on him. I still have a copy of his speech,
which says more than I can explain.

'When I came to England,' he said, 'as one of many
refugees from Hitler and after eight months in concentration
camps, all I had in my pocket was seventeen shillings and
sixpence. It was all I was allowed to take, and my law qualifi-
cation from Vienna was not worth the paper it was printed
on. My knowledge of English was nil, my prospects still less. I
felt the pain of being "amid the alien corn". The feeling of
deep depression would not leave me. When I went into the

street and saw all the strange words above the shop windows, I had an unbearable feeling of profound loneliness.

'One summer morning these feelings miraculously disappeared when my brother took me to Petticoat Lane. It wasn't a grand shopping street, certainly nothing like Bond Street. But for me it had something very special. I looked around and suddenly stopped in my tracks. I stared in amazement because I had discovered something that instantly filled me with a feeling of warmth and trust – and a hope that I had not known since leaving home. What I discovered were the names over the shop windows. Looking down on me were all the good old familiar names, like Goldberg, Finkelstein, Rosenthal and Oppenheim.

'I underwent an indescribable transformation. It was almost instinctive, and it was wonderful. I was no longer depressed, no longer alone, because I suddenly saw I was surrounded by my own people. The Goldbergs, the Finkelsteins and all the others may have spoken English, but they also said "*Shema Yisrael*" – like me. They were Jews like me, and I was sure they had something I was absolutely convinced of: a Jewish heart.'

Despite all outward appearances, Siegfried Tisch, who now called himself Fred S. Tysh, had inwardly remained Salomon the Jew. Nobody had been able to rob him of his spiritual home, and from this he seemed suddenly to take strength for the future and resolve to begin a new – his third – life.

He went on learning new English words each day, and writing them in a notebook. 'I think I shall soon be writing lyrics again,' he said. His determination was impressive, but I had my doubts. Many German writers were working hard to master a language that would never be theirs. Most lived from hand to mouth, depending on support from refugee organizations or the PEN club. Fred had no job, either. He thought of working in his brother's firm, which made labels for Harrods and Liberty's, but his English needed to be much better, and in any case he had no work permit. The foreign section of the Home Office was very hesitant about issuing these. On no account should the Jewish refugees streaming into the country take jobs from British workers.

In July 1939 the Germans set up in Prague the Central

Office for Jewish Emigration under Adolf Eichmann. The principle was similar to that obtaining in Vienna: the Jews should leave the country, but first they were fleeced as far as possible by confiscating most of their remaining possessions and on top of that imposing a *Reichsfluchtsteuer*, a tax for leaving the Reich. Father wrote that he was having a lot of problems with the 'tax business'. His and Mother's letters wavered between hope and resignation. 'One must accept whatever comes,' wrote Father. 'When will the sun shine for us again?' asked Mother, adding that she hoped 'peace would break out'.

Nevertheless my parents sent two cases ahead to London. The keys came by post with a list of contents on a long, narrow card on which my father had drawn up in his neat hand items for his new life: 2 nightshirts Fritz, 1 pair of shoes Grete, 1 pair of slippers Fritz, 14 pairs of stockings, 6 handkerchiefs, 1 brassière Grete, 2 silk blouses Grete, and various other things. As circumstances required, it was a modest list, and Fritz Lönhardt did not realize that he would never see again the things he sent me.

My parents also sent valuable linen, the damask tablecloths, the linen sheets, the napkins edged with lace, and the bedclothes with the monograms 'GW' and 'GL'. As I opened the vulcanized fibre suitcase and found the things from my childhood, which I felt were exuding the smells of that time, I veered between joy and pain. The hope that I would soon see my parents safe mingled with mourning for the loss of our past.

But now it looked as though we all had a future. Thanks to Franz Kind, Father had got a post in the chemical industry in Hull in Yorkshire. He was looking for a job as a seamstress for Mother, who had begun earning a little extra money as a dressmaker in Prague. She had been told, she wrote, that she could take her sewing machine with her. I even managed to find my parents a small furnished flat in Hampstead. The Lavers had offered to advance me money. Now everything needed to be arranged quickly because the danger of war was growing by the day.

But progress in Prague was slow, especially with Father's tax affairs. Many documents from his firm were missing, and he had not enough money for the exit tax. Time was working against us.

On 1 September 1939 Hitler's troops invaded Poland. 'We must have patience,' warned Father in a letter to me next day. 'If I can get to you,' he wrote, 'it will be possible for Mother too, sooner or later. We can only hope the world settles down.' He had come to realize, he wrote resignedly, that an individual person is of 'absolutely no significance'. If they didn't come safely through this momentous event in world history, it was because God or Providence intended it so – 'and we must accept this'.

The next morning, 3 September, Britain and France declared war on Germany. The Second World War had begun.

At 11.30 a.m. the sirens started wailing. Everyone knew the sound from exercises, but this time I hardly heard it, I was so deaf and clogged up inside. Large cylinder-shaped balloons rose into the sky over the rooftops to force enemy aircraft to fly higher. The fear of a poison-gas attack was tangible. As the sirens howled, people sought safety in shelters and cellars or even in doorways. I was alone at home with Mr Laver. His wife had gone to Wales with the children the day before. As we parted, the children cried and cuddled me. 'What will happen to Ilse?' they had asked. My friend Susie had meanwhile left for New York with her parents, and Kathlyn had gone back to Ireland. And so Mr Laver and I stuck it out alone in the coal cellar with gas masks at hand.

Although on this and later occasions the wail of the sirens proved a false alarm, my hopes already lay in ruins. All prospective countries of refuge had immediately shut their borders, including Britain. In Prague, where my parents sat on packed suitcases, the half-open door closed again. If the war had started three weeks later, they would probably have got out. Bina's mother was also trapped. She too had packed her cases in Vienna, having got an affidavit for the USA. It had become worthless overnight.

I hated being shut up in the coal cellar, where there was nothing to do but sit and wait for the all-clear. Meanwhile, one's mind spun one's thoughts into frightening fantasies in which one could get completely entangled. The sirens wailed almost every night. The whole city lay motionless in the darkness like a black giant We had to draw blackout curtains or blinds. All theatres and cinemas were closed.

Every morning the phone rang. Fred called to find out whether everything was all right. Hearing his voice did me good, and it comforted me to know that his winter voyage to Shanghai was off the agenda. 'I really don't want to leave you in London,' I heard myself say. 'I'm worried about you.'

'Look,' he said gently, 'if I die no one else is affected. But you are responsible for your sister. You must leave London. I'll write every day and come and see you.'

The thought of Fred dying made me panic. And suddenly I knew what this feeling, which had at first been mixed with pity, was all about: I had fallen in love.

In wartime love blossoms differently. Sometimes it is based on fear, sympathy or loneliness. It may be less free, but it is often stronger and more unconditional. It was in those war years that some of the best marriages among my friends originated.

Fortunately I was too busy preparing for my departure to worry about exploring the life of my soul. The Piggotts had already gone lock, stock and barrel to Reading, and I followed them in a few days. I hardly had time to register that this was yet another farewell. The Lavers' house, where I had felt so at home, stared at me from its bare windows as though with vacant eyes, and all life had left it.

Reading, a town in Berkshire, in the Thames valley about thirty miles west of London, didn't especially appeal to me from the start. I would have liked to turn right around at the station and go back, because my reception by Lady Piggott was not at all warm. I was shown to a little room without heating and an old sagging bed. 'The comfortable times are over for all of us,' she announced with a shrug.

What I received was hardly decent human treatment. For the first three days, I ate with the family. Then Lady Piggott thought it would be better if I took my meals in the kitchen. These meals got more and more meagre, and I often gave my portion to the dog, a huge, dribbling monster. Instead, I began peeling the potatoes thicker and ate the skins. I did the same with apples.

Fred's letters were a welcome support. He really did send one almost every day – and always in rhyme. They were love poems, and I have never had more beautiful ones. Sometimes they were screamingly funny and made me laugh, sometimes full of earnest feelings, tender and longing.

At first I insisted that Fred write his letters to me longhand. I still notice people's handwriting; it says a lot about them. When I had had a number of letters from him and found his writing sympathetic and expressive of a strong character, he was happy to hear that they might now be typed. He needn't always bother to write poetry, I wrote. 'That shows how little you know me,' he replied. 'It's much easier for me to write poetry than prose.'

Marianne sent postcards from the convent in Dublin. She still found academic work hard, she wrote, but she was one of the best at sport and needlework. She had also found a nice friend. 'Just be brave and fight your fear,' Father had written to her shortly before, asking dear God to bring us all together again.

We sent one another letters of encouragement, saying we were fine and expressing concern for the others. Mother tried to hide it, but she was always worried that Marianne had enough to eat and had warm clothes, and that I was treated well. Father always urged courage, especially to Marianne. 'Try hard to get over your fears,' he wrote in November 1939. 'We must do the same.' Mother asked Marianne how she got on in geography and history – as though there was nothing more important.

Our cousin Hans Frank, with whom we used to play in Grandfather's garden, had emigrated to Denmark, she wrote. Grandfather was not doing so well in Türmitz; he was so weak and had been refusing to eat lately. I was terribly sad about this. Yet it was typical of Grandfather's stubbornness. He did not wish to live in a world that had ceased to be human. And so he found his own way of speeding his exit from it.

Father was still hoping to be able to leave for England soon. His visa had expired, though, and the case was still with the Central Office in Prague. Many Jews had now emigrated to Palestine, Father wrote, but he himself was doubtful about a future there, where his expertise wouldn't earn him a penny. The Jewish community in Prague was offering courses in agriculture for those going to Palestine, but he thought he was too old. Above all he and Mother wanted to be with the children, and this decided him against all other possible countries. As it turned out, it was the wrong decision.

Mother had told me that the wife of her cousin Oswald Richter had also landed up in Reading. Her husband, the well-known Viennese social democrat, had been murdered in Buchenwald concentration camp in January 1939. The widow was given 'heart and circulation defects' as the official cause of death. Maria Richter and her daughters Renate and Liane lived in a rented flat in the centre of town. I visited them as often as I could. Maria sometimes lent me her typewriter so that I could write letters to London and Prague more quickly. My parents regularly complained that I didn't write enough, but I was usually simply too exhausted, and dropped like a stone into my bed.

Lady Piggott treated me like a menial. I often had to get up in the night and fetch her a glass of warm milk because she couldn't sleep. How should she? She shared the double bed with the stinking giant of a dog, while her husband spent the night on the *chaise longue*. I always held my breath when I brought her anything because I couldn't bear the dog's smell. It was probably because of this slobbering creature that she had left London. There, pet owners had had 100,000 cats and dogs put down in the first days of the war, presumably to save them from dying in a gas attack.

The Piggotts' daughter was hardly more charming. She kept borrowing my clothes without asking, including the beautiful reversible coat that Mother had had made for me. She never brought it back, saying it had been stolen at the office. To replace it, she gave me an old worn coat with about as much style as a workman's overalls.

'It's the fault of you Jews that we are at war,' said Lady Piggott. No doubt there were some who thought this. Sometimes I felt she wanted to punish me because her life no longer ran the comfortable course it had previously.

There were widespread job losses. Taxes had risen, petrol was rationed, and there was a coal shortage. But the big dance halls in London had reopened, Fred reported, and people were queueing to get in. After the initial anxiety died down, some theatres reopened. Despite all pessimistic predictions, not one German bomber had appeared.

Although most people realized that this was just a postponement, thousands of evacuated children came back to London towards the end of the year. Despite official advice, more and more people, Fred told me, took to leaving home without their gas masks. Only the night-time blackout was generally maintained. Under the black veil of night the aspect and extent of the city lay hidden. Now unrecognizable, London could well have been just a collection of wooden huts by a silvery river, as it had been 2,000 years before. The streets became mysterious, unknown places, and every night there were accidents as people tripped over kerbs, sandbags or other obstructions, or were knocked down by cars, which had only a tiny light inside.

London's Christmas illuminations did not deserve the name. Only in the main streets were 'glimmer lights' allowed. They were more like lighting for an emergency rear exit than festive light. At night most shop windows were yawning black mouths. But who was in the mood for Christmas anyway? Mother especially sounded very depressed. It was her forty-seventh birthday on 3 December, but there was little celebration. Malva Schalek, the painter, visited her with Emma Richter, my mother's aunt. Malva was now living with her brother Robert in Prague. Father had given Mother presents of sweets, a blouse and a pair of slacks, and money for presents was now pretty well exhausted. Mother had been very depressed lately, Father admitted in a letter.

She worked from early to late as a dressmaker, and said that this was the only thing that could distract her from gloomy thoughts. She was very worried because Marianne had suddenly decided to leave school. She thought she couldn't stand it another day, and Mr Collins, the nice lawyer from Dublin whom I had got to know in my first job at Mrs Citron's, offered to take her on as a nanny in his house. This made Mother very unsettled. And she probably suffered even more because her hands were tied, and she could only look on as things took their course.

'I would never have thought I would be so afraid,' she wrote to Marianne. 'What will happen to my little one now?

You have been gone almost a year, a sad year for me. I often think I could have you with me, and you could have learned something here.' My father wished us, for Christmas and the New Year, that dear God might give us strength, 'so that we can all be together again some time'.

It was bitterly cold in the last days of the year. In the evenings, Sir Henry Piggott sat by a meagre fire and knitted. Yes, the MP actually knitted woollen balaclavas for British sailors, warm headgear that covered the whole face except for the eyes, mouth and nose. I was useless at knitting but nevertheless, when I had finished my work and could force myself, I tried to knit a pullover. I would much have preferred knitting myself something to cover my whole body because I was freezing the whole time.

Everyone complained about the hard winter; a coal shortage meant that there was little with which to warm oneself. Fires could be lit only for a short while. Otherwise one had to make do with warm thoughts. My room was unheated, and every morning the water in the enamel washbowl was frozen solid. I could hardly sleep at nights from the cold. My feet were painful even though I put on all my stockings. I was so thin from chronic shortage of food that the cold seemed to gnaw directly at my bones.

One morning I discovered flat, bluish painful lumps on my feet and under my arms. They were chilblains, as the GP I consulted discovered. He certified advanced under-nourishment, and gave me a letter for the Piggotts threatening to report them if they did not feed me properly and put a heater in my room. They promised to do both, but Lady Piggott's manner after this was icier than the harsh winter.

I just wanted to get away, back to London, and was longing to see Fred. How happy I was that he came to see me at Christmas. We sat in my room, in which the Piggotts had now actually put a wood stove (temporarily, anyway; later they used it to warm the garage so that their car started better in the mornings). Fred gave me some crimson lipstick. Lady Piggott would probably have boxed my ears if, as the maid, I had run around the house during the day with painted lips. But that evening I put it on, and Fred beamed with happiness. How beautiful I was, he said, and how happy he was to have found me and that I had taught him to laugh again. 'My mother,' he said, 'would eat you up with love.' Said by an orthodox Jew, that is a huge compliment.

Late that evening Fred sat down at the typewriter I had borrowed from the Richters and wrote a poem for the New Year. I had never seen him working, and I was struck by how skilfully he hit the keys. The verses he wrote that night are the first ones where he used English. In a way they point to the future, because they start in German and continue in English – like a parable of the life of Salo Tisch, who was now resolved to meet the unknown future as Fred S. Tysh:

Und wieder einmal kauft man 'nen Kalender
Und hofft, man fängt ein neues Leben an.
Die Seele ist ein grosser Scharlatan
Und hüllt sich gern in festliche Gewänder.

Man sieht sich noch bei früheren Silvestern:
Man war vergnügt, gesichert und zu zweit.
Das scheint heut' eine ganze Ewigkeit –
Und wenn man rechnet, war es fast noch gestern.

Für uns besteht die Welt jetzt nur aus Schienen,
Doch keiner weiss, wohin sein Train ihn führt.
Das Herz ist kalt, es fröstelt und es friert
Und man sitzt doch an glühenden Kaminen.

Die Stephansturmuhr hat in früher'n Tagen
Dem neuen Jahr gesagt: Non, hoppla, renn!
Jetzt hören Wiener und Berliner den Big Ben.
Und beide wissen wir, wie viel's geschlagen.

Doch trotzdem lassen wir den Mut nicht sinken.
Wer leben will, der sagt dem Leben: Ja!
Denn wie's auch immer sein mag – wir sind da
Und da ist schliesslich auch ein Grund zum Trinken.

Whatever fate may bring, we've got to face it,
Whatever days may come we're not afraid
There are lots of things to be repaid

There is still something and we must replace it.

But let's forget. This year's last light is falling,
Few minutes till and then it's got to go.
Now nineteenhundredforty comes: Hello!
Once more a year begins and life is calling.

8 London Blitz

In my garden the first violets are struggling through the moss towards the early spring light. I love seeing them each year. When they have grown into clumps, I pick a handful and put them in little vases around the house. They are soon followed by cowslips, primroses, little narcissi and lilies-of-the-valley. Sometimes snowdrops or red tulips creep out of the earth, reminding me that I planted bulbs there in the autumn. These little surprises give me special pleasure. I can't imagine life without my garden.

For some years after the war when we didn't have a garden, I used to buy two small bunches of flowers every Monday from an old flower seller at Turnham Green tube station. Mrs Smith had a face as rugged as the Cornish coast and a voice not much softer. She was a stubborn old lady, so much so that when Britain adopted decimal currency, she stuck to 240 pence to a pound.

'I'm too old to learn this decimal system,' she said to me once, after she had sent an American who insisted she use it complaining on his way. 'If they don't like it, they must buy their flowers somewhere else,' she said. I laughed. 'Oh, by the way,' she added, 'I meant to ask why you always buy little flowers like violets and lilies-of-the-valley instead of big bunches of flowers.'

I hesitated, and then told her that I put the flowers in front of framed photos of my parents. 'My parents were killed by the Nazis, and they have no graves,' I said. 'So I decorate their pictures with flowers the way other people decorate graves.'

Her face suddenly softened. 'Oh dear,' she sighed. And then she said, 'Darling, would you do me a favour and always come to me when you need fresh flowers? And I don't want you to pay for them.' From then on, two little bunches were waiting for me every Monday, and the old lady would not take a penny for them. 'It's the least I can do,' she said.

Some months after that, the flower stand was empty. Mrs Smith had died suddenly, they told me, and nobody knew where she was buried. I was devastated. I would have liked to take flowers to her grave. It would have been the least I could do.

I still put a little fresh bunch of flowers each week in front of my parents' photos. I must have got the habit from my mother. She wrote that in their little flat in Prague there were always vases of flowers or greenery in front of pictures of my grandparents, Marianne and me. It was a way of being close, even if she could not be with us.

In the early years I put the photographs of my parents within reach of my bed. I often gazed at them a long time before falling asleep, and spoke to them in my thoughts. Sometimes I even prayed to a God whose existence I more and more doubted. But praying consoled me.

Fred prayed in secret. I think he did not want me to see the depth of his faith. Sometimes he spent ages in the toilet. There were not many other ways to be alone in the crowded conditions we lived in at that time. When he came back, he said he had asked for help for me and Marianne and his and my parents and all the other people that he loved. Fred's brother Mundy, who had not been notably God-fearing until then, began to pray around that time.

I imagine that everyone secretly prayed in their own way that the world would come to its senses, and that they would be together again with their loved ones. Fred rushed from one official agency to another, trying to help his parents get to Palestine. But his efforts always failed one way or another. Well over 100,000 Jews had so far left Vienna, and about 60,000 still lived there. Thousands of Jewish apartments had been compulsorily vacated, and the tenants expelled from them driven together in the second, ninth and twentieth districts. If tenants did not leave their flat, their furniture was thrown onto the street, and they were arrested and sent to a concentration camp.

Over half of Vienna's Jews now lived in the second district, the Leopoldstadt. Jews from elsewhere in Austria were forcibly settled in Vienna. Since January 1940 they had been allowed to use only Jewish shops. A curfew was imposed from 9 p.m. They had long been banned from going to the Burggarten, the Prater and the park at Schönbrunn. Fred's father used to like walking in the public gardens on Sundays. Now he was deprived of this. He and Taube Tisch lived 'at home' in a tiny space with other Jewish families.

Since the outbreak of war, emigration from Vienna had also slowed to a standstill. In the spring of 1940 the Palestine Office there was closed. Fred was as depressed as I was. Sometimes one had the terrible feeling of moving towards the last square on some huge games board, only to be grabbed by a gigantic hand and put back at the start, however far one had got. It was emotionally draining.

Rejections showered on us from everywhere. Oslo, where I had written to ask about immigration for my parents, fobbed them off with an indefinite delay. Father now hoped for help from a friend in Florence called Strittmatter, with whom he had corresponded for some time, and whom we disguised in our letters under the name 'Guglielmo'. As direct entry to Britain was not possible, he was looking for a country 'where we could take up temporary residence while waiting for confirmation of our visas to join Ilse', Father wrote to Strittmatter. Perhaps it would be possible in Italy, he asked, and could he find out? 'On the whole, life would be more bearable if we knew what the future held,' remarked my father. He was in constant inner turmoil, he said, living for the day, and never knowing how he would get through tomorrow. He would be forever grateful for his friend's efforts. 'You don't know how refreshing your letters are, as we are just not used any more to warm-heartedness and loyalty.'

Mother, whom we called 'Mutz', suffered most from not being able to share in her daughters' everyday lives. She sent Marianne a list of twenty questions, saying, 'We are very interested in everything that concerns you,' and she was afraid that they would become strangers to one another. She wanted to know how it was leaving the convent, and about Christmas, whether Marianne had started having her periods, what her school report was like, and whether she knew any young men in Dublin or just nuns. She asked me about Salo, whether he was kind, and whom he was like. Our parents asked us to send them photos when they discovered that pictures without any writing passed the censor. 'It's all so sad,' complained Mother. 'When I am too troubled people try to comfort me by saying that anyone should be happy if they have got their children away ... My idea of happiness is rather different.'

Even if most of the letters we got from our scattered friends and relatives now did little for our confidence, they nevertheless brightened the day by strengthening the bonds between us. Little else remained of our past. From time to time a small parcel came, to be opened with a mixture of joy and sadness. For my twenty-fifth birthday Mother sent me a flower broach made from velvet and a pin cushion, which she had made herself. Marianne, who now hoped to join me soon, sent a home-made picture puzzle. None of us could afford presents any more.

A few days after my birthday, news of my grandfather's death reached me. He wanted to die, and had refused food for four months because, Mother wrote, he could not 'bear these evil times any longer'. At the end no words came from his dry lips, only tears running silently from his dying face. Mother was not allowed to go to the funeral in Türmitz. She did not even know where her father was buried, she wrote.

Though I had expected the news, it hit me very hard. Opa Gustl, who came right after my parents on my toilet paper list of those I loved most, who had shared confidences with me and whose beard had always tickled me, had been the first to go, leaving behind the threatening unspoken question: who would be the next to follow him?

Father tried even harder to get out. He wrote to his former representatives in Sofia and Stockholm, and not a week passed without his asking whether I had had any success. It was a long time since we had heard anything from Strittmatter. I should enquire about Palestine, China, Bolivia and Santo Domingo, Father suggested, and mightn't Ireland be interested in a technical expert? 'Ilse,' he wrote, 'think and act, search and find if you can.' I had been doing just that for months. I wrote to consulates and refugee organizations and talked to all my friends and acquaintances, but nobody was interested in a sixty-one-year old factory owner who had been forcibly retired and now had nothing more than his technical knowledge. As far as my parents were concerned, the Nazis'calculations were right. They had been robbed of their place in society; now, as poor Jews without means, they were not welcome in any country. My mother's brother Herbert tried as best he could to emigrate. He had been released from prison, and was living with his sister and mother in Türmitz, working as a day labourer on a construction site. Jewish life in Aussig had ceased. The remains of the outer walls and the ground floor of the burnt-out synagogue there were bought a little later by the meat firm of Robert Houdek, who made sausages in this once sacred place.

Father wrote that he had to sell the house in Türmitz to pay the tax for Mother and himself. But he was afraid he wouldn't get a lot for it, too little in any event for the fares to travel abroad, often amounting to around $1,000.

What could I do? Whatever happened, I must return to London as soon as possible. In Reading I could do nothing, and I wanted in any case to be closer to Fred. He raised little further objection to my return. After all, there were still no air raids.

Fred seemed to have a firmer grip on things with every day that passed. I could hardly believe it, but he was on the point of writing a text in a totally strange language, not a simple undertaking, and one at which, having lost their readership, their native setting and often their subject matter, a number of great exiled German writers had failed. Being an author isn't easy, a Jewish exile once said, but being a Jew makes it worse. Being a Jewish author is almost a minor tragedy. But what if, on top of everything else, the Jewish author is from a country with another language?

As before, Fred, who was still being helped financially by his brother, spent every penny on going to cinemas and theatres to develop a feel for English. His senses, rather blunted up to now, were resharpened as he started to master the peculiarities of the Anglo-Saxon tongue. 'Just imagine,' he wrote to me, 'I've found a street in London called the "Seven Sisters Road". It cries out to be set to music.'

It was Fred's first English title. 'Seven Sisters Live in Seven Sisters Road' described, as one might well suppose, seven sisters, each with a particular characteristic. He sent me the draft to Reading to go over. From then on I was always the first to read his work. If I laughed, he was happy; if I didn't, he rewrote it. This time, I laughed.

The song was published a few months later. Fred had got himself an English agent, an English Jew by the name of Fred Glass, and had run into the composer Hans May again, with whom he had worked in Vienna. Like some other émigrés, May had started a business, a publishing firm called 'Schauer & May'. So, after only six months, Salo had succeeded in a new language. 'Seven Sisters' was his first hit in a foreign country.

Fred bought himself a new suit with the royalties. Probably his external appearance now represented for him his triumph over the humiliation of having had to wear a threadbare camp uniform for eight months. In any event, Fred always set great store by being impeccably dressed. Even when he was short of money, he made a special effort to keep up appearances, which meant so much to him. He had labels made by his brother's firm sewn into his suits. 'Harrods', it said proudly on the left inside breast pocket. Fred enjoyed a bit of malarkey.

Fred owed some of his first work in England to the ex-Viennese pianist Hans May. His real name was Johann Meyer, and he was almost twenty years older than Fred. May had already composed film music before emigrating in 1933 and, because this occupation is more readily transferred to another cultural milieu than language, he had been able to get established in exile. And so an unexpected opportunity opened up for Fred to write English lyrics for May's music for the film of the play *The Stars Look Down*. He wrote the text for *Starlight Serenade*, which was also to be a success.

As in the old days, Fred sat all night at the piano with Hans May, inventing English rhyming schemes. At Easter 1940 he sent me, in Reading, a painted egg with a card saying: 'I cannot come *zu* Easter, Producers *sind* big *Biester. Doch sei nicht bös*, I beg, and have *statt mir* this egg!' How could I possibly be angry?

Working at his old passion again gave Fred unexpected energy, although because of his concern to be secure, he kept his sense of reality. 'I can't live just from writing lyrics,' he said. When he finally got a work permit and his brother offered him a job doing the accounting in his textile firm, he agreed immediately. Juggling figures suited him as much as juggling with lines of poetry. And so, it seemed, he had now re-established his life on a firm basis, with the three basic props of logic, religion and art.

Meanwhile I also had good prospects of employment in London. A number of families wanted me as a nanny, and wealthy refugees – there were some – were looking for a cook. Paul Friedländer, my rowing companion from Aussig, suggested I work as a chauffeur; he was doing well at it. I myself wanted most of all to work in a hospital. In my head I had compiled carefully thought-out plans with which to confront a collapsing world. I wanted to find a two-bedroom flat in London with somewhere to cook for myself and Marianne, who ideally would undertake some training or other, and sub-let a room with breakfast and evening meal. Such facilities were in demand, as there were many bachelors from the Continent who couldn't even fry an egg. I reckoned that with the cooking, I could earn somewhat over the odds. During the day I would work, and in the evenings we would at last have a home for the two of us, which was what I most dearly wanted.

At the beginning of May 1940 I applied to work as a nurse at St Mary's Hospital in Paddington. I was accepted straight away and told I should start on 1 July. How happy I was! London was like a silver lining in the dark days. I would do my favourite work, have my own flat, Fred would be there, and soon Marianne too. And perhaps we would have some money over for Father and Mother when they were in England. At first, we agreed in our letters, we daughters would care for our parents.

The darker the present was, the more I tried to imagine a bright future. Age subverts this outlook. At twenty-five, despite all the worries, the future seemed huge and full of promise. But the more time one has behind one, the less one clings to the future.

On 9 April 1940 the Germans invaded Norway, on 10 May Belgium and Holland. In London, Chamberlain resigned, and made way for the new prime minister, Winston Churchill, whose first speech promised his country 'blood, toil, tears and sweat'. On 15 May Denmark, occupied by Hitler's troops without resistance two days earlier, surrendered, and just two weeks later Belgium gave up the struggle. The Germans now marched on Paris.

'All our friends think that trying to get to another country on this continent is impossible and inadvisable,' wrote my parents. 'Soon no country will be able to ignore what is going on and stand idly by.'

Even Tony, ever the professional optimist, who was keeping the wolf from the door by working as a film extra following the collapse of his beauty business, raged, 'The Germans are making too much progress for my taste.' When Tony's humour was laced with irony, you could be sure the situation was serious. All the same, I still set my hopes on Strittmatter. No other prospect was left.

On 4 June Churchill's historic speech was broadcast on the wireless. There cannot have been anyone in England who did not hear the news once or twice a day. When Churchill spoke, people stopped talking in the pubs or interrupted their work to listen. I was standing at the stove as his voice came from the wireless in the kitchen. 'We shall fight on the beaches, we shall fight on the landing grounds, we shall fight in the fields and in the streets, we shall fight in the hills,' said that voice. 'We shall never surrender.' It had none of the irascible bawling of Hitler's speeches, and it moved us to the core. The speech transformed the mood of the country. Churchill appealed for courage and unity in the struggle against the enemy, and we, who spoke the enemy's language, felt we too were being addressed. We dearly wanted to help inflict damage on Hitler's Germany. I was happy that I had applied to work in a hospital. Looking after wounded soldiers seemed more sensible than putting up with the hysterical moods of my employer.

In recent weeks Lady Piggott had stopped my wages because, in my increasing nervousness, I had broken a piece of crockery. A cup had fallen down which she claimed was very valuable. Feeling guilty, I sent the shards to Ferdinand Rauter in London, asking him to buy a new one. He did so, and told me he had got it at Woolworths for a few pence.

At this eventful and stressful time there was a letter from Strittmatter. He had managed to get my parents transit visas, he said, and they must leave straight away. They could stay with him, and he would guarantee their financial position. The heavens opened. I was never again as relieved as at that moment. I sent a telegram to my parents in Prague. Father replied with a sentence that has stayed in my memory. 'We put our fate in your little hands, Ilse,' he wrote, adding that they would leave Prague on the next possible train and would get the tickets that very day.

The next day, 10 June 1940, Hitler and Mussolini concluded a pact. Italy entered the war on Germany's side, and all chance of escape was lost. Once more, we were too late by a whisker. My little hands had been helpless.

Perhaps I feel even more despair today than I could then that this window to freedom slammed closed after opening a chink. At the time, one never quite gave up hope, and got through each day with some small remnant of confidence, hoping that the war would soon end, that Germany would haemorrhage economically, and that my parents would eventually manage to come to me.

But events were very dispiriting. On 14 June the Germans entered Paris. On 22 June, Britain's last remaining ally announced its surrender. A few days later I had a letter from the hospital in Paddington telling me with regret that I could unfortunately not take up the job, as it was not allowed for refugees from an enemy country to nurse wounded soldiers, who had returned in their thousands from the Continent. It was feared that in a state of febrile delirium the soldiers might reveal military secrets.

And so my plan for my own flat and a job in London was shattered overnight. As there was no question of withdrawing my notice to the Piggotts, I turned to the Hochwalds, who offered me temporary accommodation in London. Josef Hochwald, who was married to a cousin of my mother, had dealt in textiles in Brno, and now, using old business contacts, made quite a good living dealing in English wools and tweeds. I accepted his offer gratefully and spent my first weeks in London with his family in Golders Green.

Uncle Josef was very generous. 'You need something to

wear,' he said, and told me he would give me the material and the name of a good tailor. 'But you'd better take your Fred,'he advised. 'The tailor is notorious for fondling his female clients.'

Fred attended the first fitting with watchful eyes. I had ordered a costume in grey tweed. The tailor fussed around the waist with his chalk, and without warning suddenly sketched in large breast pockets on the jacket. It was really not necessary to emphasize my size D by adding them. 'I said I didn't want pockets there,' I objected immediately. The tailor nodded obsequiously. 'OK, no pockets,' he said, and before I knew what was happening he was rubbing his big hands over my breasts to erase the chalk marks. Fred had been too slow, but he was good enough to settle the bill.

London had become no easier for Jewish refugees. Now Britain stood alone, fear of Nazi spies spread like the ubiquitous fog. The newspapers had reported a year before that the Gestapo had infiltrated Jews into the country as spies, causing an extraordinary paranoia about a fifth column among the British people, who are normally so sensible. The fears were stoked up by Churchill after he came to power when he proposed it would be best to put 'enemy aliens' and suspect persons behind barbed wire. After France's surrender the tone got shriller, and Churchill gave the order, 'Collar the lot!' and sealed the fate of thousands of Jews.

We were divided into two camps: 'friendly aliens' and 'enemy aliens'. In order to classify them, the refugees were ordered before tribunals set up around the country and exhaustively questioned. I had been through the tribunal in Reading, and released as a 'friendly alien' because I had left Czechoslovakia before Hitler's invasion. Refugees from Germany and Austria were classed as 'enemy aliens'. Fred and his brother were 'enemy aliens', and of course Tony from Halle. 'Enemy aliens' were *prima facie* suspect. It was thought better to lock up a thousand innocent people than let one potential Nazi spy slip through the net.

The first wave of arrests began on 15 May, when 2,200 men were taken, most of them from areas under military restriction. By mid-July 12,000 Germans and Austrians were behind barbed wire. Some avoided arrest for a time by a simple trick.

It soon got around the refugees that the men from Scotland Yard always came for people between 6 and 8 a.m. in the morning. What was simpler than to get up earlier and be somewhere else when they knocked on the door? And so that summer crowds of Jews were to be seen at first light in the parks. Fred and his brother got up at 5 a.m. and spent the early hours on Hampstead Heath. Tony too stuck it out for a time, wandering around Hyde Park. After a while he found it silly. German air raids were expected any day, so spending the war outside London would be 'the healthier variant'. 'I'm not good at this heroism game,' he said. So he stayed at home, and two days later he was arrested, not thinking he would be sent to safety on the other side of the world.

I had no idea what had happened. The earth seemed suddenly to have swallowed him up – like many others. Friends often disappeared. In a few weeks more than 27,000 refugees were interned. It was done in a very British manner, not at all like the way the Germans went about it. There were no mass transportations, only individual arrests, the police usually showing especial courtesy and consideration. Not that this lessened the absurdity of it all. The last democracy in Europe was putting behind barbed wire thousands who had fled from Hitler, most of them with little more than their own skins. The times were really out of joint.

Even Ferdinand Rauter was politely arrested and interned. Shortly before, I had heard one of the recitals he gave at the National Gallery. He and Engel Lund had performed for almost nothing: entry cost one penny. In October 1939 Rauter had been the first Austrian musician to appear in the National Gallery – with the walls bare because all the pictures had been removed. He and Engel Lund had omitted German folk songs from their programme 'Folk Songs of Many Lands'. Their message of international friendship was the same as always, but somehow the moment did not seem right.

After his arrest, Ferdinand Rauter was sent to a holding camp near Bury, where he was elected camp leader. And what did this camp leader do, who was convinced all his life of the soothing effect of music? At night, as he and his fellow prisoners crept under their blankets, Ferdinand sang them lullabies.

And with a professor of music, he sang two-part songs by Schubert and Strauss. Many of the prisoners wept.

On the Isle of Man, where Rauter ended up, there were at least a couple of old pianos and a handful of other instruments. Nearly 14,000 people were interned on the island, almost all of them Jewish. They could move freely, and lived in boarding houses where English people used to go for their holidays. Among the internees were many scholars and musicians, and so a rich cultural life soon began to flourish behind the barbed wire. Improvised universities sprang up. Academics gave lectures. There were concerts and recitals, theatre productions, art exhibitions and further education events.

Ferdinand met a number of performing musicians and composers there from Germany and Austria and performed music with them. From their co-operation evolved the Refugee Musicians' Committee, which concerned itself not just with strengthening solidarity through shared music-making, but with getting work permits for refugee musicians – sometimes against the opposition of the British Musicians' Union. The committee was able to recruit the famous pianist Myra Hess as their champion. As a friend of the royal family, she had excellent contacts, and helped with getting engagements. Ferdi was apparently one of those people who are always able to make the best out of the worst situations.

In this way, he was rather like Tony, who had drawn a short straw where internment was concerned. He had first been sent to a reception camp on an old racetrack, and then taken to Liverpool. There he found himself on the troopship *Dunera*, which sailed for a two-month voyage to Australia on 11 July 1940.

Conditions aboard the *Dunera* were inhuman. As they were tossed about in storms in the Irish Sea, the prisoners hung on the deck rail being sick into the water. Only Tony stayed upright. He was never seasick. On the very first day he sought out the butcher on board to see whether he needed help. Asked what he knew about the butcher's trade, he answered, 'Not a lot, but I bet I'll learn it all in two days.' And so he spent the voyage from Liverpool to Australia as a butcher's assistant, with the advantage that he always had enough to eat, and didn't have to go short all day below decks, where the stink, the overcrowding and the heat were unbearable. Tony had to cut up halves of pigs and cows and carry them along the swaying deck. Thus it was that half a cow went overboard. There was a high sea running, and Tony had to make a choice: 'The cow or me.' The cow was already dead, he thought, so he dropped it.

In Australia the prisoners had to build their own camp in Hay. This time Tony offered his services as a building foreman, and once again got the job. He was given plans and survey equipment that he had not the slightest idea how to use. When the chief military engineer took over a few weeks later, he blew up when he compared the wooden barracks with the plans. Everything was wrongly sited. 'You built it in the wrong fucking place,' he yelled at Tony. Tony wasn't going to put up with that. 'For the starvation wages you pay us, you damned well take the place the way we built it,' he shouted back. Afterwards he said he had never felt as free as at that moment – as a prisoner in a camp somewhere in the Australian Outback.

Fred had a dread of being interned. Just the word 'camp' brought the most horrendous pictures to his mind. His relief when he was finally told that, having been in a concentration camp, he would not be arrested, was overshadowed by his even greater fear of a German invasion. After Dunkirk and Hitler's announcement of preparations for Operation Sealion against Britain, this fear was almost paralysing the country.

One evening Fred and I sat listening to the news. Fleets of German aircraft had begun raiding RAF bases. Sometimes you could hear the dull echo of bombs falling in heavy raids. The air war was being fought outside London, but it was only a matter of time before it raged over our heads. Over 100,000 children were evacuated again from the capital. Soldiers set up barbed wire in the streets, houses were barricaded and street signs and signposts removed to confuse the enemy if there were an invasion.

Fred's face hardened, and I saw the colour drain from it. 'I must tell you something,' he said as the news ended. He spoke slowly, weighing each word carefully and uttering it painfully. 'I've got hold of a revolver,' he said. 'I've hidden it well. If the Germans come, I'll shoot us all. First you and Marianne, and then myself. And God will forgive me.'

I went rigid with horror. 'What do you mean; I don't understand,' I stammered. 'Why do you want to kill us? I don't believe the Germans will invade. Britain isn't quite alone. We've got all the exiled governments with their armed forces here in London, the Czechs, the French, the Belgians, the Norwegians.'

Fred seemed not to hear. 'If the Germans come, we're finished,' he said to himself. 'I won't stand it a second time. We wouldn't survive anyway.'

Sometimes Fred was frightfully gloomy. Sometimes I sensed that my laugh would never light up the remotest corner of his soul, where it was always night. I could understand him, but I was quite different myself, and I had no intention of dying without a fight. No, I was determined to join the Home Guard, a sort of civilian army that had been forming for some time in all parts of London.

It was said that at first the exercises of the Home Guard were very amateurish, and that, lacking proper equipment, they had sometimes been armed with spears from the props stores of London theatres. But this did not affect morale. It brought the British people together, from housewives to down-and-outs. Children played 'English and Germans' in the streets instead of 'cowboys and Indians', and had a grand time.

One gets used to the presence of death surprisingly quickly, adopting a shoulder-shrugging fatalism and escaping into black humour, which the British demonstrated in abundance. It is strange that today, when I often go to more funerals in a month than to the theatre, the omnipresence of death troubles me more than it did in the war.

I was only a few weeks with the Hochwalds. Their care for me was touching, but I didn't want to go on being a burden. One day I saw an advertisement in the paper for a job that sounded made for me: 'Jewish refugees seek Czech cook.' I applied and was engaged on the spot.

I landed up with four Jewish émigrés from Prague, all about thirty, and with the same background. They shared a large apartment in Vivian Avenue in Hendon near Golders

Green. They had been fur dealers in Prague, and had apparently earned enough money not to have to starve in exile. I don't know how they did it, but they seemed even here to be well connected with the black market, and brought home delicacies that the likes of us, who now had only food on ration, could only dream of. They brought in whole hares, pheasants, ducks and venison, not to mention hefty wines and fine cheeses.

'Just say what you need,' they said, 'and we'll get it.' They often ordered complete dinner menus, stuffed roasts with dumplings and cabbage with dessert to follow. Sometimes they sat at table late into the night, smoking, playing poker and emptying a bottle of red wine an hour, almost like young Regency blades. They could be like little children, fighting over the food. 'He's got more than me,' one complained, fumbling around on his neighbour's plate. 'If I don't see proper table manners, you'll all get semolina pudding tomorrow,' I warned them. The threat was enough.

They seemed to want for nothing – except female company. Their wives – all except one were married – were still in Prague, and they wanted to get them out. The idea of living celibate lives in the meantime didn't appeal at all. One in particular had set his eye on me, and tried to pinch my bottom at every opportunity. Sometimes he knocked on my door in the middle of the night. I didn't open, of course.

I didn't tell Fred a word of this. He would certainly have insisted that I give notice. And everything considered, I was fine. There was usually enough left over from supper for me to take something for Fred. As far as bodily sustenance went, we both managed quite well. Hunger, at any rate, was one thing that didn't afflict us.

Every Sunday afternoon a refugee orchestra played in the large ballroom at Bloomsbury House. Tea, coffee and cakes were free, and they played English and Viennese waltzes and, tangos. The Hungarian Isidor, who had fled from Vienna, and had the appropriate surname of Geiger, slipped between the rows of tables playing the violin. Like the other musicians, he performed for no fee other than a warm meal.

Fred was a wonderful dancer, and could tango with great style. He didn't like the waltz. But he was also determined our *pas de deux* would not be disturbed. When a young man asked me for a waltz, Fred said, before I could open my mouth, 'The lady doesn't dance.' I had to laugh. It was Fred's way of showing his love.

In such places, where old friendships were renewed and new ones made, the refugees tended to keep to themselves. Their London diaspora centred on Swiss Cottage, Hampstead, Chelsea and Kensington, and they went to the same places in their leisure time. In the Café Cosmo in Swiss Cottage one met only Austrians and Czechs. I often went there with Bina. The Czech Club, known for its good dumplings and the fact that one could talk politics without being disturbed, was the favourite meeting place for the Sudeten Germans.

In Hampstead there was the Freier Deutscher Kulturbund, which Fred avoided as he wanted nothing to do with German *Kultur*, even in its Jewish émigré variant. He much preferred going to the Austrian Centre, founded by Austrian refugees. It was not only homesickness that drove the Austrians there, but the need to distance themselves publicly from the 'Anschluss'. The Austrian Centre, which was started in a shabby house in Westbourne Terrace, made exile more bearable for many refugees.

The little Austrian island contained a library with a reading room, a restaurant with reasonable meals, lecture rooms, English classes and debating clubs. A favourite place to meet was the Laterndl, which belonged to the centre, a typically Austrian cabaret theatre that was a little bit of Vienna in the middle of London. Fred met Paul Knepler, Lehár's librettist from Vienna, there again. With his son Georg, he had taken over as director of music at the Laterndl. By day, Georg worked as secretary in the Austrian Centre, and in the evenings played the piano accompaniment for the cabaret performances in the Laterndl. It goes without saying that people felt committed to seeing their native culture wasn't forgotten. Fred, too, having quickly made friends with Paul Knepler, sometimes suggested text ideas for sketches. It was one of the few opportunities he had to write in his mother tongue. They played pieces they wrote themselves, as well as the *Threepenny Opera* and a lot of pieces by the young Viennese writer Jura Soyfer, who died of typhus at twenty-six, a few days after Fred's release from Buchenwald.

In the 'Blue Danube' the Viennese cabaret artist Peter Herz let fly at the Nazis so wittily that the *Völkischer Beobachter* once threatened, 'We shall get our hands on these cheeky lads in the Finchley Road who dare to ridicule us, and we shall divert the 'Blue Danube' into a concentration camp.' Peter Herz wasn't impressed. His compèring was very popular. Fred and I liked going with friends. Humour was our weapon against the Nazis, and we resisted them with our laughter. It was all we had.

I would have liked to have Marianne with me. She wrote unhappily from Dublin, where she was now an *au pair* with a family, complaining that she did not get enough to eat. 'I've got very thin,' she wrote, adding that she wanted to come to London at last. I still tried to comfort her, and began sending her ten shillings a week to buy food.

I was also very worried about my parents. I had had no news for months. The war had cut off mail contact. From one of their last letters I gathered that Marianne Bauer visited them most days. Marianne, an old Aussig rowing companion of mine, worked as a nurse in an ophthalmic clinic in Prague. Although she had straw-coloured hair and watery blue eyes, and looked the ideal Nazi BDM-type, she was in fact the illegitimate daughter of a Jewish woman. Her mother had committed suicide when Marianne was still a child, and she had been adopted by her uncle, a lawyer in Aussig. She had moved to Prague before the annexation of the Sudetenland, and had a German boyfriend there. She was very happy with him, and the two of them talked of getting married. A few days after the Germans entered Prague, however, he left her.

I shall never forget what Marianne did for my parents. Several times a week she brought them a warm midday meal. She got it in the clinic and somehow smuggled it out under her white nurse's apron, taking a big risk out of friendship for them. If she had been caught, she would have lost more than her job. But it was reassuring to know that people like this were in contact with my parents.

On the night of 7/8 September 1940 the London blitz began. At four in the morning several hundred German bombers appeared, filling the sky and bringing a foretaste of hell The bombs fell mostly on the docks in east London and on the Surrey docks, where millions of tons of timber were stored. In no time there was a blazing conflagration. A thousand fire hoses were in action trying to tame the inferno. There were several hundred dead, and that was just the start.

From now on, the bombers came every night, and often by day. On 10 September, what was thought at the time to be one of the worst fires was started in St Katherine's dock, where there were huge warehouses in which paraffin wax was stored. The flames shot over 6,000 feet into the air, and the paraffin streamed like lava everywhere and lay as a wax covering on the Thames. Of the seven-storey warehouses there remained only a pile of smoking ashes.

I wasn't afraid. Not for my life. I feared for others, especially for Fred. Whenever possible, we rang each other every morning to make sure the other was still alive. I was allowed to use the fur dealers' telephone, and Fred shared a line with his brother. But the lines were often broken, and sometimes we had no news for days at a time.

Fortunately Swiss Cottage, where Fred was living with his brother in a small flat, was spared air raids. Only once did an errant bomb fall nearby. I was visiting Fred that evening. We were sitting with Mundy and his girlfriend in front of the fire playing cards when it went off. At that moment a cloud of soot burst out of the fireplace, apparently from the enormous pressure wave from the blast. It covered the whole room with a layer of soot. The whites of our eyes flashed in astonishment in our black chimney-sweep faces, then white teeth as each of us laughed at seeing the others' faces. We spent until dawn cleaning up the soot from all over the place. It is hard to imagine now, but at the time we could hardly stop laughing.

Being in constant danger of one's life breeds an almost devil-may-care courage that is hard to find in times of peace. Once we survived the first few days, we began to feel safe, even invulnerable. Most people felt this. When a German parachute bomb came down, people would often run to where they thought it would land, ignoring the danger. German parachute silk was said to make good blouses.

Between September and mid-November the German planes came every night but one, when bad weather prevented an attack. Worst of all were the clear nights. On 15 October the scene was lit by a full moon, and more than 400 bombers dropped over 500 tons of bombs on the city. That night alone 400 civilians died.

In central London Buckingham Palace, the Tower, Madame Tussaud's, the Natural History Museum and the Zoo were hit. In the West End, many of the exclusive clubs lay in ruins. Oxford Street was so badly hit that we thought we wouldn't be able to go shopping there for months. But only four days later the shops were open again, many with a Union Jack flying defiantly above the wrecked building. A heavy bomb had buried itself deep in the earth in front of St Paul's cathedral without going off. With great courage, disposal men dug their way to it, recovered it, and took it to Hackney Marshes, where the explosion tore a crater 100 feet deep. They were awarded the George Cross or the George Medal, new awards that the King had created for acts of bravery by soldiers and civilians.

The people celebrated these heroes from their own ranks and the war brought everyone together in a lay army. In the Home Guard there were scouts and pensioners, civil servants and businessmen, young mothers and old people – all volunteers, and all unpaid. I worked as a messenger for the Home Guard in Swiss Cottage. Twice a week I was on duty all night. There were four of us accommodated in little tin huts hardly bigger than a summerhouse. We slept, as far as sleep was possible, on mattresses in our day clothes. There was a kettle for making tea, but that was all. In front of the hut stood a Home Guard sentry, keeping track of where the bombs fell. Most were First World War veterans, who did not get excited easily. Whenever a bomb exploded nearby or flames were seen rising, the sentry woke us up and sent us off on bicycles to the nearest centre, where the hit was recorded. I have never cycled faster than on those nights. As a 'friendly alien', I was allowed to ride a bicycle. For 'enemy aliens' it was forbidden.

My heart was in my mouth as I raced through empty and darkened streets while the sky reflected the fires around and the droning of the planes, the thuds of the bombs, the chatter of anti-aircraft fire and the wailing of the sirens made up a cacophonous chorus. As I went, pride drove out fear, because at last I had the feeling of really doing something against the hated Nazis. However small my contribution as a cycle messenger might be, for me every stroke of the pedals was a blow against the enemy. I really flourished when I was on duty.

Many thousands were bombed out in the first weeks. They were put up in schools, gyms or tube stations, and looked after by mobile kitchens. People slept on tube platforms on straw sacks or mattresses, whole families taking to life underground.

Most cinemas and theatres in the West End opened again in October 1940, often bringing performances forward so that people could be home when the raids came. Fred and I saw *Gone with the Wind* in Leicester Square. I cried throughout, of course, Fred pulling one handkerchief after another from his jacket and giving it to me without a word. He seemed to have got to know me very well. We often went to the pictures, where the world was better than it was outside.

My four fur dealers were pretty stoical, especially where my safety was concerned. As soon as the sirens started wailing, they took the lift down to the shelter in the basement and left me behind, saying, 'Ilse, make us a pot of tea and a few sandwiches so we don't starve down there.' I got good at making sandwiches very quickly, and the tea was quite weak, as I didn't leave it long to draw. You don't feel so comfortable in a fourth-floor kitchen when the whole city around is shaking with explosions.

All the same, I usually made a few extra sandwiches so there was something over for other people. The dealers didn't mind. Somebody in the shelter always had some cake or a few apples, and it was taken for granted that everything was shared.

In the cellar they called me 'Miss Cheerful' because I always had a stock of Jewish jokes ready. Most of the inhabitants were Jews, who made up most of the population in Hendon. We were often doubled up with laughter while the world was being blown to pieces all around us. It was a sort of put-on laughter, a little too loud and resonant, which covered the tension that one usually tried to hide and the exhaustion from constant sleep deprivation. We usually sang, too.

Everywhere in air raid shelters people sang to ward off fear and the noise of exploding bombs. I sang Czech songs, and together we bawled out English folk songs. All over England people sang 'We're Going to Hang Out the Washing on the Siegfried Line' to defy the Germans, whose defensive line in the west was called the Siegfried Line. The name Siegfried stood for all they hated about Germany. It was a good thing Fred had dropped the name.

Most air raid shelters also kept out clean air as well as bombs, and they stank dreadfully. The underground stations assured one of a good draught of fresh air, and were opened as shelters soon after the first raids. Some nights they held over 170,000 people. But even there, in supposedly safe buildings, people were killed by structural collapse, floods or were crushed in a panic.

Our cellar held people from sixty flats, and there were only four toilets for us all. In no time, body smells were added to an atmosphere you could cut with a knife. The children slept or played on the floor, part of which was laid out with mattresses. Babies were breastfed. Many women knitted. One taught me a pattern with reversed stitches, and I started to knit a winter pullover for Fred. 'When you've finished, the war will be over,' said Fred drily. He knew I was no great shakes at working with my hands. I wanted to prove him wrong, and every time there was an air raid, I worked on it like mad. A few weeks later when he tried it on, it came down to his knees.

My talents lay elsewhere, I thought. I found an ad in the paper by a vet who was looking for a Czech cook who could also help him as a veterinary assistant. He offered twice my present salary, and I gave notice immediately. The vet, who lived only a few blocks from the fur dealers, was called Edgar Lustig, and was very happy when I served Czech food, which he had been missing badly. The 'Herr Doktor' couldn't have everything of course, only what was allowed him in the 'ration book'.

Many people brought their pets to his surgery to be put down. Animals were not welcome in the air raid shelters, and fewer and fewer people could manage to feed them. It was now forbidden to give cats and dogs food fit for human consumption. So hardly a day went by without Mr Lustig administering some four-legged creatures a fatal injection. Sometimes the phone rang as he was in the middle of it, and he handed me the syringe to finish the job. I had learned to give injections as a nurse. But those had been meant to heal; these were fatal, meant to protect the animals from going through what might be in store for their owners. What a crazy world.

Two days before New Year enemy bombers returned to London. In the previous weeks it had been quieter, and the city had breathed with relief. The Germans had turned their attention to other cities, attacking Birmingham and bombing Coventry until nothing was left but a skeleton.

And so they came again. It was the first Sunday after an amazingly peaceful Christmas, and a deceptively quiet day. London slumbered. The firewatchers were not at maximum readiness, and the fire tenders on the river could not manoeuvre properly because the water was so low. The city was unusually vulnerable and would pay a heavy price. Fifteen hundred fires burned that night, most in the City. They spread to form two massive conflagrations such as London never saw again in the whole war.

As if by a miracle, St Paul's cathedral survived, although hit by twenty fire-bombs. But around the cathedral lay a ruined landscape that was still smoking and smouldering days later as Fred went back to work. The office block was still standing, but he saw a lot of men standing helplessly holding their briefcases in the rubble that covered their former work places. And some of them even turned up there again the following day, as though they were hoping that Destiny would intervene.

One got used to clambering over mountains of rubble on the way to work. Fred often looked in the evening as though he had come from a building site. A grey powdery dust covered his hair and clothes, as it lay over the whole city. Undismayed, he brushed his suit every evening and polished his shoes until they glistened. 'Why do you bother?' I once asked him. 'By tomorrow evening it'll all be just as dirty again.'

Fred paused, as though painfully upset. 'What do you

mean?' he said, shaking his head. 'I'll never let the Germans make me dirty. Even if I have to brush myself down from head to foot every hour that God sends.'

And so we each fought in our own way. I cycled through the air raids and Fred wielded his clothes brush against the Germans. It didn't seem to hold much promise for a famous victory.

9 Home Thoughts

This morning I woke up early. It was still dark outside, and the cold night air came through the open window. It blew over my face and brought me back to London. That night I was in Bohemia, in our house in Türmitz, but everything was different. The place was deserted. Where furniture once stood there were blank spaces like wounds on the walls. Mother and Father were not there, and Marianne had gone too.

My home never stops haunting me at night. Exiles' dreams, they call them. My friends have them too. Like a group of travellers sharing the same experiences, we gather in the waiting room for a nightly journey to our past. In the daytime, when reason keeps fear under control, our mental pictures of home are more cheerful. Sometimes the idyllic valley of the Elbe flashes before my eyes, sometimes the splendour of the flowers in Grandad's garden or the elegant streets of Prague. At night, horrors break in. I often dream that Father and Mother are being taken away before my eyes. I want to cry out and hold on to them, but my limbs won't move and my voice is dumb.

In the first months of my stay in England my home was in my dreams every night. During the war, circumstances were not conducive to such nocturnal melancholy. Sleep in the air raid shelters was too shallow to dream. Fred, with whom I sometimes stayed overnight, had worse dreams than I if he slept at all. Sometimes he cried out or woke up in horror, covered in sweat, and I had to talk to him for a long time to calm him down and bring him back to present reality. It was not only his own traumas that plagued him; he was tormented above all by thoughts of his parents. Uncertainty over their state gave rein to the worst fears.

The first rumours of a forthcoming 'resettlement' in Poland circulated among Vienna's Jews in January 1941, throwing people into sheer turmoil. A little later, the first Jews were deported from the Aspang station to the *Generalgouvernement*, the central area of Poland under German occupation law. The lists of names were compiled by the Central Office for Jewish Emigration; the Jewish cultural community was in charge of informing those selected and caring for the internees in the assembly camps. After five transports the deportations were temporarily stopped. The system of annihilation had still to be fully worked out.

There were hardly any signs of life from Father and Mother. Letter mail between Prague and London was still forbidden, and all my parents could do was write sporadically to New York, where my friend Susie Meyer, the Lavers' erstwhile governess, had gone with her family. The USA was still neutral. My parents always wrote that they were fine, and were trying all they could to leave the country. Fred too heard from his parents in Vienna via friends in the USA that they had had to move to a Jewish house in Grosse Schiffgasse. He did not realize it was to be their last address.

None of us, I am sure, could imagine how hopeless the situation was for those left behind. I know today that my parents' fate was as good as sealed by then. At the end of 1940, the Jews of Prague had been made to transfer all their savings to blocked accounts. They had already had to hand in gold, silver and jewellery. Now they were allowed to withdraw only minimal sums from the account, and the amounts were always being reduced. My parents had become simply too poor to afford to leave, like thousands of other Jews.

My desire to have Marianne with me grew ever stronger. The air raids were now rather less severe, and I again dared to plan beyond the next day. If Marianne were here, we could live together and make a home for ourselves. However I would have to give up my job as housemaid and look for work where I didn't have to live in. For a time, I was reluctant to give up the well-paid position with Mr Lustig without the firm prospect of something else, until outside events forced a decision on me.

It should have been a special evening. Mr Lustig had invited his neighbour for her birthday. Before I came, she had often cooked for him, and he was grateful to her. Mr Lustig's father had bought a hare on the black market. Although I was not keen on roast hare – I was too upset at the sight of the animals – I made an honest effort to produce a tasty dish from this expensive meat. I stuffed the hare, which I had marinated earlier, with herbs, and cooked it in a red wine stock. Soon the whole house was filled with tempting odours, reminding me of meals on feast days at home in Türmitz, where the cooking smells wafted from the kitchen like delicate banners waving in the breeze.

As I was about to serve the food, still buried in thought, I heard Edgar Lustig say, 'Ilse, I forgot; we could obviously use the good Rosenthal service this evening.' Even before I could reply, the neighbour said, 'Oh don't bother, Edgar. Where Ilse comes from they eat with their fingers. How should she know any better?'

The sauce boat slopped over as I put it down with a jerk. Tears of anger filled my eyes, and I stormed out of the room without a word. I wanted to run into the street and get right away, back to a past that no longer existed. I phoned Fred and told him tearfully what had happened. He promised to come straight away.

Mr Lustig had rushed after me in the meantime to apologize for his guest's rudeness. It was too late. An hour later Fred was at the door, and said to my employer, 'You will understand that Ilse will not work for you any more under these humiliating circumstances. I give notice on her behalf.'

As I saw Fred standing there, apparently composed but inwardly raging, I knew he was offended as much as I, who could not utter a word. Did everyone think like this about us émigrés? Didn't they know we had had the same living standard as them, and that it took a measure of courage to have lost everything and start again from nothing?

Certainly, most British people knew it very well, for in general the climate changed and refugees did not encounter the sceptical attitudes common at the start of the war. Everyone now realized that interning émigrés was sheer nonsense. There had even been official protests, and the internees slowly returned from the camps. Ferdinand Rauter had been released in December, after someone had certified that he was an 'eminent musician', and was working again.

The country needed the refugees – and it needed the women. Because the men had joined the armed forces by the thousand, replacements were urgently sought. The papers were full of advertisements for book keepers, commercial and sales staff and the like. The war, it seemed, was a more powerful force for female emancipation than the suffragettes had been. Suddenly women were breaking into male domains. They drove buses, were waiters and worked in the Home Guard with the same easy self-assurance as they did behind bank counters or in the fire service. Some housewives even learned to shoot. Bina had found a job as an interpreter at Selfridges and advised me to apply. I urgently needed work, so I took her advice. The woman I saw there turned out to be only mildly interested.

'Sorry,' she said, 'But just now we have nothing. Come back next month.' When she saw my despair, she must have taken pity. 'All right' she said, 'as you're here, fill in one of these forms. Say what training you've had and where you went to school.'

I did as she asked, and handed her the completed forms. She cast a quick eye over them, paused, then reread them more carefully. 'You speak four languages?' she asked. 'You had commercial training and ran a company? And you're a trained nurse too?' I nodded. 'Wait a moment,' she said, and disappeared into her boss's office.

He soon came rushing out and shook me vigorously by the hand. 'Miss Lönhardt,' he said, 'we would take you on the spot, but there is really nothing free at the moment. But I have a suggestion: we'll pay you a full salary from next week but you don't have to start until a month's time when a position is vacant in accounts. We can't let such a well-qualified young woman as you go.'

The praise gave me a warm feeling, and countered the sense of not being valued that I had had in my recent jobs. At last I had the prospect of office work that suited me, and which, at two pounds ten shillings a week, was better paid than anything until now. I could afford a room of my own, and Marianne could finally come to London.

Fred was delighted. 'Let's go dancing this evening,' he said. 'We must celebrate.' We went to the Austrian Centre, I wore my grey costume with no pockets and he ordered half a bottle of wine to mark the occasion. We danced a slow tango. Fred drew me gently against him. 'So suddenly I found love,' he sang softly in my ear, and, encouraged by my flattered smile, went on, 'I found love right in front of me; when we danced and I looked at you, love came out of the blue. So suddenly did my heart sing a melody.'

'What's that?', I asked. 'A new song?'

'Do you like it?' asked Fred.

'Oh, very much, but that's because I take the words personally.'

'So you should,' he said and smiled. 'Who do you imagine I was thinking of when I wrote it?'

Shortly afterwards, Hans May's firm Schauer & May published it. It was played on the radio and several London dance bands took it up. Jack Payne, who had become famous as leader of the BBC Dance Orchestra, was among those who played it. It was not long before Fred and I danced the tango-foxtrot and the orchestra played his song 'So Suddenly'. So suddenly his life was transformed.

Mine too changed. I had finally found a little flat in Goldhurst Terrace, which I shared with two Jewish women refugees. Eva, who was from Danzig, also worked at Selfridges. Friedl, the other one, came from Berlin. She had been a buyer for KaDeWe, the famous 'Kaufhaus des Westens' store, and had a sure sense of taste that overcame even wartime deprivations. I had found her through an ad on the blackboard in the Café Cosmo. In London she earned her living as a dressmaker.

I liked our *Dreimäderlhaus*. The rooms were furnished with only the bare minimum, but it was ours. It reminded me of my time of freedom with Traute Fehres, from whom I had not heard for ages. In the evenings, Eva, Friedl and I sat together for hours, telling one another about our homes and our parents.

We had all come to England without them, Fred, Bina, Paul, Eva, Friedl and many others. Most of us had heard nothing from home for a long time. Secretly we all lived with the feeling that we would never see our fathers and mothers again. The Nazis had made us a generation without parents, orphans in exile.

In February the Luftwaffe made Hendon, where I had lived before, a wasteland in one night. In March the Café de Paris was hit and a number of people were killed. It was a favourite place for émigrés to meet, and Fred and I had been there several times. I had the feeling the bombs were coming closer.

Following the dreadful fire in the City in December, firms were obliged to set up fire watches in their office buildings. Fred volunteered as a firewatcher. At nights, as the bombs rained down, he stood on a roof opposite St Paul's cathedral and tried to see with binoculars where they hit and where fires had started. The reports were then passed by field telephone to an information centre. I was always anxious about him when he was on night duty, but I said nothing. It was Fred's way, touching though it was in its relative passivity, of fighting the Nazis. I did not want to talk him out of it.

After I had started my job at Selfridges, Marianne could at last join me. It put my mind at rest knowing that I could take care of her. Even if I could not get over feelings of guilt, which have stayed with me to this day, at not getting my parents out, I was very happy at least to have my little sister with me again.

This time I got to the station in good time to meet her, but I hardly recognized her. She had grown and had cut her hair. But that wasn't it. Marianne looked terribly ill. Her formerly slim neck was inflated like that of a toad; for the rest, though, she was as skinny as a rake. What had happened to her?

'Mein Kleines,' I said, stroking her hair, 'didn't they feed you in Dublin?'

'Oh, Ische, I don't want to talk about it,' she said, and snuggled against me. 'All that matters is, I'm here at last.'

Later, though, she told me that with the money I always sent her, she had bought only biscuits and chocolate. I was horrified. She should have got herself fruit and vegetables. 'But I was so lonely, and I felt so dreadful, and chocolate made me feel better,' she said. 'Don't scold me, Ilse. I'm with you now, and if you cook for me I'll soon be well again.'

It was a vain hope. Marianne, I was told by a doctor I consulted, had a dangerously enlarged thyroid gland caused by under-nourishment. 'You must have it operated on,' he said earnestly, clearly concerned. 'Do you have the money to pay for it?'

He might as well have asked whether I would like to rent a part of Buckingham Palace. I didn't have a penny to pay for an operation. But Marianne needed treatment, there was no question of that. How could I get the money?

I called Erika, a friend of Mundy's, who was a doctor in a hospital for women in London. She made an appointment with a colleague, a surgeon named Mr Joel. 'We have to remove the growth as quickly as possible,' he confirmed. He called Marianne in at the start of the following week. The operation lasted two hours. Mr Joel would take nothing for it.

People like this were a light in the darkness in the war, people who without thought or hesitation helped and shared and gave. Of course there were others, who looted bombed houses or took rings from the fingers of the wounded. The great mass of British people, though, were united in a fellow feeling that no bombs could destroy. Almost every morning somebody gave me a lift to work in a private car. As the buses and the tube were always overcrowded, this courtesy soon became commonplace. Anyone with room would pick up people at bus stops going in their direction.

Marianne stayed at home on her own for the first few weeks, recovering from the operation. Across her neck, now a normal size, was a flame-red scar. 'Nobody will look at me,' she complained. 'I look as though someone has tried to cut my throat.'

I bought her a lot of scarves and coloured chokers that matched her clothes and covered the scar. Having shot up, she needed new clothes urgently, and fortunately I got a 20 per cent reduction working at Selfridges. Marianne looked very pretty in her new blouses and dresses, quite the young lady. Lately she had started using lipstick like me. Gradually her looks came back.

The transformation did not escape Fred, and he was concerned like a father who sees his daughter maturing. 'Your little sister will soon be seventeen,' he said to me. 'Don't you think you should tell her about the birds and the bees? I can't imagine they taught that in the convent.' I put his mind at rest. I had long ago talked to her, and she was very well informed on all aspects, despite her Catholic education.

More than ever I felt a motherly responsibility for her. Although I did not let her see it, my hopes of rescuing our parents declined day by day. What was reported about Germany on the radio and in the papers was nothing if not disheartening.

In April 1941 the Palestine Office in Prague was closed, shutting the last bolt on the door. The last illegal transport to Palestine had left the Protectorate almost half a year before. In Warsaw the Germans had herded 400,000 Jews into the ghetto and cut them off from the outer world. They had created another huge ghetto in the former Polish city of Lodz, now renamed Litzmannstadt. There was no more news of my parents.

I had their photos in a small case that I took with me during air raids. We continued to spend many nights below ground. It was all new to Marianne. At first she probably had a youthful sense of adventure, but soon she had seen and heard enough of the shrill whistling of falling bombs, the anxious waiting for the nerve-shattering explosions and the flames rising into the sky. On 16 and 19 April the raids were especially bad. German dive bombers chased over the city, flying low above the rooftops with piercing shrieks as they dropped their bombs. It was a night of hell.

In the morning London lay like a stricken monster, disfigured by open wounds. Whole streets lay in ruins, churches were destroyed, houses had disappeared. In Mayfair, between Marble Arch and Grosvenor House, there was not a building where the windows were not broken. In the two nights more than 2,000 people had died, and almost 150,000 houses had been damaged or razed to the ground.

Three weeks later, on 10 May 1941, there was a bright full moon in a clear sky over London and the Thames was very low. Although conditions were ideal for an attack, nobody expected one because the last three weeks had passed off so peacefully. It was to be the worst night of bombing in the war. Westminster Hall was set on fire, the House of Commons and Big Ben were hit, and all Thames crossings between Tower Bridge and Lambeth Bridge were impassable. Almost 1,500 people died.

In the morning one saw many men going to work unshaven. Exhaustion and deprivation began to show in people's faces. One in six people had lost their homes. And yet few lost heart. Londoners were creating a legend, and everyone bore up with courage, decency and all the humour they could muster.

Shop owners whose premises had been hit the night before put up a sign over their smashed shopfronts saying: 'More open than usual'. Outside a church was written: 'If your knees are shaking, just kneel on them!' In the air raid shelters people made jokes about Hitler and sang songs mocking the Germans. The prolonged bombing, it seemed, had removed class boundaries and destroyed class consciousness, and every blow only increased the sense of unity. 'Stiff upper lips' had softened and the British became talkative and open. Sometimes their mood was euphoric. Constant threat ennobled ordinary lives, and gave mere day-to-day survival a touch of the heroic.

People kept cool heads, and every day stories made the rounds that showed the *sang froid* of ordinary citizens. All over London psychiatric wards had prepared to handle huge numbers traumatized by the war. But hardly anyone came to the clinics, and some were closed down for lack of demand. There was no hysteria in London, suicide rates dropped, and the incidence of serious drunkenness halved. Calmness and composure marked what they now call 'Britain's finest hour'.

The English seemed to forget their traditional reserve. Total strangers spoke to one another in the street and parted on good terms. Because of shortages, food had replaced all other topics of conversation. One week there was a shortage of onions, another week of cheese. Whenever I could, I exchanged my tea coupons for cooking ingredients. Actually, it wasn't allowed, but few people took any notice. Because the British cannot do without their tea even in times of great deprivation, I could always get a few extra coupons for flour, sugar and butter for making pastries and dumplings.

And now I also had the ration books of two Czechoslovak bachelors for whom I cooked Czech meals every evening. They collected them themselves and paid me a few shillings a week for the luxury of being served the cooking they knew from home. Whenever some of their coupons were left over, we could use them for ourselves.

Our fellow tenant Friedl had lately shown lively interest in my cooking. Shortly before she had met, in the Austrian Centre, a soldier in the exiled Czechoslovak army. He was from Bratislava, and seemed keen on Czech cooking. He was really charming, said Friedl, and she would like to invite him to come some time for supper. Sadly, her skills in this direction went no further than making sandwiches. In spite of this, we invited Bandy, as he was called, and I cooked. Although the weekly meat ration had been halved since February, by bartering coupons I had got enough for a *Wiener Schnitzel*, which I did with roast potatoes, followed by poppy-seed dumplings. It was a feast, and, as we agreed, Friedl pretended she had made it.

Bandy was worth taking the trouble to ensnare. He was both brave and warm-hearted. When the Germans invaded Prague, he fled to Poland on his own initiative, crossing the mountains on foot and walking through the woods as far as the coast at Danzig, from where he got to London and volunteered for the Czechoslovak exile army.

Many Jews fought against Hitler in Britain. Thousands of Czechs joined armed forces in France, Britain, the Middle East and the Soviet Union. Some had previously formed small resistance groups, and some had returned from Palestine to fight the Nazis. Jewish soldiers were not always very welcome. They were not nearly as nationalistic as the Czech professional officers, who had been through the strictly patriotic military academies. They could hardly speak Czech, but usually adjusted better to the culture and language of the lands of their exile than the nationalistic Czechs. Many professional soldiers regarded the Jews as 'undesirable elements'.

Bandy was one of about 4,000 Czechoslovak soldiers in Britain. The independent Czechoslovak Brigade, as it was called, based near Chester, was about 30 per cent Jewish. Among them were many former reserve officers, now serving as ordinary soldiers for seven shillings and sixpence a day. Because of a surplus of officers, they had been demoted in favour of the non-Jewish officers. There were constant complaints that Jews were treated as second-class soldiers. A petition was even sent to the exiled President Beneš, and Bandy must have spoken about it often.

That evening, though, there was another topic of conversation: Friedl's magical skills in the kitchen. His eyes misted over as Friedl served one delicacy after another. 'And you did all that?' he asked. Friedl nodded with eyes downcast, and I blushed. But Bandy seemed not to notice. He took a fourth helping of roast potatoes, and his face glowed. When he saw the poppy-seed dumplings and smelled the brown butter, he burst out, 'Friedl, you know, I haven't eaten these since I left Czechoslovakia.' He promptly lapsed into silence as he annihilated as many dumplings as he could, one after the other. Friedl and I counted quietly. He managed nine.

After that Bandy always came to eat with us when he had a day off. He seemed not to notice the fraud. One morning Friedl came to my bed in tears. The evening before Bandy had taken her to a dance and asked her to make herself especially pretty. She had tried on one dress after another and tripped around the flat like a frightened chicken, all her sense of taste having deserted her.

'What's happened?' I asked. 'Has he left you?'

'On the contrary,' she sobbed. 'He's asked me to marry him.'

'But that's wonderful,'I said. 'Did you say "yes"?'

'Of course I said "yes".'

'So what's the problem?'

'Don't you understand, Ilse? When Bandy finds out that I can't cook like he thinks, he probably won't want to marry me.'

Clearly it was time to serve up the truth. Sooner or later he would have seen through our game. Friedl hesitated a bit, but at their next date she revealed the creator of those Czech dishes. Bandy's face froze. For a long while he said nothing. Then he burst out laughing. 'Do you really suppose I thought you had cooked them?', he asked.

When they got married some time afterwards, Friedl asked me to be her witness. It was an unusually happy marriage.

The war gave a special impulse to romance, and sometimes it seemed all London was in love. Fate brought many of the émigrés together too, their similar pasts binding them more than an unknown future.

Eva, the tenant from Danzig, got to know my rowing companion Paul Friedländer at one of our suppers. Paul had given up being a chauffeur, and was training as a pilot. Eva and Paul hit it off straight away. She was captivated by Paul's humour, though not with his new occupation. But Paul dismissed all worries with his 'you can't keep a bad man down' attitude. His wish to fight Hitler was greater than the fear that one didn't want to be constantly thinking of in any case.

I had found an applied arts college in Chelsea for Marianne. Its director was a Czech called Matoušek. Marianne, who had applied submitting a portfolio, soon became his favourite pupil. Sometimes Fred and I took her dancing with us. Since the Germans had concentrated their attention on Africa and the Soviet Union, and the air attacks had decreased, one could risk it again. Many theatres and cinemas re-opened in the West End, and the throng of people starved of entertainment and culture was enormous. Fred, Marianne and I went whenever we could to the cinema. We saw *The Grapes of Wrath*, *Rebecca*, and Charlie Chaplin in *The Great Dictator*. German cinemas at the time were showing *Jud Süss*.

In the pictureless National Gallery the daily lunchtime concerts continued, with frequent appearances by Ferdinand Rauter and Engel Lund. Long queues stood at the entrance because the concerts, started by the pianist Myra Hess, had become one of the country's most important cultural institutions. British and foreign musicians often appeared together. For continental artists, the engagements were important in giving them a start to their lives in exile. For the audiences, often more than a thousand, the works of Beethoven, Bach, Schubert and Brahms, of all things, were symbols of British resistance to the Germans – and at the same time tokens of a noble and unconquerable world. Fred and I went to some of the concerts, which were always sold out. I have never since known an audience that listened so earnestly and with such attention and applauded with such enthusiasm and gratitude.

Perhaps music was so indispensable because it strengthened the feeling that all the privations people suffered were not in vain. When the Queen's Hall was bombed and all the

London Philharmonic Orchestra's instruments were destroyed in the fire, Londoners offered their own instruments, so that the music could go on. From then on, the orchestra played with borrowed instruments in the Albert Hall, where Fred and I heard them a number of times. Fred knew the corpulent figure on the conductor's podium from days long before, from the time he used to perform facing the public. It was Richard Tauber, who conducted for a fraction of his former appearance fee.

Music did not make anyone rich, but it enriched people's lives and freed them for a while from reality. When a dance band played 'Red Moon over Havana', Fred asked me to dance. The words were by him, and the music was by Fred Prisker, a refugee from Saaz, who had never been inside a music conservatory. He had been a jeweller, and first started composing in exile. Fred thought that his namesake had real talent, and the success of 'Red Moon over Havana' showed he was right. Since Geraldo, whose band was one of the best known in the country, had included it in his repertoire nobody doubted it any more.

Whenever he had unexpected royalties, Fred always took me out shopping. He was very generous, and gave me clothes and shoes. I am sure he would have lent me money, but I didn't want that. I had managed until now to take care of my sister, and I wanted to go on doing so. At the time, though, it was not easy. After Marianne moved in, the owner of the house had raised the rent considerably, and Marianne, who had not stopped growing, needed new clothes every year. Money was unusually tight.

Regretfully, I decided to sell a few items from home. Marianne was horrified when I told her, but there was no help for it. We needed the money. When I opened the case my parents had sent me, I felt queasy. It seemed a betrayal to sell these things, some of which were from my mother's bottom drawer, but it was better than going begging to other people.

The continental tablecloths got a good price. Wealthy Britons, and there were plenty of them, paid up to ten pounds for a large tablecloth with lace inlays. And I took Father's golden pocket watch, which Tony had brought from Prague, to a jeweller. I took it out one more time and listened to its gentle ticking, as I had often done as a child. Tears ran down my face. The jeweller inspected the whirring wheels through his monocle lens. It had a Swiss movement; Father wore only Swiss watches.

Since September 1941 he and Mother had worn the yellow star, like all Jews in Prague. All over Hitler's Germany the anti-Jewish restrictions and impositions became harsher. The war distracted from the atrocities taking place. Emigration from Vienna was stopped at the start of August, and a month later the Star of David was introduced. The chattels confiscated when the Jews were 'resettled' – the furniture, carpets and pictures, clothes, linen and china – were taken to the Vugestap offices in the Bauernmarkt and sold off cheaply to authorized *Volksgenossen*. By mid-1941 the Nazis had collected more than 4 million Reichsmarks in this way. Since the start of September there were further rumours of more imminent deportations. They were denied by Adolf Eichmann.

Meanwhile the Jews in Prague were deprived of most ration allowances. Clothing, sugar, fresh fruit and vegetables, cheese, fish, tobacco, soap and canned food were withheld from them. Jewish doctors, teachers, lawyers, translators, engineers and countless other occupational groups were unable to practise their professions. Jews had to surrender their driving licences and were not allowed to move into new premises, but had to lodge with other Jewish tenants. Since the beginning of the year, telephones had been disconnected in all Jewish households.

Father and Mother were now trapped. As Jews, they were forbidden to enter public parks and swimming pools, theatres and cinemas, and they could shop only in non-Jewish shops at set times, in the mornings between 11.00 and 1.00 and in the afternoons between 3.00 and 3.30. Certain streets were out of bounds for Jews, as were the banks of the Vltava between the railway bridge and the Hlavka bridge. From September 1941 Jews could use only the post office in Ostrovní Street in the 2nd district – between 1.00 and 2.30 in the afternoon. All other post offices in the city were barred to them. I wonder how many days it took before one could send a letter from there, because since September Jews needed written permission from the Central Office just to leave their own district. Their lives were one long obstacle course.

My father must have handed in the letter to Susie Meyer in New York at the post office in Ostrovní Street. He included photos of himself and Mother, asking that they be sent on to me. Did he sense these were to be the last pictures of the two of them?

Susie sent them to me immediately by airmail. It was now mid-October. 'Your parents look very good on the photos,' she wrote in English, saying it made her very happy. 'I hope they stay like that until the "butcher of Berchtesgaden" – as he is called here – is eliminated. And that will surely be soon. Then we shall all meet again.'

I was moved by Susie's concern to encourage me. But one had only to look at the sunken faces, the vacant eyes and the shadows around them to doubt her words. Mother had forced a smile that only enhanced the sadness of her expression.

A good week later another letter arrived from New York. Susie's father Ernst wrote 'in great haste'. It was 26 October 1941. He had heard from a local firm that a telegram had come from my parents, saying, 'Get urgently visa Cuba and boat tickets.'

He made immediate enquiries. Ernst Meyer wrote: '$2,800 is needed, of which about $1,000 will be returned on entry. As your parents must know I have no means and there is no chance of my raising this amount here, I assume I should forward this telegram to you and ask for Babyson's help, bearing in mind that they can't contact you directly. Once the money is here, the visas will take two or three weeks, and it should be plain sailing. Several thousand telegrams like this have reached here from Germany and the Protectorate, and you can imagine the activity here.'

I was in extreme need; $2,800 was an unimaginably large sum, a fortune so unattainable that I despaired. Nevertheless, I contacted Franz Kind in Manchester. Babyson, who had helped us time and again, didn't fail us now. It would take a while, he said, but he would try to raise what was needed as quickly as possible.

The weeks passed painfully quickly, and since the telegram there had been no more news of my parents. I got no proper sleep. A peculiar sense of alarm raged in me, and made me restless. I felt something was wrong, and I could barely suppress my attacks of panic by reason or exhortation to hang on. I tried to hide them from Marianne, who was in any case more pessimistic then I was.

Since the air raids had stopped, London was in a strange sort of limbo. The city drew shallow breaths, not yet really relieved, but with shoulders hunched. A strange flakey mood spread. The blitz and the constant bombing had taken up all our attention. Merciless as it was, it had made Londoners heroes, and led them to forget the broader war. Now they were painfully aware of it again. The British were still sure of victory, but how long would it be in coming, and for how many would it come too late?

The money arrived in November. Franz Kind transferred it to me in pounds, but there was now the problem of getting it to the right place. No contact was possible between London and Prague, and we were dependent on the refugee organizations in America, which were hopelessly overworked. I wrote to Hans Simon, my grandmother's nephew, who had in the meantime also emigrated to America, and asked for his help. Perhaps he could advance the money and we would transfer it to him afterwards.

On 7 December 1941 the Japanese attacked Pearl Harbor, and four days later Hitler declared war on the USA. In Britain this was seen as the turning point in the war. A German victory now appeared almost impossible. I dared to breathe a sigh of relief – until the reply arrived from Hans. He had got my letter only on 11 December, he wrote, the day Germany declared war on the USA. The same day the Cuban government had announced that no more refugees from Europe would be allowed into the country. He could not think what to do. 'We can only be resigned,' he wrote. It was all terribly sad, and I had his deep sympathy.

I was distraught. Why was it that all our attempts at rescue failed at the last moment? I did not realize that in any case there had been no sense in all the struggles of recent weeks. It was already too late because the decision to wipe out the Jews in Europe had already been taken, and the mass murder had already begun. It was too late because Father and Mother were no longer in Prague.

On 26 October, the day their telegram arrived in New York, Fritz and Grete Lönhardt were deported to the Lodz ghetto in Transport C, one of the first transports from Prague. Hence the flood of telegrams to New York. In panic the Jews had tried once more to get out. It was nothing more than desperate scratching at a closed door.

A few days later, on 7 November 1941, Taube and Isaak Tisch too had left their 'home' in Vienna's Grosse Schiffgasse. I learned this only two years ago because a relative of mine undertook some research on the subject, and I also have the residence registration forms of Fred's parents from that time.

The Tischs, the Central Office for Jewish Emigration had informed them and thousands of others on pre-printed postcards, were to go to the assembly camp at 2a Sperlgasse. There they spent several days. The building had been a school, now there was an electrified fence around the outer walls. One day Taube and Isaak Tisch, like all the prisoners, had to pass by several tables where the functionaries of their destruction sat. At the first table their documents were checked and their passports and identity cards taken. At the second table they had to list their assets in duplicate and sign that they were making them over to the Gestapo. Money and valuables worth more than 100 Reichsmarks had to be handed over. At the last table their keys and ration cards were taken. After this, all that people had left was a bundle of belongings.

Sixteen days later, on 23 November 1941, the eleventh transport, with at least a thousand men, women and children, left the Aspang station in Vienna. Isaak Tisch and his wife Taube were in the trucks. Originally the prisoners were to be deported to Riga, in what had been Latvia, but the transport was diverted to Kaunas in Lithuania and handed over to the third Einsatzkommando. This was a mobile murder unit, recruited from ex-Gestapo men. Supported by local collaborators, its members had set about 'cleansing Lithuania of Jews' in June 1941, killing 130,000 people. Immediately on arrival the deported Viennese Jews were driven into Fort IX, a part of the old tsarist fortifications of Kaunas. There were many 'volunteers' from Lithuania who carried out the orders of members of the Einsatzkommando. On 29 November, they shot a thousand men, women and children from Vienna. There were no survivors.

Fred never learned that his parents were among the dead that day.

10 Richard Tauber

My son Ian has asked me to get myself a washing machine with an integral drier so that I don't have to go out of the house to do the laundry. I'm not sure it makes much sense to start with something new at my age. Over the years I liked going to the launderette. It often gave me the chance to talk to a neighbour or acquaintance on the way. But I can understand Ian. He is worried about me after what happened.

When I was in the launderette recently there was a young man with his four little sisters. He trampled around in his boots on the washing machines, and his sisters copied him. The youngest was no more than three, and I could not bear to see how clumsy she was, and likely to lose her balance. 'Take your sister down,' I said to the lad. 'She could fall and hurt herself.'

The young man came up to me, but he didn't look at me as he said he could not understand my awful accent and I should mind my own business. He was obviously angry. When my washing was dry, and I went to load it into the little trolley, he took the pram his sister had been sitting in and pushed it against me as hard as he could. It all happened too fast for me to grasp what was happening. The collision opened a vein. Blood poured out, and I tried applying an emergency tourniquet with a newly washed nylon stocking. I was quite alone. The attacker and his sisters had gone.

Would it have been better to say nothing? And did I have any chance of defending myself against that arrogance that sometimes goes with physical superiority?

Why did so many say nothing, then? And could the Jews have fought back? We have all asked ourselves these questions countless times. Could our parents, even if they didn't fight back, at least have escaped? Maybe, maybe not. It makes no difference to the guilt felt by of those of us who survived. There is no acquittal.

The question of resisting was put to the few survivors of the Lodz ghetto and the concentration camp that followed. 'If you're starving, you don't revolt,' was the answer one of them gave to young German schoolchildren who asked. Human imagination, I think, was bound to fail faced with the Holocaust, which was literally unimaginable and concealed by deceptions and false hopes, including no doubt the hope that one might survive by conforming. When the truth began to dawn, it was too late to do anything. 'Terror', a Jewish survivor once said, 'was the best camp guard.'

Yet there was resistance. Minor acts, such as ignoring Nazi restrictions, fleeing or hiding; desperate acts, such as suicide; or determined acts, such as resisting openly. In August 1940 there was even a hunger demonstration by the occupants of the Lodz ghetto. It was brutally put down. After that there were repeated hunger protests, until the Elder Mordechai Chaim Rumkowski declared a state of emergency in March 1941.

I learned later from a survivor that my mother had been told that she could wear her best clothes in the ghetto, and so had packed all her smartest things. Perhaps she and my father, being among the first to be taken from Prague, really thought they would have a different and a better life in Lodz. The Jews had been told this at first.

Many years ago I bought a massive documentary volume about the Lodz ghetto. I still find it difficult to read it for more than half an hour at a time, so I read it in small steps, taking what was unbearable in tiny doses. I also tried to imagine Father and Mother there and to grasp it all. I couldn't.

In those October days of 1941, 20,000 deportees arrived in the ghetto from Vienna, Prague, Frankfurt and Luxembourg. Marianne Bauer, the nurse who had smuggled food to my parents, went with them to the assembly camp in Prague. My parents had said nothing, she told me later. They held hands all the time. Marianne helped them to carry the heavy suitcase in which they had packed what they had been advised to take. A spirit stove and warm underwear, gloves and ear muffs, dubbin and candles. The cases had to be labelled with names and destination, and they had to bring completed forms. The closer they got to the assembly camp, a collection of shabby huts near the Holešovice station, the denser was the mass of people going there. The deportees wore the yellow star on their breasts and carried their transport number round their necks. Most were older people. Almost all were well dressed.

Marianne Bauer embraced my parents in farewell. They should write soon, she said, and she would send them parcels and if possible money. Grete should try to work as a dress-maker to earn something. And as soon as the war was over, they would both be able to join their daughters.

When the war ended, 253 of the 5,000 or more Jews deported from Prague in October 1941 were still alive.

My parents went through a bureaucratic process lasting several days, similar to that to which Fred's parents were subjected before being taken from Vienna. Under cover of darkness SS guards and Gestapo men escorted the Jews to Holešovice station. Only once did they make the mistake of taking the Jews there in daylight. The procession of old people, young people and small children had caused a commotion. The people of Prague who encountered the long line of deportees were visibly moved at what they saw. Men demonstratively took off their hats and many women cried.

Aunt Hilde, my mother's sister, was in the first transport, A, from Prague to Lodz with her husband Robert, Hans's father, on 16 October 1941. Those deported from Prague in transports A, B, C and D had an average of 50kg of luggage and were allowed 100 marks each. They did not find accom-modation straight away in Lodz, and had to wait in schools and disused warehouses, and many wandered through the ghetto for weeks looking for a room. On 5 November they were followed by over 5,000 Sinti and Roma, who were shut up in the so-called gypsy camp. On 1 December 1941, almost 163,000 people were living in the ghetto. Typhus broke out.

That same month, in Chelmno, just 70 km west of Lodz, organized mass murder was begun using carbon monoxide. By 12 January 1942 all the Sinti and Roma still alive in Lodz were deported to this, the first Nazi extermination camp, and killed in closed vans with the exhaust gases from the engines.

By the end of May, 55,000 had died like this. A month later a bare half of those deported to Lodz were still alive. The others, the 'unproductive' Jews, were murdered in Chelmno. For a long while no one was sure what had happened to the victims. The Nazis had disguised the deportations as 'resettlement', and no one knew what had happened to those selected. But when the clothes of the people sent to Chelmno began coming back in dribs and drabs to the ghetto any doubts about their deaths were at an end.

Only those who worked could hope to survive. The occupants of the ghetto worked for their lives twelve hours a day, six days a week. The city had previously been a centre of the textile industry, and Rumkowski offered to resume production for the German authorities, and manufacture textile and leather goods to ensure food for the inhabitants. He hoped that the Germans' economic interests in cheap slave labour would moderate their intention to exterminate them. This reckoning did not absolve Rumkowski of the requirement placed on him by the Nazis to send the children, the old and those unable to work to their deaths to preserve a slight chance of saving at least a few of the others.

Lodz had the longest-existing ghetto. One of its main customers from now on was the Wehrmacht. In a very short time, production in Lodz was raised, but the food rations allocated by the Germans remained so meagre that many people died of hunger.

The amount of food one was allocated depended on work. Anyone who did not work was condemned to starve to death sooner or later. Many began to sell their clothes or anything they had been able to save for a loaf of bread, some fat, a piece of soap, anti-louse ointment or toilet paper. It was not allowed to pay in Reichsmarks. The Jews had to surrender any they had for ghetto money, which was no more than a receipt. Outside it was worthless. In any case, there was no 'outside' any more.

Mother and Father lived at first at 27 Franzstrasse, a long street cutting right across the ghetto from north to south. A card from Mother shows that she later moved to 40 Sulzfelderstrasse. Brzezínska, as it is called in Polish, was in the southern part of the ghetto, and ran at an angle to the ghetto boundary. At the eastern end it was cut off by the boundary fence, and the rest of the street was not accessible to Jews. In the west, it ran into Hohensteinstrasse which, as a major thoroughfare across the city, could not be blocked off, and could be crossed by Jews only at certain times. Later, wooden footbridges were built at crossing points, and one of them appeared on the ghetto stamps. I have often tried to think what it must have been like for Mother to go to the other part of the camp. Probably one had to keep moving, but would have had time for a brief look into the other world below, on to the main road and what purported to be the civilized world. Down there were trams, and in them sat other human beings.

In February 1942 I got news that my parents were in the ghetto and were well. Direct contact with them was not possible, but they could send postcards to relatives in the Protectorate. The ghetto had its own postal system. On German orders, the Jewish censorship forbade the use of Polish and Hebrew, and demanded clearly legible writing.

The time for long letters was past. People sent brief messages, which were forwarded by the International Red Cross. The content was strictly controlled. One was allowed only twenty-five words, it was forbidden to say that somebody was in the army or where he was, and one could not mention details of radio or any other news reports or results of enemy action. Even the names of towns could not be given. Violating these rules meant that the messages, on flimsy paper, would not be forwarded.

Twenty-five words are not many, a sign of life but no more. It was often a month or two before messages arrived, and even then they might be misleading. In May I had a Red Cross message from Grandma Hedwig in Aussig. She was now in a 'home for the elderly' in Schönwald in the Erzgebirge, with her daughter Trude and her son Herbert. I had learned of this, and that Herbert was 'in charge' of the home, shortly before. It struck me as odd. Trude was only forty-eight. What was she doing in a home for the elderly? And why was Herbert in charge of it? He had always been a builder before.

The brief message from the home in Schönwald was written in capitals. 'Health still good. Your parents well. Last post 20 April,' it said. It was signed: Grandma, Trude, Herbert Israel Schnitzer. It was not their writing; they had at best dictated it. But I took comfort from the words. I was inclined to believe them; perhaps I wanted too much to be comforted. Anyway, at least I had news. Fred had none from Vienna. He was very despondent, and some days his spirits were so low I could hardly reach him.

Fred sought refuge in his religion, going regularly to synagogue. On Friday evenings he celebrated the start of Sabbath with his brother, with whom he still shared a flat. I often sat with them, quietly and reverently. Fred spoke the prologue to the Sabbath meal in Hebrew, with multi-syllabic words that were still strange to me. He wore a *kippa* and *tallit*. He spoke the *kiddush*, the blessing, over a beaker of wine. If there was no wine, he spoke *kiddush* over two loaves of bread. I listened to the hurried words with their ritual rhythm. At such moments Fred was Salo again, Mundy was Moishe, and the world seemed intact.

But of course it wasn't. The Royal Air Force had begun raiding German cities, bombing Lübeck in March and Rostock in April 1942. At the end of May, over a thousand bombers, more than ever before, attacked Cologne. There were many dead, but I felt little sympathy. The only good German is a dead German, the British said. I could understand their hatred.

Refugees from the Continent were asked to send in photos of their home towns showing factories and industrial buildings, especially ones that might be munitions works. I sent a few views of Aussig, knowing they could be used to plan bombing targets. It was not a treasonable act against my own country. That country had ceased to exist. Bandy and Paul were now flying missions over German cities, bombing the country that spoke their mother tongue. They did it from deep conviction.

The strange paradoxes and coincidences that war produced seemed to attract Tony by magic. In the midst of a city of eight million people, and after a year and a half without news of him, I ran into him. Even this disordered world is sometimes reassuringly small, and in Swiss Cottage, where I met Tony, perhaps especially so, as thousands of Jewish refugees lived there. I was waiting for a bus when suddenly someone tapped me from behind on the shoulder. 'Is it you, Ilse?' asked Tony. He looked more mature, perhaps because of the uniform he was wearing. His eyes had hairline wrinkles that fanned out when he smiled.

He was able to smile again. 'You haven't changed,' he said. 'But you have,' I told him, looking at his shoulder flashes. 'I see you're fighting for Britain now.'

'No, I'm not.' Tony suddenly became serious. 'I'm fighting against the Nazis. I would have joined any army to do that.'

He had returned from internment in Australia a few months before. Once even British officialdom had cottoned on to the idea that Jewish refugees from the Nazis were not an immediate threat, they were allowed to join the Pioneer Corps. Anyone who volunteered would be sent straight back to England.

He had volunteered with gritted teeth, Tony said, not having forgiven the British for first arresting the Jewish refugees and then releasing them only if they joined the army. 'And they won't even give us British citizenship for doing it,' he burst out angrily. Tony had now transferred from the Pioneer Corps to a special unit that he couldn't talk about. Much later I learned of the secret commando '3 Troop', consisting almost entirely of Jewish refugees. Only a few knew of the existence of this ninety-strong elite unit. The '3 troopers', as they called themselves, went through tough training in secret in north Wales. They had to jog for miles with heavy packs and weapons. They learned parachute jumping, creeping up on an enemy, signalling, how to use a great variety of weapons and how to interrogate enemy prisoners. Like his comrades, Tony had shed his old identity for a new one. He had had to burn all personal documents, letters and photos, and had been given false papers with an invented biography that explained his heavy German accent. Tony's cover story was very simple. His father was in the British army of occupation in the Rhineland after the First World War, and Tony had been born there.

'How is Marianne?' he asked. 'Is she still so pretty? I hope they haven't made a nun out of her in Dublin.'

Not at all. Marianne was now even drawing male nudes at art school. But she didn't seem unduly impressed, and hadn't said much about it. When I talked to her teacher, he showed me a portfolio of her work. He was happy with Marianne's performance. In the portfolio was a pencil drawing of a muscular young man who posed for the students as a nude model. It was very good, but in one particular place Marianne had used a rubber eraser so much that the paper was smeared and worn thin. When I got home I asked her why. 'Oh, that wretch, he did it on purpose,' she said. 'Every time I looked the thing was a different size, and I had to rub it all out again.'

Marianne did not yet seem terribly interested in men, much to Fred's relief. He was always worried she would throw herself away on some ne'er-do-well. When I told her about meeting Tony, though, she was all ears. She would have loved to see him again, but just now that wasn't really possible. Tony was in London only rarely.

That was another strange thing about the war. It tore friends apart, and it welded them together again as quickly. Fred's friend Paul Knepler now worked for the BBC. For some time there had been a special satirical radio programme for Austrian émigrés. Paul's son Georg was taken on as the pianist, and appeared with the actor Fritz Schrecker. At the end of the programme there was always a Viennese song, for which Paul Knepler wrote new words. He was more at home with the old language than with the new, and he often discussed his ideas with Fred. Fred sometimes wrote the words for him. The Kneplers often came to see us. Paul brought scores and his wife brought her knitting. She knitted constantly and earned a little money. I cooked for all of us. The men mostly sat together until late at night. Knepler puffed at one cigarette after another, producing a pall of grey streaks. It seemed not to bother Fred, who didn't smoke. When he was immersed in his craft, everything else was incidental.

Many artistes and musicians from the Continent got minor engagements with the BBC. Since 1940 short addresses by Thomas Mann, who now lived in California, had been relayed here, and read to 'German listeners' by German announcers. Later, Mann's voice itself was broadcast. The BBC had created the German Service at the start of the war. Graham Greene's half-brother Hugh ran it. It represented freedom and truth not only for refugees in Britain, but for millions of secret listeners in Germany. The station always identified itself by three short drumbeats followed by one long, in the rhythm of the opening of Beethoven's Fifth, and also morse code for V, as in 'Victory'. Listening to the BBC helped keep faith in the victory of justice. The British countered Goebbels's rabble-rousing propaganda broadcasts with realism and facts, even when it was to their disadvantage.

We listened to the BBC every day. Sometimes several of us gathered by the radio. The political sketches of the German Service were satirical broadsides against the Nazis, in which émigrés made fun of events and the tottering Third Reich.

The tenor Richard Tauber sang on this anti-Nazi radio. He had had British citizenship since 1940, and for a long time was the only refugee who appeared as a singer on the Home Service of the BBC. As propaganda broadcasts to Germany and Austria were extended, he was more and more often to be heard singing in German.

His voice, Fred found, was not as powerful as it had been. The damp climate seemed bad for it. Tauber was now touring provincial theatres and still conducted the London Philharmonic occasionally. Most concerts were for charity, proceeds going to the Red Cross or the British Legion. In *Land of Smiles* he was partnered by a young woman called Esther Moncrieff. She was only twenty-five, and had been his new muse for some time. His wife, Diana Napier-Tauber, who was working as a nurse in a hospital in the Scottish Highlands, seemed to tolerate it. She had enough amorous diversion herself.

Tauber lived in the Grosvenor House Hotel in London. One evening Fred got a phone call from there. I happened to be with him when the phone went. It was Tauber. He had got Fred's number from Fred's agent, Erich Glass. 'Tauber here,' droned the voice. 'Glad you're well, Tisch. I hear you're working on lyrics again.' Fred said he was, and Tauber explained his dilemma. He had written an operetta he hoped would re-create the old days of Tauber magic. The plot was worked out, the score was written, but the words! He was not happy with the English lyrics, he confessed, and asked Fred whether he could write new words for him in three weeks.

Of course Fred accepted. He put the phone down, his face red with excitement. Just imagine! Richard Tauber had rung, and the next morning they would meet for breakfast and get down to work. If only we had had something in the house with which to celebrate! There was nothing, so we raised glasses of water to Fred's great chance. I was proud of him, and even happier at what I saw in Fred's eyes. There were glistening again.

Fortunately Fred got time off at short notice. When he entered Tauber's hotel suite, where he had his own piano, the next morning, the tenor was already at breakfast. The war had not made Tauber any slimmer, and he liked to start the day with a heavy meal. On his plate was a piece of Spam glistening with fat. 'Do try this!' said Tauber, chewing away, having had another place laid for his guest. 'It's delicious, quite delicious!' Fred said he could hardly bear to look, not only because he always ate kosher himself. The scene was not very appetizing.

After that Fred preferred to have breakfast at home and go to the Grosvenor House Hotel later. He got home very late. Tauber, he said, did not work steadily. Sometimes he played other music on the piano as if on another planet. Then everything had to be done in a rush, and he got impatient if the words didn't fit the tune.

The original idea for *Old Chelsea* came from the librettist Walter Ellis, who had arrived in Tauber's dressing room with it one evening. It was said Tauber had written the music over the last few years in his spare time between engagements. Bernhard Grün, a refugee now called Grun, who had been at school with Alban Berg in Vienna, had contributed some of the music, writing the lighter bits, while Tauber indulged his penchant for sentiment and drama. Fred was to write the words for all Tauber's songs.

Tauber could now reach the high notes only with difficulty. It was easier for him with words ending with an 'ee', he explained. Fred should think of as many 'ee' endings as he could. Me, knee, tree, she, tea, sea, he, flee, key. From now on Fred collected these words for the *Heldentenor* and entered them as usual in his little notebook.

Old Chelsea is set in the eighteenth century. A struggling composer falls in love with a pretty young milliner – a *mésalliance* drawn from Tauber's own life. Tauber intended to give his lover, Esther Moncrieff, a small role as an aristocratic lady. He himself played the composer, and the milliner was the twenty-two-year old Carole Lynn.

It was very hard to speak to Fred in those few weeks, while he was writing the words for eight of Tauber's songs, all of them of course about love with a happy ending. Tauber seemed very happy with Fred's lyrics.

From now on Fred joined the tenor's close circle of friends. Tauber invited us to his own concerts, and sent tickets for others with VIP reservations. He could use only a few of these himself, especially now the rehearsals for *Old Chelsea* were starting.

Once, Fred had to see Tauber again in his dressing room after a performance. I was to come too, and for the first time I saw Tauber offstage. He had taken off his shirt, and underneath he wore a corset sodden with sweat from conducting, and from which piles of flesh were bursting. Any glamour he still possessed came off with the tailcoat.

Fred had told him that I cooked good Czech food, and Tauber insisted on being invited. He missed the cooking from home perhaps hardly less than he missed its now stifled cultural life. We entertained him several times. He came alone. On the rare occasions meat was to be had, I made beef goulash with dumplings, otherwise there were the puddings that Tauber loved best of all, such as *Kaiserschmarren* made from a single egg with apple purée, *Quarkpalatschinken* without *quark* or *Böhmische Dalken*, flat dough cakes with jam on very thin dough. Tauber sweated when he ate as much as when he conducted, and he showed the same fervour. He was especially taken with my dumplings. I don't know how many of them he could eat at one go, but I know that he eventually bestowed a title on me for my services. He always called me 'Schnappula', his name for things and people he liked.

We lived divided lives, between glittering evenings and nights heavy with fear, tossed between hope and resignation, between a sense of normality and utter turmoil.

In June 1942 I had a letter from an acquaintance in Aussig.

Ada, as she was called, said she had had 'indirect' news of my parents. Both were said to be well and in good spirits. Father had apparently found work, and was earning money – that was of course the best medicine; it took one's mind off things and gave one a sense of satisfaction. Grandmother was still in the home for the elderly run by Herbert.

At that time, Father had been dead for four months. He had died on 7 February 1942. In the Lodz ghetto people were dying so fast that burials could not keep pace. The dead were carried constantly from the mortuary. Every day there were a dozen burials going on at the same time in the cemetery, a muddy field at the edge of the ghetto. The graves there were narrower than wooden planks, two cubits wide. The ritual washing of bodies was forbidden. There were no coffins. The dead – men, women and children who had died of under-nourishment and disease – were wrapped in scraps of paper and laid between two boards. Many of the adults had taken their own lives.

People had no opportunity to mourn the dead. They couldn't even inform the next of kin. My cousin Hans sent a Red Cross postcard in July from Denmark saying that his parents, Robert and Hilde Frank, and my father, had been 'resettled' but he didn't know where. 'Resettled' is an unusual synonym for 'dead'. Hans's parents were no longer alive either. His mother had had an accident with a spirit stove and died of burns. Her husband Robert had starved to death.

Shortly before, a postcard from my mother had reached Prague. It was one of the pre-printed cards from the ghetto giving name and address but without any personal message. The cynical formulation merely read: 'Grete Lönhardt residing here at 40/60 Sulzfelderstrasse is well.' It did not occur to any of us that Grete Lönhardt was now a widow because her husband's name was missing from the card.

She must have been anything but well. But she knew that she must do everything she could to give the impression of being healthy and fit for work. As I now know, at the end of August 1942 there was a round-up in the ghetto. All the inhabitants were driven together and paraded in front of a selection group. Mothers had tried to escape with their children and had hidden in cellars but were tracked down with Alsatian dogs and many were shot on the spot. That day 17,000 people unable to work were picked out and sent to the extermination camp. Among them were more than a thousand men, women and children who had come to Lodz from Prague.

Mother was not one of them. I heard that she was always well groomed, and perhaps that is why she survived so long. She always coloured her cheeks by moistening the ersatz coffee bags, and had tidy hair and clean clothes. She never had a torn seam or a hole in her dress. As it was almost impossible to wash clothes, she wore dirty items inside out until they too looked dirty. She had also taken her clothes in. Everyone in Lodz soon needed this done, so bad had things become.

It must certainly have helped that Mother was a good seamstress. I don't know what work she did, but skills like this were in demand in Lodz. Just in the street where she lived there were five workshops making straw shoes, two cobblers and a place that made caps. Mother was now living with Else Glaser, whose husband Erwin had died in July 1942. Else was a nurse. Her husband, who had had a doctoral degree in law and came from Brüx, was for a long time legal adviser to my father's factory. The Glasers had shared a room with my parents in the ghetto, along with other families. They lived in a tiny space in Room 60 at 40 Sulzfelderstrasse. Some rooms in the ghetto had thirty people in them.

After their husbands died, Else and Grete slept in a single bunk bed. The other had to be freed for new occupants. They comforted one another and promised that if one of them survived, she would visit her friend's next of kin and tell them all that had happened. They were both determined to survive.

Meanwhile forces from around the world were assembling in London to fight Hitler. Every day saw the stream of foreign soldiers swell. In Piccadilly one saw French and Polish uniforms, and members of the Canadian, Czechoslovak and Brazilian forces. Most noticeable were the Americans. For GIs London was not just a co-ordinating point. Many American troops based in the provinces visited London on leave. Because of their white helmets, the American military police were called 'snowdrops'. Some street crossings were sprinkled with white snowflakes.

With the Americans in the grey, battered city, there was a different mood in the air, a self-indulgent amusement-seeking mood that lies easier with an invited guest, perhaps, than with the burdened host. Many Britons viewed these ambassadors from overseas with some reservation. Until now, it had been they alone who, like David, had defied enemy might, and now the Americans had come and stolen the show. American soldiers had better weapons, better pay and a different air. The British observed drily that they were 'overpaid, over-sexed and over here'. People sneered at English girls who went out with GIs and restaurant owners who kept their best tables for the well-paying customers. What was never in doubt was the readiness of the Americans to help and the importance of their contribution.

There were still sporadic raids by the Luftwaffe – mostly in retaliation for devastating British raids on Berlin and other German cities. These raids bore no comparison with those of the year before and, although steps were being taken to guard against worse attacks, the cellars of bombed-out buildings being converted into water reservoirs and steel water pipes laid all over the place to deal better with possible major fires, the city for the present was no longer seized with fear.

The première of *Old Chelsea* in Manchester drew nearer and took up much of our attention. Fred was nervous and made me nervous too. Tauber was also feverish. It would be the first time he had sung in a musical he had composed himself. For the first night Fred had had a black dress made for me with satin sleeves and an elegant shawl collar. It cost a fortune. Every one of the shining buttons was worth the price of an evening meal. When it came to money, Fred had the soul of an artist. If he had it, he would spend it as naturally as he saved it when times were lean. At present he was doing well. He had written the words for 'Tell Me, Teacher', a lively foxtrot which was often heard on the wireless, and that brought him some nice extra income.

I liked going shopping with Fred because he had sure taste and an exact idea of what he liked me to wear and what not. 'I want other men to turn round and look at you,' he used to say. I am sure this was not a sort of pride of trophy with him, but a feeling of triumphing over those who had tried to take everything from him. 'It's no great achievement falling in love when you've come out of a concentration camp,' I once quipped thoughtlessly. Fred was very hurt, and I immediately regretted it.

Tauber had reserved a small suite in a four-star hotel only in Manchester for the première. I had never stayed in a de luxe hotel, let alone in the middle of a war. A little ex-cook accounts clerk staying there seemed like the Cinderella story being played on the stage that night. The pile of bouquets and good-luck telegrams that were sent to Fred at the hotel only served to increase his nervousness.

We sat in the front row, and saw Tauber throw himself with verve into his role and sing more brilliantly than for a long time. The songs 'My Heart and I', 'There are Angels Outside Heaven' and 'If You are in Love', which he sang with passion, earned particularly long applause. There were fifteen curtain calls, and Fred was called up on to the stage. Our eyes met, and for a moment there were just the two of us, lifted up on waves of applause as though swimming on them. I was unbelievably proud of him.

A newspaper critic wrote that the music was so memorable that some of the songs would still be being hummed in a year's time. 'My Heart and I' was in any case unforgettable because it was played for months on the wireless. It became the greatest hit Fred ever wrote in England.

Without him knowing, I got a clipping service to collect all the reviews when the show went on tour to Birmingham, Bradford, Liverpool, Edinburgh, Coventry, Nottingham and other cities. In spring 1943 it was to be given at London's Princes Theatre. The reviews were very positive, and Marianne stuck them into a hand-bound album with black hard covers, adding photos and sketches she had done herself, and gave it to Fred some months later as a Christmas present. His best gift, though, was the one he had given himself by succeeding on his own in re-creating his glory days.

The war seemed to have become more distant, and to be taking place mostly in the headlines that reported battles in the Caucasus, at Tobruk, El Alamein and Stalingrad. And then suddenly it burst devastatingly into our lives. I shall never forget my boss's look when he came up to me one day in October. He had just heard that Paul Friedländer had been shot down by enemy aircraft over the Channel. Our own Paul, who was always laughing, our cheeky, irrepressible Paul, was dead. He was only twenty-eight.

'You must give Eva the news,' my boss said. 'You're her best friend.'

Eva worked in the same department as me at Selfridges. She was sitting at her desk, engrossed in paperwork. It was terribly difficult to go to her. Until then, I had never had to break news of a death. I don't think there is any right way. The horror can't be given in doses, and there is no way to avoid the finality of those three words.

'Eva,' I said softly, taking her in my arms. Eva had seen my tears, and I felt her body stiffen with tension. 'Paul is dead,' I said, and held her tight. 'He was shot down over the Channel. He died a hero's death – for all of us.'

Eva's legs gave way under her. She had fainted. I knelt weeping beside her, held her head and tweaked her cheeks helplessly. I think I was crying not only for Paul but with foreboding for all those others I had by that time, in October 1942, already lost.

Just a few weeks earlier, the BBC's German Service had relayed a broadcast to Germany by Thomas Mann, in which he accused the Germans of systematic mass extermination of the Jews. Now they could no longer claim to know nothing about it. Since the Wannsee conference, in January 1942, which had decided on the 'final solution' of the Jewish question, there was no more doubting Hitler's intention.

And yet the crime was done under cover, kept from the public and cleverly hidden. The so-called Schönwald Old People's Home in the Erzgebirge, where my grandmother, Herbert and Trude had been sent, was actually, I now know, an internment camp for Jews. The Nazis also called the camp in Theresienstadt the Reich Home for the Elderly. Before their deportation there, those about to be sent were told about the Bohemian clean-air resort called Theresienbad, where there were gardens and walks, pensions and villas. My grandmother, who was taken there from Aussig in the first transport on 23 November 1942, won't have believed it because she knew the old fortress town from younger days. But could she possibly have imagined that almost 60,000 people would be penned up there in an area of less than a quarter of a square kilometre, and that each of them would have to make do with about two square metres of living space, and that all of them, whether doctors, professors, rabbis, lawyers, industrial directors, bakers, housewives, secretaries or artists would have to do menial work? That every imaginable disease – scarlet fever, diphtheria, jaundice and TB – would rage there because of inadequate nourishment and overcrowding? Grandma's brother, Armin Simon, an accountant from Vienna, had been sent to Theresienstadt shortly before, and perished within ten days. Many of the other older arrivals also survived in the inhuman world of the camp only briefly. The painter Malva Schalek was already in Theresienstadt. Aunt Trude and Uncle Herbert, my mother's sister and brother, also went there, before being sent on to their deaths. Uncle Otto and Aunt Olga, my father's brother and sister, were taken to Theresienstadt at the very end. Their 'mixed marriages' did not save them.

Many years later, I learned that my old schoolfriend Traute Fehres was in the records section, where the deportation lists of Jews from Aussig were compiled. With their administrative zeal, it was an easy matter for the Nazis to retrieve the names of all the Jews from the the card index of the town's inhabitants, as their cards were stamped with a 'J' and had two red index tabs. The card index is now in the Usti municipal archives. I was told that Traute had removed the index cards of the Jewish families she knew and burned them. I have never had this confirmed, as I could find no trace of her after the war, but it sounded like the Traute I knew.

Fred was depressed by the dull sense that his parents were no longer alive, as he had had no further news of them for a year. Perhaps it was not knowing what had happened that made him strangely unprepared to talk of our future. We had been together for nearly three years, but he had never talked of an engagement, let alone marriage. 'Is it because of all the dreadful divorce cases you had to deal with in Vienna?' I asked him eventually, swallowing my pride. 'Do you still think that all marriages have to end like that?'

Fred did not answer straight away. He sat without speaking, as if chewing over my words. Then he said, 'Look, darling, I've found with you what I thought I'd lost for ever. I wouldn't want to live any more without you. I mean that seriously. If you died tomorrow, I would end my life as well.'

His strange, if forceful, way of paying me compliments, sometimes brought tears to my eyes. 'Of course I want to marry you, and spend the rest of my life with you,' he said. 'But it's not the time. We don't know what has happened to our parents. And it wouldn't be good for you, a "friendly alien", to become an "enemy alien" by marriage. You'd lose a lot of privileges. Let's talk about it when the war is over.'

He was probably right. It wasn't the time. Also because of Marianne, who was not yet old enough to stand on her own feet. I preferred to have her live with me a while longer, and she herself didn't want to leave me. Because our landlords had raised the rent to more than we could afford, we now had to look for a new flat. The housing shortage meant that market forces were driving prices horrendously high. Many bombed-out families were looking for somewhere new to live, and refugees and soldiers all needed a roof over their heads.

Everything Marianne and I looked at was far beyond my means. It got us down. Finally, though, we unexpectedly found a flat we could afford in Howitt Road near Hampstead Heath. It belonged to a deaf couple who lived on the ground floor. We had to sign an agreement that we would wake them if the air raid warning went, and take them to the Anderson shelter in their garden. And so we got the first-floor flat, in which the two of us lived.

Marianne was now eighteen, and had grown into an attractive young woman. This had not escaped Tony, who met her several times in London when he was on leave, and was obviously very interested in her. He had even told her the truth about his activities with the commandos. This amounted to a declaration of love because the secret could be revealed only to those closest. Tony often spent nights in enemy territory. His boat anchored off the coast of the Continent, and he and his comrades would paddle in rubber dinghies over the dark water, and creep ashore to photograph enemy positions or steal up on German patrols, silently overpower them, and take them back on board. There they were met by men in British uniforms who interrogated them in faultless German. Tony said that most of the German prisoners talked freely, apparently relieved at not having to be part of Germany's *folie de grandeur* any longer.

If Marianne feared for Tony, she did not show it. She was in any case much more buttoned-up than me, and rarely showed her feelings. I often guessed what was going on inside her. I thought she liked Tony very much. The two of them shared a past that had been cut short. Tony's mother, now also in a camp, and our Aunt Olga had been best friends. Our fathers had studied chemistry together at university. Marianne and Tony had been delivered by the same midwife, and had known one another since they were small. Similar backgrounds and experience often gave rise to deep, often unspoken understanding.

Nevertheless, Marianne did not want to be tied down, and time and again sent Tony off with a flea in his ear. I wasn't sorry; she was young enough to take her time. But it got Tony down, and at some point he gave up. Compared with Operation Marianne, his nocturnal activities against the enemy were child's play. Contact was broken off.

Marianne finished at art school and started working for a Czech firm making and selling hand-painted wooden craft articles. She did not earn much, though that was not terribly important, since in February 1943 I had found a well-paid job in accounts with the Post Exchange, known as the 'PX', the shop for American troops in Oxford Street. I was responsible for the financial transactions and the special sale of valuable articles like watches and fountain pens. In the office I shared with the commanding officer there was a safe with a code only I knew.

Materially, things were improving. On Fridays, staff were allowed to buy damaged tins of food from the attached commissary store at half price. On top of that, Willy Eichberger sent us Care parcels from California. Willy was the son of Armin Simon, my grandmother's brother who had died in Theresienstadt. He had been an actor at the Burgtheater in Vienna, and – another strange coincidence – had appeared in the film *Burgtheater*, for which Lengsfelder and Tisch had written 'Sag beim Abschied leise Servus'. In Hollywood, which he had reached in time, he now worked as an actor under the name of Carl Esmond. He seemed to be doing well, and sent us luxuries like canned pineapple, peaches and excellent pâtés, smoked salmon, asparagus, coffee, chocolate, biscuits and the inevitable chewing gum.

Everyone with relatives or friends abroad asked them to send food parcels, as rations were still very meagre. Londoners dug up almost every unused patch of ground to grow fruit and vegetables. Peas, beans and lettuce flourished in the inner court of the British Museum, and in many places people had hens in their gardens. Hyde Park police station had eight pigs.

Marianne and I managed well enough without a garden. I earned ten pounds a week tax-free with the Americans. But that was not my reason for applying for a job with the army and before – in vain, as it happened – with the Red Cross. I wanted to do something to fight the Nazis. Even if my contribution in accounts with the Americans was very small, it was my way of contributing to the 'war effort'.

It was now spring 1943. The Germans had surrendered at Stalingrad, and the allied area bombing offensive spread to the whole of Germany. By day American bombers droned over German towns, by night the British. At sea, too, the Germans sustained big losses. From the military point of view at least, a corner had been turned.

Hans wrote from Denmark that he had still had no news of his parents. He heard from Theresienstadt that Grandma had left and Uncle Herbert was fine. As so often, the authorities hid their atrocities behind lies like this, and we believed them because we grasped at anything that left a sliver of hope. But Grandma had not left; she died in Theresienstadt the day before my birthday.

I have often wondered whether she met her niece Malva Schalek in the camp. Malva had secretly made dozens of charcoal and watercolour drawings of the inmates and their everyday life in the camp. Many of those she had painted portraits of in their old, peaceful surroundings, she now painted again in the inhuman world of the ghetto, and for some it was to be the last picture of them. Some of the pictures arc to be found today on the Internet. When I saw some later for the first time, my eyes sought out familiar faces, but I did not recognize anyone.

I have never been able to drop this automatic habit of looking for people I know in photos from the camps. Many years after the war, I saw in the Spiro Institute, the Jewish cultural centre in London, a documentary about Lodz. In a sequence only a few seconds long, I thought I had seen my mother. Much excited, I told one of the assistants of the institute. They treated me with great understanding, and offered to show me the film again privately. A little later, after days spent in a highly nervous state, I sat on my own in a small, darkened room, hands screwed up together from inner tension. I feared meeting my mother in the reality of the ghetto, which I had never been able to grasp completely, and at the same time I wanted nothing more than to see her for a last time as a living person. When the sequence came up, I asked them to stop the film. They went through the scene several times in slow motion, where a good-looking, dark-haired middle-aged woman was to be seen. It was definitely not my mother. I was immensely relieved, and equally disappointed.

In April 1943, according to Elder Mordechai Chaim Rumkowski's report to the German authorities, 85,884 people were in the Lodz ghetto, of whom 80,784 were working. Those unfit for work Rumkowski had allowed to be 'settled elsewhere'. The old, the sick and children were sent in their thousands to be gassed in Chelmno. Ninety-five per cent of the work contracts were from the Wehrmacht for uniforms and other items, but private firms like Karstadt and Neckermann also profited from the forced labour. My mother, Hans wrote, was in good health. The fact that my father's name had not been mentioned for over a year I had long seen as an ill omen.

Fred still had frequent nightmares, and woke up wailing. And the sound of rain drumming down still triggered a traumatic state. I knew better now how to handle it. I always had a mild sedative to hand – an almost laughably hopeless attempt, of course, to fight a symptom whose cause lay deep in his soul and could never be removed.

At least he was flourishing financially. The royalties from *Old Chelsea*, in which Richard Tauber performed almost seven hundred times, were streaming in, and further commissions were not slow in coming. Berhard Grun asked Fred for lyrics for 'In Queen Victoria's Days', and the composers Alec Blewis and Fred Pisker provided music. Fred wrote English words for Tauber for a piece by Tchaikovsky, a ballad called 'No More I'll be Singing'. Tauber made a successful record of it. Fred hardly used his rhyme notebook now, as his command of English was growing rapidly.

Sometimes it was tempting to forget the war and give way to the illusion of normality, but sooner or later reality caught up. It was in the late summer of 1943, the end of a warm, bright summer, that the news reached me that my father had been dead for almost a year and a half. He was the first from my family of whose death in the camps I learned. I wrongly supposed or hoped that all the others were still alive.

I was in shock for days. Endless scenes from our past together pushed their way into my thoughts. I saw father's face as he told me that I was adopted, as we sat together by the wireless and heard Hitler's election victory, and as he ran panting after me as my train left Bodenbach station and we parted for the last time. I thought of his heart-felt, encouraging letters and his recurring fear of having to leave us on our own. All these pictures in my mind were overshadowed by one thing: the knowledge that it had profited him nothing to have seen this evil coming.

11 Holocaust

Yesterday a small parcel came from Germany. A dentist friend in Wiesbaden sent me a dozen miniature bottles of *eau de cologne* and lots of little tubes of toothpaste, which she thought someone like me, who likes travelling, would find useful. I get post almost every day from Germany, where many relations and friends of mine live. I like Germany now.

It wasn't always so. It was many years before I developed a relationship with the country – which was never my home but the country whose language I spoke – that was not marred by hatred and mistrust. I would probably never have taken the path of reconciliation if I had not been forced to by the expulsion of my relatives to Germany from Czechoslovakia. Aunt Olga, my father's sister, who was taken to Theresienstadt by the Nazis and survived there until the ghetto was liberated, was expelled by the Czechs in 1946. Her son-in-law Hugo, who had refused to divorce his 'half-Jewish' wife, Dorothea, and had been held by the Nazis for several months in an 'educational work camp' near Kassel, was repeatedly imprisoned by the Czechs after the Red Army came. He and his wife landed in a punishment camp for Nazis in Lerchenfeld, just outside Aussig. Because he refused to wear prison uniform with a sewn-on swastika, he was kicked and beaten until his wife no longer recognized him.

The Czechs' fury at the Nazis, who had desecrated and abused their country, cheered on by a majority of the Sudeten Germans, was understandable. But sometimes they were so blind in their urge for revenge that they created new injustice. This could reach absurd heights, as with my cousin Hilde, Aunt Olga's daughter, who was unable to marry on three occasions because of official prohibitions. The first time, when she had fallen in love with a German in 1934, they could not marry because he was a Reichsdeutscher and she a Czech with Jewish relatives. It was the same story when she tried a second time, after the Sudetenland had been taken *Heim ins Reich*. After the war, she fell in love with a Czech Jew, and was not allowed to marry him because now, in the eyes of the Czechs, *she* was a German.

After the war Aunt Olga applied for Czechoslovak citizenship but was refused. She was at least allowed, as a former victim of the Nazis, to take some of her furniture with her to Germany. Most Sudeten Germans were allowed only 50kg of luggage. Hugo, who had once owned a factory, left Aussig with his wife and daughters shortly after his release. Aunt Olga and Hilde followed them later. They lived in poor circumstances in the Bavarian cathedral town of Freising, and in the years after the war I used to send them parcels of clothes for the growing girls, and food, coffee and cigarettes for Hugo. Many of my friends who still had relatives in Germany sent Care parcels to the former enemy country. The world had changed.

For Fred, however, the guilt of his tormentors remained. After leaving Vienna, he never again visited Germany or Austria. When his friend Paul Knepler told him in 1955 that he and his wife wanted to return to Vienna, Fred was furious. 'How can you go back to a country of murderers?' he asked, and was outraged when Knepler did what he had said he would do. Four years later Fred received an invitation from the Raimund Theatre in Vienna to a new production of *Warum lügst du, Chérie?*, offering to meet all his travel costs and pay for a first-class hotel if he would attend the first night and come on to the stage at the end. He refused, and wrote back to the organizers, 'For me, a country that forced my parents to scrub street cobbles with toothbrushes is dead.' The wounds he carried were as if cut in stone. He even refused the money he was offered as compensation for his time in concentration camps because 'This money has blood on it.' It was a large amount, and we could really have done with it, but Fred could not be persuaded. 'Money cannot undo anything,' he said.

He reacted similarly to my intention to visit Aunt Olga and her family in Germany. 'It's still crawling with Nazis over there,' he said. Sometimes we talked all night about it. In the end he accepted that I wanted to see my aunt again. She was the only close relative from Türmitz who had survived Hitler. I was on no account to speak to older Germans, Fred made me promise, and I kept to this the first time I went.

Later, starting in the 1960s, my work in the book trade took me to the Frankfurt Book Fair. Even then I still felt a vague unease meeting older people. Lingering suspicions and thoughts that they might have perpetrated or aided Nazi crimes began to fade only as that generation disappeared. Occasionally I was asked how I spoke perfect German. When I explained, some people reacted with understandable embarrassment, but others were quick to stress that they had had nothing to do with the Nazis.

My English is still coloured by a foreign accent. In my first years of exile, it was even stronger, however much I tried to get rid of it. Every sentence I uttered declared that I was not English.

Ernest Hemingway noticed my un-English pronunciation when we fell into conversation in spring 1944. Hemingway, who had enjoyed worldwide fame since the publication of *For Whom the Bell Tolls*, had shortly before followed his wife, Martha Gellhorn, to London, and was always dropping into American army HQ. Wherever he appeared, the attention of bystanders followed him like the wake of a ship. This happened in the PX, where he came to shop, like any other American soldier.

I asked him for his autograph and exchanged a few polite words with him. 'You have a German accent,' he said, as he casually scribbled his signature on a piece of paper. 'Are you German?' I said that I wasn't, and that I came from the Sudetenland and had fled to England before the Germans came.

'Are you Jewish?' he asked. I nodded. Hemingway found that 'interesting'. He was working on a piece about the German occupation of Czechoslovakia, he said, and asked whether I would have time to go to lunch with him in the officers' mess, as there were several questions he would like to ask me.

Of course I had time. Over the next few days we met for lunch three times in the officers' mess. I always had a warm meal, but Hemingway never ate, and made do every time with a drink. He asked every possible kind of question, about Henlein's party, about Jewish cultural life in Bohemia, about my parents, and how the last five years had been for me. My speech often faltered because I was struggling to find the right words, and sometimes because I was choked with tears. Hemingway was very friendly and attentive. He scribbled notes endlessly in a little book, and after an hour or more asked for the bill. Finally he said that I had helped him a lot, and wished me and my family well. The book, or whatever it was he planned, never appeared though.

The times ordained other priorities. In the London of April and May 1944 there was only one topic of conversation, and everyone was discussing it fervidly and speculating wildly. It was the imminent allied invasion of France. The scenarios that were envisaged were not reassuring. London would be bombed day and night, some predicted. Others saw Londoners condemned to a prolonged mole-like existence in the air raid shelters. Thousands of French refugees would overrun the city. In mid-May the speculation suddenly stopped, and at the end of the month, seemingly overnight, all military uniforms disappeared from the city. Hordes of soldiers from different armies assembled in the south of England for D-Day. The few remaining GIs in the headquarters where I worked had tension written all over their faces, a tension that pervaded the place like a painful continuous high note. Outside the military bases, in the pubs and the streets, people seemed less impressed by the historic significance of D-Day. On 6 June, on the day more than 150,000 soldiers landed at dawn on the coast of Normandy, it was business as usual in London – as usual, that is, as the state of emergency had become. Everyone thought that the Luftwaffe would retaliate, but the first week passed uneventfully. The Germans retreated, and the allies advanced rapidly. My disquiet remained. Would they be in time to save countless Jews from being killed? I did not know whether or not Mother was still alive. There had been no sign of her for over six months. Perhaps she was no longer in Lodz.

A week after D-Day, the first V1 hit London. There had been rumours of a new German weapon for months, and here

It was. In the following days, hundreds of these flying bombs rained from the sky. Every night Marianne and I woke our deaf and dumb landlords and crept with them into the Anderson shelter in the garden. They didn't hear what we heard. The unmanned V1s flew with a pulsating rhythmic sound, and those on the receiving end gave them the onomatopoeic name of 'doodlebugs'. Before they fell, the chugging sound stopped, and at most fifteen seconds later there was an explosion as they hit the ground. Those seconds were the worst. Scared stiff and helpless, you waited for the explosion, not knowing if the bomb was directly overhead, and sometimes diving for cover at the last moment – a reaction that became instinctive, and made Marianne decades later dive under a table when a helicopter flew over her house in Canada and the clattering of its blades briefly faltered.

As the V1s appeared above the roofs of London at all times of the day and night, they disrupted the day and ruined sleep. The sirens wailed constantly, and everyone ran to the shelters, back to work, back to the shelters again, and so on, on some days a dozen times. The British people met this fire from the skies with composure, reckoning it to be the last throes of a doomed enemy. A million allied soldiers had landed on the Continent by the end of June, and were advancing towards Germany. In the east, soviet troops were forcing the Wehrmacht back.

We know today that the news of the Wehrmacht's defeats trickled through to the Lodz ghetto because an underground group risked listening secretly to foreign stations on a home-made radio. Mere possession of a radio was punishable by death in the ghetto. A day after D-Day just such a group was caught red-handed by the Gestapo at 9 Mühlgasse, and all its members were executed. The leader, a Zionist, killed himself to avoid falling into the hands of the Gestapo.

After the news had spread, there were demonstrations here and there in the factories in the ghetto, and some dared to stay away from work or to go slow, as though this would hasten the German collapse. In recent months there had also been repeated cases of soup strikes. Young workers especially had often dared to refuse the watery brew, but they were helpless against the deportations.

After the Warsaw ghetto was closed down and almost all its inhabitants exterminated, Lodz was the last surviving ghetto on Polish soil. Now that Soviet troops were approaching, it too was to be emptied. On 23 June 1944 deportations to Chelmno resumed, and once more the council of elders had to organize the transports and get people to the assembly points. There was talk of 'resettlement in the old Reich'. In July, thirty-one postcards from people supposedly transferred to Leipzig arrived in the ghetto. They were all postmarked 19 July 1944. They were well, people wrote, they were living in comfortable barracks and re-united with their families. Many in the ghetto took hope from this. But in fact, not one of the 7,000 people moved out between 23 June and 14 July 1944 had ever reached a town. The transports went without exception to the extermination camp at Chelmno, where they were all gassed.

On 22 July 1944 a telegram came from my cousin, Hans Frank. He had left Denmark in adventurous circumstances. Members of the Danish underground had taken him and other refugees at night by boat to Sweden. Via Stockholm, he had shortly before reached England and joined the Czechoslovak exile army. His message came as some relief for the moment, bringing, as it did, the first news of my mother for a long time. He had heard from Aunt Olga's daughter, Hilde, that Grete was well, Hans wrote.

But Aunt Olga, who had always believed she was protected by being married to a non-Jew, was deported with fifty-seven others from Aussig to Theresienstadt at the start of the year. She was now widowed, and so endangered. Jews from mixed marriages were often sent to a camp immediately after the death of their non-Jewish spouse.

It had been known in London for some time what was happening in the death camps. The gas chambers were no longer just a rumour after prisoners who had succeeded in escaping from a concentration camp confirmed them to a stunned world. In mid-July the BBC had broadcast a report about this. Several Jewish organizations asked for allied bombers to attack the extermination camps or the railway lines leading to them, but the defence ministries in London and Washington turned down all requests.

At the end of August the Lodz ghetto too was dissolved.

One after another the workers in the various factories were told to go to the Radegast railway station. Hans Biebow, the German head of the ghetto administration, made a speech ordering people to report for the transports and promising work and better food. In the days that followed, almost 68,000 people were deported to Auschwitz-Birkenau. Most were gassed the day they arrived. Mordechai Chaim Rumkowski, the Jewish elder, was taken there on 28 August 1944 and gassed. This mass exodus took place in secret, without the knowledge of the outside world.

Marianne hardly spoke about either our mother or our father. It was her way of avoiding pain, and I respected it. One can't live with fear all the time. Each of us tried in her own way to make life go on. Fred's songs dealt untiringly with love, and conjured it up in a 'Serenade for Two', a 'Skirt Waltz' and the waltz 'My Most Romantic Memory'. He wrote mostly dance numbers, some for new publishers, and some lately under the *nom de plume* Irving Lennard. I was flattered at his appropriating my surname for the purpose. It was a discreet way of showing his affection.

We hardly went dancing any more ourselves. Since our parents had been deported it didn't seem appropriate, and with the renewed bombing people tended to keep to their own four walls again – if they were still standing. Many theatres and cinemas closed for lack of patrons. Shortly before, Fred and I went to a recital by Ferdinand Rauter and Engel Lund in the National Gallery. Even they played to empty rows. Because of the flying bombs a good two-thirds of the usual audience stayed away.

Rumours of the new V2 rockets increased day by day. At the start of September there had been a huge explosion in Chiswick that made a massive crater. The mysterious explosion, it was whispered, had been caused by a new German wonder weapon. Speaking openly about it was unpatriotic because it would have confirmed for the Germans their unimaginable destructive effect. It was only in November that Churchill made a public statement, admitting their enormous power.

There was no protection against the V2s. They shot out of nowhere so fast that the sirens could give no warning. Most of them hit the East End and the northern edge of London.

Although, despite their power, they killed relatively few people, some days over ten thousand buildings were damaged, some of them reduced to rubble. Dampness and cold crept into damaged houses through temporarily covered roofs and broken windows. Special teams were out all over the town doing at least emergency repairs. In many places wooden and metal huts were put up as temporary refuges.

On top of this, London had its worst winter for fifty years. The whole city seemed to have caught a cold. Marianne lay in bed with bronchitis and a high temperature, packed in layers of warm underclothes, and Fred fought 'flu for weeks. A feeling of malaise gripped people in London and spread like a depressive epidemic. The country had been at war for five years. Hopes that it would end within months of the Allied invasion were not fulfilled. The constant bombing, loss of sleep, shortage of food, the bitter cold and the increasing destruction all added to the general depression, which was worse still that Christmas. Hitler had massed remaining German forces in the Ardennes for an offensive to break through the allied front and gain a German victory. The attack started on 16 December, and managed to dent the Allied line. Germany's unconditional surrender now seemed far in the future. Instead of the war being over by Christmas, as we had hoped, there was news of ever more bloodshed.

Fred did not celebrate Christmas Eve anyway, and Marianne and I were hardly in any mood to either. We accepted an invitation from Erika, the doctor who had arranged Marianne's thyroid operation, to cocktails on Christmas Day evening. Because alcohol was so scarce, there were only non-alcoholic drinks. Through the bold assistance of a store worker at the PX, I managed to contribute a few cans of valuable orange juice. As an employee, I was entitled to buy damaged goods at half price. Annoyingly, though, our latest consignment of fruit juices was in faultless condition. When the store man saw my disappointment, he asked how many tins I had wanted to buy. 'Four,' I said. At this, he took a hammer from his tool cupboard and four cans from the shelf, and dented each one with a smart blow. 'There, now they only cost half,' he said, gave a conspiratorial wink, and wished me a Merry Christmas.

But it was not a happy one. It was one of the saddest, as it probably was for most Londoners too. War-weary, worn down by anxiety and deprivation, we began the New Year a week later with scant hopes. Sometimes I didn't dare think about my mother, or I would have had to admit that her chances of surviving were less every day.

On 17 January 1945, Soviet troops entered Lodz. In the abandoned ghetto the Russian soldiers saw emaciated figures crawling from underground hideouts. There were about 870 of them, inhabitants of the ghetto who had belonged to the last 'clearance squad'. Shortly before, the Gestapo had directed them to dig nine massive graves in the cemetery. Sensing that they had dug their own graves, they had not appeared at the last parade, but hidden themselves in prepared places they had dug under the earth. Most were men. Grete Lönhardt was not among them.

Ten days later, on 27 January, the Red Army liberated the extermination camp at Auschwitz, where there were still 7,600 prisoners. At the time Lodz fell, the count of prisoners in Auschwitz was a good 66,000, but, with the exception of those unable to walk, they had been sent off on a death march towards the west.

I applied to the Central Tracing Bureau in London, which had begun working with the British Red Cross two years earlier. Relatives of those who had disappeared in Hitler's empire were besieging it by the thousand. They were all told they would have to wait for months. Fred and his brother had also initiated inquiries there about their parents. People also tried to get information via Bloomsbury House.

The bombing of London was gradually falling off. Now allied planes droned overhead at night on their way to Germany. On 3 February Berlin had its heaviest raid ever, and on 13 and 14 February the British bombed Dresden to the point of extinction. More than 35,000 people died in the city, which was filled with refugees.

On 17 and 19 April 1945, Aussig had its first serious raids by British bombers. The centre of town, the main church and the shops on the Teplitzerstrasse were badly hit. A paint factory and the stores of a chemical plant along the railway from Aussig to Teplitz were set alight. Stretches of railway line were destroyed, and the local Nazi Party headquarters was completely burned out. As late as 30 April, teachers from the secondary schools were ordered to supervise the building of tank barriers among the villas in the smart part of town. Anti-tank ditches were dug on the right bank of the Elbe, and in the town park, already disfigured by trenches for people to take cover in during air raids, foxholes were now dug. Aussig, my lost home, remained loyal to the Führer, who that very day fired a bullet into his mouth in his Berlin bunker.

Those weeks and months were the hardest of my life, because the defeat of Germany and the liberation of the concentration camps brought the whole truth to light. At the end of April London cinemas showed a film about Nazi atrocities in the camps at Bergen-Belsen and Buchenwald, which had been liberated by then.

'We ought to see that,' said Fred, with almost defiant decisiveness.

'I don't think that's at all a good idea,' I responded. 'The pictures will torment and torture you more than what you have already seen. You won't be able to sleep a single night even with sleeping tablets.'

But Fred was not put off. 'I must see the whole truth, don't you see?', he said. 'It doesn't help to avoid it. I must live with it for the rest of my life, so I'd rather know.'

Fred never spared himself these things. He was obsessed all his life with learning all about the Holocaust, as if knowing numbers and facts would make it easier to grasp the unutterable, and to come to terms with it in his own life. I have not spared myself the truth either, but a protective instinct let me to filter out and repress and forget the worst details over time. Otherwise, I don't think I could have gone on living.

And so we went to this film. Long queues snaked in front of the cinemas, and it was hours before we got in. Fred and I sat together, but we did not hold hands, perhaps because when we face the greatest horror we are in any case quite alone. I do not remember individual scenes. I only know that at the end the audience sat in shocked silence, in a way I had never experienced before in a cinema. The silence was total. No one spoke on the way out because there were no words for what they had seen.

The pictures haunted me for weeks, weeks when I lived behind a wall, unable to get on with the simplest everyday things. I had to have time off sick, and had to force myself to eat a little. Neither of us could eat much. We slept badly because of the horrific scenes that came in our sleep. Perhaps, like Marianne, we shouldn't have seen the film. She had refused to go with us. 'I don't have to do that to myself', she said.

I often wondered how Fred could retain any of his creativity with all these tortured thoughts. Shouldn't his ability to write, being one of the disciplines most affected by mental anguish, simply have withered away? How could he go on writing about love when inhumanity on a scale hitherto unknown was being exposed? Our first reaction after all is surely to fall silent and to banish all laughter. Yet at some stage something else stirs: an instinct to go on living, to carry on, laughing and crying at the same time.

Fred was writing his second English operetta. *Can Can* featured well-known music by Offenbach adapted for the stage by Bernard Grun. It was to be a lavish production under the aegis of Jack Hylton, one of the most popular bandleaders. Hylton did not skimp on *Belle Epoque* costumes and spectacular dance numbers with a ballet troupe. Fred had lots to do, as there were nearly two dozen songs in the show. As usual, he wrote them in the evenings and at weekends, and got me to read them critically.

Hesitantly we tried out another activity normal in peacetime. The streets were no longer pitch-black but, like a shimmer of hope, softly lit, and we could go out without a torch. After five and a half years of blackout, Big Ben had been illuminated again since the beginning of May. The now silent air raid sirens were removed. New iron railings were put up around the big London parks, the original ones having been taken during the war, allegedly to be melted down for armaments. Two hundred thousand houses had still to be replaced. The first prefabricated homes were put up in Tottenham. The new rapid construction method attracted crowds of interested onlookers, and soon the standard 'prefabs' were to be seen in many parts of London. Union Jacks were sold out all over the country. The pubs got deliveries of whisky and gin, many bottles bearing the label, 'Not to be drunk before Victory Night'.

On VE Day, 8 May 1945, the day of 'Victory in Europe', alcohol flowed freely and the whole city celebrated. People rejoiced, sang 'Land of Hope and Glory' and danced in the streets. Complete strangers fell into each other's arms and kissed. Yet behind it all, many of the shining faces that night were sunken with weariness.

I was in no mood for celebrating. A few days earlier I had got a letter from my cousin Hans typed by a comrade. 'I have sad news,' he had dictated, wasting no words. Did I recall old General Syrovy from Türmitz, who had only one eye but went about in such good spirits? Well, Hans wrote, he had met the same fate. He had lost an eye.

Later I learned the details. Hans had been hit by a bullet from a comrade's rifle as he was crossing a river on manoeuvres. Two other comrades had been injured by gunfire. No one could discover why the shots had been fired. Because both the other soldiers injured were also Jewish, rumours persisted that it had not been an accident, but a deliberate attack. There were a number of anti-Semitic incidents in the Czechoslovak exile army. Hans was never to recover from the shot, which had also damaged part of his brain. He spent the rest of his life in a psychiatric institution.

For him, as for countless thousands of others, victory came too late. No, there was to be no joy in victory for us. Germany had surrendered, Hitler and some of his lackeys had committed suicide, but now we had to go on living with the legacy, and with uncertainty about the fate of our relatives and friends on the Continent.

Fred thought the peace too good to be true, even when Japan surrendered following the atomic bombs dropped on Hiroshima and Nagasaki in August 1945, and the war was declared officially ended on 2 September. I believe the Nazis had succeeded in destroying Fred's native trust and replacing it with constant mistrust.

I went at least once a week to Bloomsbury House, where Jewish émigrés crowded around hoping for news of their relatives. Outside in the corridor lists had been hung, and dense crowds formed in front of them. The lists gave, alpha-

betically, the names of surviving Jews in Hitler's former Reich.
One felt the tension of those standing there hoping to find
one of their loved ones on the lists. This would affect the
course of their lives. Some in their dejection had collapsed
and were huddled on the floor; others cried with relief and
joy because they had found familiar names. I thought I could
hear my heart beating as I searched the lists. There was no
Lönhardt under 'L', so I tried under 'S'. There I found her
names: 'Schnitzer, Grete' it read, black on white. For further
information one had to ask in the office of Bloomsbury House.

A Grete Schnitzer had survived. I know it would have been
wiser not to get my hopes up too high, but I could scarcely
contain myself. For a moment I had a vision of a door spring-
ing wide open, giving me access to a bright new future. In
tears I phoned Fred at his office to tell him. I was bursting with
ideas, and he could hardly dampen my euphoria. I would rent
a flat for Mutz, nurse her back to health, cook for her and take
care of her. We should want for nothing.

Fred warned me that nothing was sure yet. I had left all my
mother's details at Bloomsbury House, and they had
promised to let me know in a few days whether this Grete
Schnitzer was my mother. 'Don't say anything to Marianne,'
Fred advised me, 'or she may have false hopes.'

It was well I took his advice. Only two days later the call
came from Bloomsbury House. They were very sorry to have
to tell me that the Grete Schnitzer on the list was definitely
not my mother. Mother's details did not correspond to those
they had. There was no trace of my mother.

I should have been more sensible, and known to avoid
premature rejoicing, because it is worse if it turns out to be
misplaced. After getting the news, I was distraught for days.
To protect myself I resolved to suppress my naïve optimism
from now on. Why couldn't I ever really give up hoping, like
Fred, who had abandoned any belief that his parents had
survived? Perhaps it was wiser to live like that.

Months later I learned the whole truth. The truth came to
me, and rang at my door, and I let it in. It came in the person
of Else Glaser, the last friend to be with my mother. Else had
miraculously survived Lodz and Auschwitz, and now came to
my door in London to fulfil the oath she and my mother had

sworn, to visit those left behind and tell them what had happened.

It is hard for me to describe our meeting in any detail because it was certainly the most painful and distressing thing in my life. Else Glaser had landed in England a few days earlier. She had heard from the Red Cross in Prague that her two daughters were here. Both had married Canadian soldiers, and all four were on their way to Canada to start a new life. The girls had not imagined their mother would still be alive. One can imagine how overjoyed they all were at meeting again.

And now Else Glaser was sitting at our dining table. Marianne sat next to me, and I held her hand all the time. We did not say a word as Else told us all she had experienced, sometimes passing quickly over events, then hesitating, sometimes laughing and then weeping and shaking. She described my parents' last months, which we knew only from the briefest of messages. What she recounted during these long hours destroyed our last shred of hope.

She described how Mother had coloured her cheeks using the chicory bags, how she managed to look neat and healthy despite the lack of essentials like soap and water, how she always tried to keep Father's spirits up, and how miserably he had died so soon after arriving. Else told how she and my mother comforted one another after their husbands died, sharing a bed, and resolving to survive, if only for their daughters' sakes.

A rumour had circulated in the ghetto, Else said, that widows were being sent to the gas chambers, so Grete had gone through a formal marriage, solemnized by the Jewish elder, soon after Father's death to a doctor from Bodenbach called Hanak. Actually, as we later discovered, Mordechai Chaim Rumkowski had married inmates of the ghetto by assuming rabbinical powers. A list of Lodz prisoners shows my mother entered under the name Schnitzer Hanak.

According to Else, she and Grete had been taken to Auschwitz the same day, after the ghetto had been almost entirely emptied. Trains rumbled non-stop from Lodz to Auschwitz. My mother, Else said, and her *pro forma* husband Dr Hanak had gone on the morning transport from Radegast station. She herself had gone that afternoon.

Else said that she had been taken aside by a Russian prisoner who had been detailed to assist. A number of captured Red Army soldiers had volunteered to work as guards and auxiliary police in the extermination camps, and were known as 'Travnikis'. The man told her, she said, that she was going to certain death, like almost all those arriving from Lodz. The chimneys of the crematoria in Auschwitz were smoking night and day, and the dead from the gas chambers were stacked in front of them like piles of timber. The man whispered that he had two passes of German women that would allow her to escape, and that he could direct her to a nearby convent where she could find cover and refuge.

Else had tried desperately to find my mother. But it was hopeless because in the chaos of the arrival platform, with thousands milling around like terrified cattle awaiting slaughter, with whistles piercing the air, children crying, dogs barking and guards yelling, where people were falling down or being kicked to the ground or killed by blows from rifle butts or shot, where everything that was human, every civilized impulse, was pointless and lost for ever – because in this hell there was not a familiar face. Elsa learned that all those in the morning transport had gone to the gas chambers

Else said she took another woman with her, and fled that night. Only a handful of people, I now know, ever managed to escape from Auschwitz. Most were quickly caught and executed. I have not been able to find any documented account of Else's story.

I do not know to this day how Else managed to get out, but it seems she was able to reach the convent a few miles away, where she said she lived hidden in a cellar until the end of the war. The nuns apparently fed her and died her hair blond so that she had a chance in case her presence was discovered. At the end of the war she returned to Prague, where she learned her daughters' addresses in London.

I do not remember everything Else told us. At the time her account numbed my mind, and I asked few questions. I just listened, helpless and aghast. Later, after years of not talking about the subject, some questions occurred to me, but it was too late.

Else's flight can be traced, at least in part. The convent

must have been the Seraphite Convent in Auschwitz. It still exists. Sister Bogdana, one of the oldest members of the order, founded at the end of the nineteenth century, confirmed that the sisters had hidden escapees from Auschwitz in the cellar until the end of the war. The cellar was in a neighbouring house separated from the nuns' dormitory by the convent garden. A tiny window at eye level gave on to some ploughed fields behind. Over the years a good dozen people who had escaped from the concentration camp had hidden there, and the nuns had fed them. Amazingly, this act of Christian valour, undertaken on the authority of the abbess at the time, who later left the order, finds no mention in the copious documentation on Auschwitz. She had never spoken about it before, said Sister Bogdana, who was then a young nun and is now almost as old as I am.

I could not ask Else Glaser about this any more. She died of a brain tumour only six months after arriving in Canada, and I soon lost contact with her daughters. In any case, she could not have answered the question which all survivors like me ask, the question what it was like for my mother in those last seconds of her life. Whether anyone held her hand, some stranger, a companion in death herded in with her to die. Or was she was totally alone among thousands of the condemned, in that fraction of eternity that I can never know?

.

12 Life Goes On

Now, just when the days are getting shorter, the festival of light is drawing near. Every year we celebrate Hanukkah, my son, his family and I. For eight days we gather in my son's house every evening to light the candles. At sunset, as the first star appears in the sky, Ian will light a candle on the eight-branched candelabra and speak a Hebrew blessing, as his father always did. I shall fry *latkas* and *krapfen* in oil, in remembrance of the oil in the temple of Jerusalem that never ran out.

Both my granddaughters love Hanukkah, not only for its cheerful ceremony, but because they get a small present on each of the eight evenings. December is the girls' favourite month because not long after Hanukkah they celebrate Christmas. If only because of the many prezzies they get in their multi-culti home, they find it 'goody, goody'. They are not brought up in a strict Christian or Jewish faith. Their parents think it important that they learn about both cultures and traditions, and want them to make up their own minds about God.

Fred would probably not have approved of this liberal approach. His piety admitted only his Jewish God and owed nothing to rationality. It was astounding that a mind as logical and intellectual as his took so little account of any doubts about a world of belief not amenable to proof. I recall his extraordinary reaction when I told him proudly many years ago that I had an organ donor card. Fred was not at all pleased. 'And how will it look when the Messiah comes, and the dead appear before Him, and you have no kidneys?' he asked. He was completely serious.

My faith was never as strong as Fred's, and now, in the evening of my life, my doubts about any life afterwards have only grown. It would be lovely to see again those who died before us, and I envy people who can wrap themselves in this consoling trust, but I incline increasingly to my father's agnosticism.

Out of respect for his attitude, I avoided discussing religion with Fred. Secretly I often wondered how he could believe in God's omnipotence when He had allowed the murder of six million Jews. But with Fred, it would have had rather the opposite effect. The more horrifying the reports of Nazi crimes that slowly came to light after the war, the more he seemed to be immersed in his faith.

It took months, and often years, until we discovered the fate of our various relatives. Uncle Otto and Aunt Olga, my father's brother and sister, had survived. Uncle Otto worked as a camp doctor, and Aunt Olga had got by as an assistant in the kitchens disposing of kitchen waste, and had not starved unduly.

They were the only ones of my relations who had survived the camps. Malva Schalek, the painter, was deported to Auschwitz and died there. Uncle Herbert and Aunt Trude, my mother's brother and sister, also died in a camp, as did her sister Hilde and her husband Robert Frank, whose deaths in Lodz we heard of for the first time.

News of more and more deaths reached us. Fred was told that his parents Taube and Isaak had been killed on the way to Riga by gas pumped into the railway trucks. He never heard that in fact they had been shot in Kaunas by an Einsatzkommando.

It may be asked what difference it makes when and exactly how someone died in that industrialized extermination. It does, precisely because the system made its victims all the same, robbing them not only of their dignity but of their individuality, because it took first their wealth, then their labour and finally their hair and the gold in their teeth, and then disposed of them anonymously. That is why those left behind hang on to figures and dates as the last marks of the individuality of their lives. And they hang on to the material proof of their existence, pictures and photographs, a few pieces of jewellery, a book with a dedication, perhaps, that could be rescued.

One is glad to have such memorabilia, but it is heart-rending to receive them. Some months after the war ended, I unexpectedly received a large crate of things from my parents' house from a Mr Začek in Prague. Zdeněk Začek had once worked for my father, who had helped him set up his own business in Prague years before. He wrote that my parents had left all these things with him so that the Nazis did not get their hands on them.

I hadn't thought that I would ever see again so much as a teaspoon from our house in Türmitz. Father and Mother had not said a word about the hidden valuables in their letters. It was just as well, because the Nazis had strictly forbidden Jews to entrust their valuables even to non-Jewish friends or relatives for safe-keeping.

And so Marianne and I sat crying in front of the wooden crate and dug out one piece of our past after another. The carpet from the living room which my parents had brought back from Tunisia, the Meissen and Rosenthal porcelain, the Bohemian crystal glasses and the silver cutlery that we used on special occasions, the silver candlesticks, the damask table-cloths and napkins.

Mr Začek asked us to forgive him that the oil painting of my father, painted by Malva Schalek, no longer existed. He had secretly burned it because my father had looked so unmistakably Jewish in the picture, and he was afraid the Nazis would find his hide-away in the cellar and identify the contents as hidden Jewish goods from the portrait.

Malva's other pictures, the portraits of Grandfather and Mother, the crayon drawing of Uncle Herbert, Marianne and me, I got back only in the late 1980s. They were stored all those years in Türmitz, in the home of my grandfather's one-time coachman, whose family got in touch with me.

Our lives were now surrounded by familiar items from our childhood. We laid the carpet and set the table with linen and crockery from home. At first, perhaps because they had been taken forcefully from their context, these familiar objects sometimes had something that was painfully displeasing about them.

Many émigrés like us picked up the scattered fragments of their past with mixed feelings. Fred had a big crate from New York from his old friend Hans J. Lengsfelder. Lengsfelder had married a wealthy woman from New England, and worked as a music producer. He still tried writing lyrics from time to time, but he found English difficult. Time and again he tried to get Fred to emigrate to America so that the old team might repeat their erstwhile triumphs. But Fred did not want to leave London.

In the crate were all the things that Fred and Hans had hidden in the toilet window shaft in the Lengsfelders' house. Hans had actually been able to save them and take possession of them again on a visit to Vienna. As if fixed to the ground, Fred sat for days among piles of sheet music, posters and critical reviews, studying every line, singing the occasional tune to me, and sometimes secretly wiping his eyes. In these moments he seemed totally caught up in his memories.

It was similar with his parents' things, which had been sent to him shortly before by the acquaintance in Oslo who had smuggled them there in 1938. Fred was close to tears as he handled the fur coat he had bought his mother with his first royalties, the gold jewellery and the heavy 250-year-old silver Hanukkah candelabra. His hands stroked the black Persian coat as though in a trance. 'I am sure my mother would have wanted you to wear this coat,' he said, 'and it would please me very much.'

Friedl's husband Bandy, who thanks to the improvements in Friedl's cooking now had a little pot belly, insisted on altering the fur coat for me. I have never been especially keen on fur, and wore it for Fred's sake. Later, with his agreement, it went to a charity shop selling second-hand goods for orphaned children in Israel. Fred thought it was what his mother would have wanted.

When it came to giving to charity, Fred was a real Jew. He gave constantly, and could not pass a beggar in the street without giving something. When *Can Can* opened at the Adelphi Theatre in London in May 1946, what gave Fred the most pleasure was that part of the proceeds went to the Federation of Women Zionists, which cared for Nazi victims who had fled to Palestine. The fact that it was the second time a work of his had made it to London's West End was almost incidental.

Fred had gone alone to the widely praised premiere of *Can Can* in Manchester the previous December because I couldn't get time off. As with *Old Chelsea*, friends had sent piles of good-luck telegrams, Paul Knepler, as befitted a lyricist, sending his in rhyme.

Can Can got off to a good start. In Manchester, where it played to a full house every evening at the Opera House, it was extended by two weeks. After that, it went on tour to Edinburgh, Oxford, Blackpool, Coventry and Birmingham. At the same time, *Old Chelsea* too went on tour, this time without Richard Tauber, and two months after the end of *Can Can*, it was again at the Opera House in Manchester. It was not to be compared with Vienna, where two of Fred's shows were sometimes on in the same town, but for a 'language-switcher' it was, I thought, a remarkable achievement.

The posters for *Can Can* in London were as big as a garage door. For the first tour of *Old Chelsea*, during the wartime paper shortage, the advertising was rather more modest. But now everything pointed to an upswing. Marianne had shortly before got a job with a firm that decorated the walls of department stores and fire walls with huge advertisements for consumer goods. She spent all the time in the open air on scaffolding painting appeals to consumers to spend money. People in London didn't have that much money, and some had been reduced in circumstances by the war. But public attitudes had changed perceptibly. People became concerned with appearances, and tended to forget the classless solidarity that prevailed during the war.

Now they no longer faced a common threat, people worked for their own individual future. It might still be rather unclear, but at least they knew that, now the threat was gone, they at least had one. Many people got married. Fred too had repeatedly spoken of this of late, although without making any definite suggestion. I sensed what was holding him back and what he did not dare express, so I did it for him.

'I've been thinking,' I said, as we sat at our evening meal. Fred stopped eating. He had probably noticed that this phrase heralded a difficult topic of conversation. 'We wanted to get married when the war was over,' I went on. 'It has been over for a while now, and you still haven't asked me formally whether I want to be your wife, so I have sometimes doubted myself. But now, I agree we shouldn't marry. Not yet.'

Fred's eyes showed alarm. He drew a breath, as though about to respond, but I didn't let him interrupt. 'I want to suggest something,' I said. 'You once said I should go with you to the synagogue when we are married. But people would soon notice I can't read Hebrew. The service lasts two hours, and I'd be bored to death because I would hardly understand what was going on. You've told me about the Jewish holy days, and what one eats on those days. But I need to know why, and where it is all written.'

I got up and began to clear the table to hide my nervousness. His look followed me but he said nothing. 'I would like to learn it all,' I said. 'I want to learn Hebrew, I want to learn to read the scriptures, and I want to learn how to cook kosher. All those things your mother knew, that a Jewish wife needs to know. When I know those things, we'll get married, but not before.'

Fred jumped up and took me in his arms. He pressed me against him so hard that I struggled for breath. '*Mein Kleines,*' he said – he often called me that. 'That's the loveliest thing you could say. You don't know how happy you make me. I thought of it too, but I didn't want to be the one to suggest it.' His eyes were full of tears as he said, 'God must love me because he has sent me the best woman in the world.'

In Golders Green there lived a rabbi who had fled from Germany and belonged to the Reform synagogue. Fred had heard of him, and asked if he would give me instruction. I visited him in his modestly furnished flat for a whole afternoon every week for the next six months. He was a delightful, warm-hearted man with a wife of alarming ugliness, but who exceeded her husband in kindness of heart. She seemed to have taken to me in a big way. 'I shall miss you so much when you stop coming,' she always said. I put on quite a few pounds at that time because whenever I went, she made sure I had a good Jewish meal. 'Let the girl have something to eat first,' she said to her husband, and fed me carrot *tzimmes*, herring salad and other delicacies. She usually gave me a pack to take home with home-made yeast-risen pastries.

Her husband read passages to me from the Hebrew bible and translated parts into German. As the visits went on, the guttural and raw sounds of Hebrew lost their strangeness and shed increasing warmth. The bearded rabbi commented on the books of Moses and the prophetic writings of Joshua, Samuel, Isiah and Jeremiah, the Psalms and Proverbs, the Song of Solomon and the Lamentations. He taught me to read the Hebrew letters and told me to learn the 'Shema Yisrael' by heart. He explained the duties of a Jewish wife, who must care for the physical and emotional welfare of the children, while their religious education is in the hands of the husband. He explained the rituals of the holy days, the symbolic significance of the activities during Hanukkah and Yom Kippur and why flour with yeast is banned from the house at Passover. I also learned how to run a kosher household.

Fred was visibly happy over my willingness to lead a life in accordance with the Jewish faith. I am sure he sensed that I did it more out of love for him than from pious conviction, but he did not mention it. Perhaps he secretly hoped that in time I would become totally converted, although I was hardly likely to become as pious as he was.

It was then, of all times, that Fred was plagued by a conflict of conscience, caused by Richard Tauber of all people. He phoned to ask Fred to write the words for an 'Ave Maria'. Fred declined after much soul searching. 'What will He say up there?' he said, pointing towards heaven. 'As a Jew, I can't write a song for the Virgin Mary.'

But Tauber kept begging him. He knew, he said, that he was causing Fred a conflict of loyalties, and perhaps it would help if he dipped into his own pocket and doubled the usual fee. Eventually Fred gave in; not because of the money, but because of his old links with Tauber. In a matter of a few days he wrote the words for 'Pray'r in the Twilight'. With the proceeds, no doubt to appease his conscience, he bought a valuable silver and ivory *mesusa*. The tiny capsule containing the declaration of faith is fixed to the right door jamb at the entrance to a Jewish home, and symbolizes the safeguarding of the pious from sin.

It was a timely acquisition as Fred and I had found a beautiful three-room flat in Bolton Gardens, which we planned to live in after we married. In the meantime, my sister and I would live there.

Marianne was now engaged to an American sailor called Louis Meyers, whom I had met at the American HQ in

London and invited home for a Sabbath meal several times. He was a Jew, had been a newspaper cartoonist in America, and during the war had joined the US navy. Marianne liked him very much. Louis made her laugh as only Tony had been able to before, and told wonderful jokes. When he had drunk a bit, he did bold cartoon drawings of the two of us. Marianne was given big doe eyes, and I had a mouth as big as a melon – to say nothing of my breasts. He once secretly drew Fred when he fell asleep on the sofa after supper. He called the picture 'Sleeping Jew'. It looked so funny and we laughed so loud that we woke Fred.

Louis went back to the States intending to prepare everything for Marianne's immigration and the wedding, and then come and fetch her in a few months' time. When he said goodbye, he gave her a gold engagement ring with a small diamond. She was overjoyed, and I tried to hide my sadness at her forthcoming departure.

But several weeks went by without so much as a line from Mr Meyers. At first I was upset, and then angry, to have to look on helplessly how Marianne became more and more despondent by the day. Every evening when she got home from work, her first question was whether there was any news from Louis. There was none.

Weeks and months went by. It was now spring 1947. Louis Meyers did not get in touch. Only years later did we find out by accident the reason for his supposed faithlessness. Shortly after arriving home in America, Louis had suffered a major stroke, which had obliterated part of his memory. He remembered nothing of Marianne or other people or events in his life up till then. He had got married in America, and come to London with his wife hoping that parts of his life would come back to him there. I ran into them both while out shopping. He did not recognize me, and my name meant nothing to him. When I told him that he had promised to marry my sister, he was visibly upset. He had had an uncomfortable feeling, he confessed, that there was a woman waiting for him somewhere in London and he had left her behind unhappy, but he could remember nothing at all.

Marianne deadened her sorrows by working. For our new home, which would soon be the first we shared with Fred, she sewed curtains every evening and weekend; she white-washed the walls, painted the windows and put new covers on the chairs. During the day she was busy in Westminster, where she was decorating the walls in a hall where there was to be an exhibition of works by young artists.

One day Tony turned up there unexpectedly. He didn't recognize her at first in her besplattered overalls, her face speckled with paint and an old artist's hat on her head. Chance, as always Tony's closest ally, had taken him there in the course of his job as advertising manager for a London art school, and he was surprised when someone covered in paint spots ran after him calling his name. It was Marianne. She and Tony had not seen one another for a good four years. She had heard that Tony had married while in the army. I felt at the time that the news did not leave her indifferent.

'How is your wife?' she asked him. 'How should I know?' said Tony. 'I haven't seen her for over a year.' Tony confessed later that he had met casually an attractive woman where he was stationed during the war, and married her mainly because he wanted somebody to cry for him if he was killed. At the officer school he had been told that the average life expectancy of a lieutenant in action with his unit was about two hours. And he thought it was right to provide for the wife, whoever she might be, the tidy pension that the British army paid to widows. Unfortunately, said Tony, he was still alive when the war ended. He had gone to Berlin with the British occupying forces and as Senior British Film Officer had been given the job of overseeing the German film industry. He had got to know important Ufa producers and become friendly with Hans Albers. He had been back in London several months. His wife had fallen for another man, and left the matrimonial home. Tony was more upset over this than his wife's unfaithfulness. 'I don't care if she cheats on me,' he said, 'but with the housing shortage as it is, you don't just give up an apartment. It's not done.'

That evening Marianne got home very late. The change in her was apparent. Her face glowed, and her eyes gleamed as they had not done for months. 'I've met Tony again,' she said. 'He's back in London. And he's actually asked me to marry him.'

That was a little hasty, perhaps, for someone who was not yet divorced. But as far as Tony was concerned, it followed a convincing logic. 'Look,' he said to Marianne, 'this is starting to get ridiculous. We last saw one another four years ago, and before that not for another four years. If we wait another four now, I may be divorced but you may be married, and then we'll have to wait again. So let's do it straight away.'

Marianne asked for a few days to think it over. Fred and I were not completely convinced that Tony was Mr Right; to our minds, he was sometimes a bit too happy-go-lucky. But it was Marianne's decision, and she seemed very happy. A few days later she accepted his proposal.

Under English law in those days, you could be divorced only after three years. This time had not elapsed, and in any case, Tony did not have the money to pay for the divorce. Young married joy would have to wait.

My wedding, though, was getting near. We wanted to get married in August 1947, but first I had to have proof of my suitability as a Jewish wife. I was examined by six rabbis. They asked me about the Jewish holy days and various biblical passages. They wanted to know what the eight arms of the Hanukkah candelabra stood for and what goes on the seder plate at Passover. They asked whether my biological father had been a believing Jew, which I answered in the negative, and whether it was my firm intention to run a kosher household and bring my children up as Jews, which I answered in the affirmative. I had to recite the 'Shema Yisrael' and read some lines from the Torah in Hebrew, without of course understanding them. Finally they gave me a certificate showing that I was eligible to marry.

I still remember how happy I had been when I held my matriculation certificate and felt that every possible route lay open to me. This certificate, by contrast, opened up only one, exclusive way, the one to be shared with Fred, but my joy and pride were even greater than on the previous occasion.

On 24 August 1947, the day of our wedding, the summer sun shone on London, casting a merciful light over the bomb damage that was still evident all over the city. Fred wore a dark made-to-measure suit, and I had had a dark blue costume made by the 'no pockets' tailor, from fine material once again courtesy of Josef Hochwald. I would have found a white bridal dress inappropriate. I was not twenty any more, and Fred and I had not been together since yesterday.

Except for my friend Bina, who was in hospital with a broken leg, all our friends were at the synagogue. I tried to suppress thoughts about our parents. 'I'm sure they would have been happy about us marrying,' Fred said. I'm sure they would. In place of my father, whose duty it would have been to be witness to his daughter's marriage, I had Josef Hochwald as my witness. Fred had asked his brother to be his.

And so Fred and I stood under the *chuppa*, the wedding baldachin with four poles, and my heart was pounding so loud that I thought everyone in the synagogue could hear. I circled the groom seven times. The rabbi spoke the seven wedding blessings and read the richly decorated *kettubah*, the marriage contract that we later signed. My hand trembled as I wrote Dvora, my Hebrew name, there. It was the same with Fred, who signed the name Salomon. In accordance with custom, we drank from a wine goblet before exchanging rings and kissing. Then Fred broke a glass. This is done so that even in the happiest moments of life, one remembers the destruction of the temple. If the glass does not break, it is thought a bad omen for the marriage. Despite his slight build, Fred trampled it like an elephant, and it broke into many pieces. I am sure he had practised secretly at home with empty mustard jars.

We celebrated with fifty-two guests in the basement of a hotel in Paddington. As usual with émigrés, it was a fairly small reception party, not only because money was too short for a big affair, but also because some of our old friends were no longer alive and others were spread around the world. However, we had dozens of congratulatory cards and parcels from Lengsfelder in New York, from the Lavers, the sisters Sally Citron and Rosy Wine in Dublin, from Jewish relations and from artists from Fred's days in Vienna, who had emigrated to all the continents.

Mundy had insisted on paying for the celebration. After the meal he made a short speech. Then Fred stood up and delivered an apparently spontaneous poem of thanks, which caused many laughs. I was too excited to be able to recall now the details, but he thanked everyone in rhyme for the generous presents and for the friendships that had withstood all the trials of recent years. He thanked God that he could be alive on this day, and me, who had brought him back to life.

I had not been able to bring him back altogether, though, as I soon realized. Several months after the wedding he dedicated a poem to me on my thirty-third birthday. 'You're the sun that kills the blues,' he wrote, adding that he wanted to make me happy now and always. He also said that he knew his own faults. 'We have faults, we won't deny, but we will lose them by and by. At least – we'll try.'

Is it a 'fault' for someone who was in a concentration camp to be gloomy and pessimistic? Is it a character weakness that you can get rid of if you try, like poor table manners? Maybe I had secretly hoped that our marriage and living together would finally heal some of Fred's wounds. Gradually I was forced to admit to being naïve in this hope. It would take much longer, some of it longer than a lifetime.

In the preceding weeks Fred had again been very depressed, for Richard Tauber had died at the age of fifty-six. Impoverished and having lost his voice, he had died of lung cancer in his flat in London on 8 January 1948. At the end, a lobe from one of his lungs had been removed, but it was too late.

On 20 February we attended the Richard Tauber memorial concert in the Royal Albert Hall. It was full to bursting. They played compositions by Tauber and extracts from *Old Chelsea*. Fred was outraged when the soprano Elisabeth Schwarzkopf performed, as it was known she had joined the Nazi Party to further her career. At the end of the concert, the audience stood and sang 'You are My Heart's Delight' accompanied by the orchestra. Many people cried, and Fred too was moved to tears.

There were more and more farewells in the post-war years. Many émigrés set off again, and turned their backs on London. A few returned to their home countries, but most emigrated to the USA, Canada or the newly founded state of Israel.

Marianne and Tony married two years after we did and moved in together. Fred lent Tony the money for the divorce.

Life Goes On

Shortly before he had written the ballad 'Beware of April
Rain' for the much-loved Gracie Fields, and its success had
brought him big royalties.

The future, once unclear, was taking shape. Almost all our
friends were now married, and most already had children. We
had none, because Fred didn't want any. I spoke to him about
it many times, even before we married. He always avoided
the subject. And once when I forced the conversation round
to this sensitive topic, he said something that made me
speechless with horror. 'Jewish children only get murdered,'
he said.

A literally killing argument, one to which I had no answer.
However brightly the sun shone for me, these shadows would
not go. I had always wanted children, ideally a whole lot. Life
without children was something I could not, and did not wish
to, imagine. But Fred refused to discuss it. He did not want
what he had gone through to happen to one of his children,
he said. No argument, that times had changed and the danger
had passed, would convince him. It could happen again at
any time, he insisted.

As time passed, I ceased to be happy. I could hardly bear to
visit friends with children because I just longed to have a life
like theirs. In the street I went out of my way to avoid prams.
Sometimes just the sight of a baby made me burst into tears.
No one who knew me failed to see the change, including
Fred, who became very concerned.

But he probably put a good deal of my unhappiness down
to my work, which had taken an unpleasant turn since my
boss learned that I was a practising Jew. After my marriage I
had asked on several occasions for time off at Jewish holidays,
and at some stage he had asked me what for. 'I'm Jewish,' I
said, and told him that I celebrated these days with my
husband. I had not imagined there were Americans who were
anti-Semitic, but Mr Braun, as he was appropriately named,
was of German descent. From then on, he changed
completely. He put me under pressure whenever he could.
On Fridays he sent me home, saying that he didn't need me
and was sure I had the Sabbath meal to get ready, well
knowing how important Friday was for us employees, as it
was the only day we could buy goods half-price in the PX.

231

Once when I came back from lunch, Mr Braun had tipped everything in the drawers of my desk on to the floor. 'You must learn to be tidy,' he said. 'Perhaps you will learn it like this.'

I sank to the floor howling. Some colleagues helped me sort the things out again. 'Don't let him get away with it,' they said. 'You must complain to his superiors.'

I didn't. Fred thought things wouldn't improve, and I should give notice. For months I had had stomach cramp each morning when I went to the office. My doctor said I was in danger of developing a stomach ulcer if I did not change my life soon. So I gave notice, after finding a new job in a German bookshop called Barmerlea Book Sales. The shop was not far from my old place of work. I had often browsed there at lunchtimes and made the acquaintance of the owner, a Viennese Jewish woman, who was looking for someone to do the accounts.

Things would now be better, Fred hoped. To some extent they were. My stomach cramps suddenly stopped. But I still could not bear it when mothers with small babies came into the shop. They were all younger than I was. I was nearing my thirty-eighth birthday – and heading for a serious depression because of my childlessness. At any rate, that was the view of Erika, the friendly doctor who sympathized with me in my increasing misery and eventually, without my knowing, took Fred to task. 'You will lose Ilse if you deny her wish for children,' she told him. 'She has made you happy, and now you should do everything to make her happy again. If it goes on like this, she will soon be a psychiatric case.' This was surely an exaggeration, but not without effect.

In a few weeks I was pregnant. As my doctor told me the joyous news, I was so happy I fell on his neck. The more my tummy grew, the more Fred seemed to change too. He looked forward to the birth and was no doubt, like most men, secretly proud of his role. He went with me to the mother and baby shop; he helped buy a pram, a crib and nappies, and got the nursery ready. He often listened to the baby's heart beating in my tummy. For the whole of the nine months I was touched at how concerned he was for me to avoid any strain. Sometimes I felt that with the responsibilities of fatherhood he was for the first time fully committed to facing his future – and ours.

Our child was born on 21 July 1953. My obstetrician had got me into Hammersmith Hospital four weeks before it was due because he wanted to avoid complications from my high blood pressure. Fred visited me every day, and his excitement grew with my bulging tummy. The evening before the birth, he and Marianne came together to visit me. 'When it starts, I'd like to be there,' he said for the umpteenth time. I was not so keen. In those days it was not usual for fathers to be present at the birth, and Fred would only have made me more nervous. I had been warned in any case of the possibility of a difficult birth in view of my age. When the labour pains began the evening before, I did not want Fred to notice. He had announced that if necessary he would sleep on a park bench in the hospital grounds so that he could be there at the critical moment.

The labour pains came every fifteen minutes. Every time my tummy tensed I contrived some reason to laugh to distract myself from the pain. When Fred and Marianne left they did not realize that the birth had started.

The next morning it all went very quickly. It was a beautiful, uncomplicated birth. At 7.30 a.m., as the doctor on call was still having his breakfast, our child slid into the world. Our friend Erika, who worked elsewhere in Hammersmith Hospital, called Fred in his office. 'What is it?' was his first question.

It was a boy. We called him Ian because Fred wanted an initial that would remind him of his father, Isaak. Fred came to the hospital straight away. He had dropped everything, and urged the taxi driver to go faster – as though it mattered if he missed a single one of the first minutes of his son's life. The first time he held Ian, he could not conceal a slight trembling. 'I think I'd better sit down,' he said. 'Or I may drop him in my excitement.'

He kissed the baby tenderly on his wrinkled forehead. When he looked at me, his eyes were moist. But they were gleaming.

'Thank you,' he said.